# THE COMPLETE GUIDE TO PEOPLE SKILLS

# The Complete Guide to People Skills

Sue Bishop

# Gower

Published by
Gower Publishing Limited
Gower House
Croft Road
Aldershot
Hampshire GU11 3HR
England

Gower
Old Post Road
Brookfield
Vermont 05036
USA

Sue Bishop has asserted her right under the Copyright, Designs and Patents Act 1988 to be identified as the author of this work.

British Library Cataloguing in Publication Data
Bishop, Sue, 1949–
The complete guide to people skills
1. Interpersonal relations   2. Communication in management
3. Personnel management
I. Title
658.4'5

ISBN 0 566 07777 9

Library of Congress Cataloging-in-Publication Data
Bishop, Sue, 1949–
    The Complete guide to people skills / Sue Bishop
       p.    cm.
    Includes bibliographical references (p.    ) and index.
    ISBN 0–566–07777–9 (cloth)
    1. Communication in personnel management. 2. Communication in management. 3. Interpersonal communication. 4. Interpersonal relations.   I. Title.
HF5549.5.C6B475   1997
658.4'5--dc21                                                    96–37782
                                                                    CIP

Typeset in 10/12 Palatino by Photoprint and printed in Great Britain at the University Press, Cambridge.

# Contents

*Preface*                                          vii
*Introduction*                                      ix

PART I                                               1
1   Communication                                    3
2   Communicating skills                            11
3   Assertiveness                                   31
4   Neuro Linguistic Programming                    55

PART II                                             69
5   Appraisal                                       71
6   Counselling                                     83
7   Disciplinary interviews                         91
8   Dismissals                                      97
9   Empowerment                                    107
10  Induction                                      117
11  Influencing                                    125
12  Motivation                                     139
13  Negotiation                                    157
14  Poor performers                                173
15  Problem people                                 181
16  Redundancy                                     191
17  Selection interviews                           197
18  Team-building                                  209

Further reading                                    223

Index                                              225

# Preface

If you sit down and try to list every managerial function, you will see how impossible it would be to include all aspects of a manager's work – and do it justice – in a work of this size. Each facet, from absenteeism to zero-based budgeting, almost demands a work of its own. You will forgive me, therefore, for applying people skills to several selected management/team leadership functions.

Similarly, in Part I, I have concentrated on just two self-development and communication disciplines: assertiveness and Neuro Linguistic Programming. This was a conscious decision, first because I feel that the techniques involved are complementary. Secondly, I felt that to write about, then demonstrate the application of more than two communication theories, would complicate and confuse. Apologies, therefore, to exponents of Transactional Analysis *et al*.!

I have unashamedly used the pronoun 'he' throughout. In no way does this reflect my views on equal opportunities or the feminist movement. It *does* reflect my dislike of the unwieldy use of 'he or she' and 'his/hers'. In my view, this gets in the way of understanding.

My thanks to Jonathan Norman at Gower for asking me to undertake this project, and for his guidance and recommendations. Thanks, too, to Mags, for fielding telephone calls and visits while I was developing and writing this book, and as always for her patience and understanding.

*Sue Bishop*

vii

# Introduction

## Purpose

The purpose of this book is to help you to understand your own communication style, and improve your people skills so that you can then influence others by modelling good practice. People skills involve getting into the skin of the other person – trying to think how he thinks and feel what he feels. It entails having confidence in your own outcomes – what you want from an interaction – then establishing and accommodating the other person's outcomes. A manager with excellent people skills will leave every interaction confident that both parties have understood each other. Agreement is not always possible, neither is liking the person with whom you are conversing, but the essence of solid communication is mutual understanding. This book will demonstrate how mutual understanding can be achieved.

## Focus

The need for a management book on people skills lies in the rapidly changing climate of the workplace. Organizations which intend to survive – and thrive – in the years to come, will be customer focused. They will be challenged and motivated by change; creative and able to anticipate and exceed customer expectations. They will welcome technological advances and innovation. This will involve everyone who works for, or is connected with, the organization.

Such a change of focus requires a change of attitude throughout the organization, and offers different challenges to today's managers. Instead of the traditional 'manager knows best' style of controlled supervision, people-focused leadership is now required. This style of leadership involves excellent interpersonal skills; being able to communicate effectively at all levels; being able to respond appropriately to all situations; being proactive, anticipating and producing excellence in self and others.

Today's manager will not just walk the job, but talk the job, and he will need an armoury of people skills to get the best from his team. The communication skills required by today's managers and team leaders differ greatly from those where boardroom decisions were imposed on staff; where there was an army of inspectors to check for error; where a complaints department dealt with any member of the staff or public brave enough to challenge quality of product or service; where staff welfare was dealt with by a separate department. Flatter, customer-focused, empowered organizations have made new demands on managers. They need to be skilled, and will be expected to be proficient in, a wide range of functions all of which require excellent people skills.

# Belief

An excellent manager will have certain attributes and skills which can be improved upon, hopefully with the help of this book. He will believe in himself and trust in his team. He will aspire to clear and positive outcomes, yet will be flexible in the pursuit of these outcomes. Central to the thinking behind this book is the belief that success lies not in 'winning', sometimes at the expense of others, but in concentrating on the needs, opinions, and feelings of the other party to help them achieve their outcomes too. The more you understand the other person, the more likely it is for you to achieve mutually acceptable results. The successful manager will respect the other person's rights while not neglecting his own.

# Approach

This is a self-development book offering some revision for the experienced manager, and hopefully new and challenging ideas about how to improve confidence, become a more effective communicator and achieve excellence in interpersonal skills. I have concentrated on one-to-one interactions and, although there will be occasional reference to written communication and telephone technique, the emphasis is on face-to-face contact.

# Content

The book is divided into two parts. Part I gives an overview of basic people skills and offers a brief explanation of some self-development and communication theories. Its chapters cover communication, communicating skills, assertiveness and Neuro Linguistic Programming. Many of the theories expounded in these chapters are referred to in Part II, and so I would suggest that you read all of Part I before looking at the function-specific chapters in the second part of the book.

Part II gives guidance on applying people skills within specific managerial functions. The chapters are arranged alphabetically under managerial topic – from appraisals to team-building. Each chapter offers an exercise that asks you to apply your existing knowledge or to think more deeply about the subject-matter of the chapter. Whereas I hope you will read the book from cover to cover, the second part of this book is more of a reference work for you to dip into as and when the need arises.

# Part I

# 1 Communication

First, a few words about the difference between this chapter on communication and the next on communicating skills. This chapter will look at the psychology of communication; then, from the organizational point of view, the way in which information is transmitted and received up, down and across the organizational structure. It will suggest ways in which you can improve your people skills in all of these areas. The chapter on communicating skills will look more specifically at understanding and improving techniques such as effective speaking, listening and questioning.

## Communication: why things go wrong

When entering a dialogue, most of us tend to assume that our own view of the world is very similar to that of the other person. If we're from the same culture, our understanding of words and phrases will be much the same. Just consider the following scenario, however. Two people, let's call them Harry and June, watch an ocean-going liner leave port for a Mediterranean cruise. Harry loves water-sports, sailing, boats – anything to do with the water. He has made a study of ships. Watching this liner, he is relaxed, happy and invigorated by the line and power of the ship, and not a little envious of the passengers. He recognizes that the ship is flying a blue and white flag – a sign that she is leaving port, and can easily identify, by the blasts from the hooter, signals that she is leaving, is turning to starboard etc. June, on the other hand, is frightened of water and would never contemplate a cruise. She has unhappy memories of a similar occasion when she watched a liner taking her brother and family to their new home in Australia. Although happy for them, she was filled with sadness at her own loss. The visual and auditory sounds as the ship leaves harbour mean nothing to her except through this sad association.

Harry and June received the same set of stimuli, visual and auditory, but internally they decoded and interpreted the stimuli differently – they each experienced a different event. Later, when Harry and June talk about this liner – either with each other or to other people, their perception of the event will colour their understanding of it, the language they use to describe it, and so on. Consider the phrase 'What an experience!' uttered by each of them with the same emphasis, but with quite different meaning.

This example is given to illustrate how each person is unique. Every waking moment our senses are bombarded with stimuli. If we registered every stimulus equally, we would go mad. If our brains interpreted every smell, registered equally every noise, if we were conscious of every touch – the feel of our clothing on each part of our body, the pressure of sitting on a chair – all with equal force, it would be such a cacophony of 'noise' that our brains would not be able to cope.

You have the means to be selective in your response to external and internal stimuli. Your brain has to filter and interpret in order for you to make sense of this bombardment. You will be selective in your interpretation, filtering out elements which are no use to you in the current situation; factors which don't conform to your own value systems, and elements which, consciously or subconsciously, you choose to reject.

How you select will depend on a number of factors. You will be influenced by childhood conditioning, by comparison with past experience, the present context, your mood, emotional state and so on. All of this has an impact on how you perceive and consequently, how you communicate – and it is happening to you right now – always supposing that you are awake! You are continually decoding, interpreting and evaluating – and so is the other person – but they are coming from a different set of beliefs, values and experience of the world.

Seventy per cent of our waking lives is spent communicating, so it follows that most of us feel we are reasonably good at it. In fact, personal success relies largely on your ability to communicate. However, many of the difficulties which arise in personal relationships, in business, and even in international politics where effective communication is the politician's stock-in-trade, communication breakdown is often to blame for failure.

'The Government isn't listening to the voice of the people.'

Communication is not an inanimate concept. Communication takes place between two or more people, so we – you and I – have responsibilities to make communication work. The concept itself cannot be blamed for failures. If we start to look at the processes which are involved, it will become apparent not how easy it is to communicate effectively, but rather how we manage to understand each other at all, for so much of the time!

Let's start by looking at two-way communication between two people. These two people we will call the transmitter and the receiver of information. The transmitter (speaker) wishes to convey information to the receiver (listener). He will have countless thoughts about this information buzzing around in his brain, but needs to be selective in what he says and how he says it. In other words, he will encode his thoughts, choosing an appropriate form of delivery. How he encodes his thoughts will depend on many internalized factors – his attitudes and beliefs, for example, which have been formed over the years through conditioning, learning and experience. Depending on these factors, he will attach his own particular meaning to the words he chooses to use. A good communicator will also take the other person into account, and encode the message in terms which are appropriate to the receiver; in other words, suitable vocabulary and phrasing which will most accurately convey meaning. The coded message will be a mixture of verbal and non-verbal communication, and all aspects must be compatible if there is to be no confusion. Facial expression, body movement, gesture and so on have to match the words, intonation, volume and pace of the communication. All of this takes place just in delivering a simple sentence.

However, there is no point in speaking if the other person does not hear and understand the message sent. Unless the message is listened to, interpreted and understood, there is no communication, so let's look at the receiver's role in this simple exchange.

We have selective attention and selective perception mechanisms. We only respond to a few of the many stimuli being sent to the brain, shutting out others in a kind of priority system. My priority at this moment is concentrating on my notes, my thoughts about this section and my computer keyboard and VDU. This does not mean that my brain is not registering bird song, the sound of traffic outside, the fact that it is a warm day or that my dinner is cooking downstairs. If two cars crashed outside my window, or hunger is prompted by the smell of cooking, my brain will select its priorities. The desire to see the state of the crashed cars, or hunger pangs and thoughts of food, may well override my concentration on work. This sort of selective attention can interfere with encoding and decoding messages during communication. There is a difference between hearing and listening. Unless we have an impairment, we are hearing sound continually. Our brains filter sound which we need to hear from extraneous background noise. This filtering system controls active listening.

If the other person *is* actively listening, he will hear the words and register the non-verbal aspects of the communication in order to decode the message into an idea which he understands. Now the words used may have different connotations for the receiver, because everyone has their own unique experience of the world. For example, the tone of voice used may remind him of previous interactions and have a bearing on this communication. Other barriers, such as noise, may have intruded upon his own thoughts and opinions, his expectations, thinking about how he is going to respond and so on. The resulting message which is received may not be the same as the one the transmitter intended to convey.

It is every person's responsibility to check that they understand and have been understood in an interaction. Failure to do so leads to transmitters of information leaving the situation sometimes erroneously believing that all is well, when in fact the receiver has an entirely different (or confused) idea of the interaction. Communication to blame? No, the communicators. The transmitter can ask for a response to his communication – in fact, he will need often to initiate this desire for feedback where a difference in status is involved. Frequently, non-verbal signals will tell the observant transmitter that there is disagreement or confusion. The receiver should ask for clarification or reflect back his understanding of the communication if at all unsure.

In most interactions each person takes it more or less in turn to be speaker and listener, so the above scenario is repeated time and time again, each encoding and decoding the messages of the other. As you speak, if you pay full attention to the other person, you perceive their response to your communication and react with your own thoughts and feelings. The ongoing dialogue is prompted by what each of you hear, see and feel, each perceiving and responding in a similar way.

As a guide to improve people skills, keep the following in mind. When transmitting:

- choose words and phrases carefully
- respect the receiver's views and opinions (this is not the same as agreeing with them)
- use language appropriate to the receiver
- get in step with the receiver's way of communicating
- get 'into the shoes' of the receiver; how might they be feeling? What are their needs?
- be aware of the barriers to communication (any form of interference that distracts from the message)

- look for non-verbal clues
- seek feedback
- be flexible enough to respond to the other's reactions; keep in tune with the other person
- avoid jargon, verbose language or anything which might confuse the receiver.

## Communication in business

Whatever the size of your organization, effective communication is essential to connect the various parts of the whole – directors, management, employees, sections and departments, different premises and locations within the organization, and so on. Not only this, but, the company has an identity of its own – a corporate image, culture, ethos – and 'speaks' to employees, suppliers, clients, customers and the general public. Of course, the organization can't literally speak; it is the people within the organization who give the company its image, for good or bad. The brusque salesperson, indifferent telephonist or careless manager can adversely affect the company's image and destroy costly image-building advertising, however effective this is in its own right. It is you and I who are responsible for the company communicating a positive message both internally and to the outside world.

This has to come about through open and constructive dialogue, teamwork, and good team spirit with each employee aware of, being actively part of and committed to, organizational goals and visions. It means that each individual has to be responsible for setting the highest standards, because everything that each of us does, influences the organization of which we are a part. This rule applies equally to directors and post-room clerks; chief executives and car-park attendants. Everyone who works for the company is part of the system and has a duty to communicate as effectively as possible.

In order to survive and thrive, the organization must 'listen' to environmental and market forces. It has to be aware of customer needs in order to meet and then exceed them. It needs to react to change, and communicate with the outside world in order to anticipate and become proactive. The organization must communicate with its immediate environment. This means that every employee is responsible for passing information – from internal sources, customers, suppliers, the general public, competitors – up through the system so that the organization can react appropriately. In its turn, the organization – or rather the layers of management and staff – must ensure that all employees are kept informed and involved.

# Types of communication

The form which communication takes can significantly affect the attitude of those who work in an organization. The way information is passed up, down and across, will have an impact on everyone who works for the company. One-way communication does not allow for response from the receivers – at least, not initially. One-way communication includes lectures and formal addresses from (for example) the Chief Executive to all senior levels of management within a large organization. Because of the numbers involved, there is no opportunity for individuals to question, clarify understanding or to offer feedback. Most written forms of communication are one-way because no response or feedback is immediately available to the transmitter.

In organizations where direction and control are still the order of the day, formal one-way communication is still used a great deal. It gives the transmitter status and an air of efficiency. It is also a 'safe' means of communication for management because it does not allow for direct questioning or comment from those receiving it. However, there is a risk of misunderstanding on both sides, and without the facility to clarify, the receivers may well feel anxious and unsure that they have fully understood. Whereas, generally, two-way communication is seen to be the most satisfactory way of imparting information, making decisions and so on, there will be occasions, even for empowered organizations, when there is an advantage in one-way communication. It saves time. Information can be passed on to a large number of people at one go – either through the written word or by addressing a large group. If the talk is formal, with no opportunity for discussion or questions, then this cuts the time involved yet again. However, a good one-way communicator will anticipate difficulties and spend a lot of time researching his subject and his audience, predicting areas where misunderstandings may occur, and refining his report or practising his talk. This, too, is time-consuming and should be weighed against the advantages of talking one-to-one with individuals or communicating with small groups where interaction can take place.

As a manager interested in refining people skills, you must always be conscious of the needs of the other person – even if you are contemplating communication with a large number of people. Two-way communication is invariably more effective because it allows for instant feedback; hence greater involvement. It actively encourages a response from the receiver(s). It satisfies the needs of all parties because the speaker can check that he has been heard and understood, and the receiver(s) can clarify, and air their own views, doubts or suggestions. They are less likely to leave the interaction frustrated or irritated by the fact that they have not had the chance to check facts or otherwise take part in the communication. True it can be very time-consuming, and also, if addressing groups of people, threatening to an unskilled communicator. There is potential loss of control, and anxiety about loss of face, the ability to manage a group discussion or to field questions effectively, may keep some managers locked into the safety of one-way communication. However, the manager with good people skills will be as good a listener as he is a speaker, and will see the all-round advantages of adopting a two-way approach wherever possible. He will quickly develop the skills and confidence to manage group situations as well as one-to-one interactions.

## Directional communication

Internal communications should flow in three directions: upwards, downwards and laterally. It is essential to the health of the organization that there is a free flow of information upwards, from lower levels to higher. In this way information from the outside environment can be used to the benefit of the organization. For example, sales representatives in the field will learn a lot about competitors, and this information needs to be filtered through to top management. If there is a free flow of communication between subordinates and their bosses, throughout the organization, management at every level is aware of issues relevant to the work of all employees. Effective people skills will involve creating an environment where your staff feel free to express themselves without fear of ridicule, retribution – or just being ignored.

Organizational mission statements, policies and major goals, quality and performance standards and so on need to be passed downwards from the board of directors through the various levels to all employees. In this way there is the potential for everyone to share the same vision; for everyone to pull together and in the same direction to strengthen the organization. An issue you will need to consider is how much to pass on to your subordinates – for their own and the organization's good. There are bound to be times when there must be some restriction of information. A proposed management discussion of cutbacks, for example, would only cause discontent to the rank and file and could produce unwarranted anxieties. Provided that generally you have created an atmosphere of mutual trust, most staff will accept that there will be times when there are good reasons for information being withheld.

Lateral or sideways communication across departments and between sections and locations completes the effective communication loop within the organization. Here it is your responsibility to communicate with managers at a similar level. It is to everyone's advantage to share knowledge, information and expertise.

Companies often have communications problems because they have no provision for information to flow upwards or sideways. Co-ordination between departments becomes difficult when the left hand is unsure of what the right hand is doing, and senior management loses the opportunity of tapping into the ideas of employees working at a lower level in the organization. However, as has already been stated, it is the responsibility of everyone to make communication work within the organization. Whatever position you hold presently within your company, you can have a positive effect on good communication practices by becoming better informed, and passing information in an appropriate way across, up and down the organizational structure.

As a manager, you may need to consider why there might be difficulties or blockages in the communication process in your organization. Are your subordinates reluctant to express opinions and suggestions? Have they had unsatisfactory experiences of offering ideas which have been ignored, rejected or dismissed? Might they fear the impact on their career prospects if they 'rock the boat'? Do you, in fact, give them every opportunity to contribute fully to the work of your team? What can you do to further openness with individuals within your team? How can upward communication be encouraged?

Do you pass information up the organizational structure? Do you feel free to offer suggestions to senior management? Do you ever openly disagree with a managerial decision when you feel that the organization might suffer as the result? Can you admit to your boss that you have a problem? If the answer to any of these questions is 'no', then you need to look at ways and means of increasing your confidence assertively to communicate upwards.

Do you discuss goals and visions with other department heads? Do you know their priorities, and do they know yours? Do you trade ideas for interdepartmental improvements? Do you exchange and disseminate information and ideas laterally, across the company?

One final word about the dangers of not having open communication channels within an organization. The main problem is the grapevine. If clear, unambiguous information is not transmitted in an appropriate way, rumours take hold and messages become distorted as they are passed from one person to another. Rumours cause uncertainty and anxiety; morale and motivation suffer. Therefore, it is far better to communicate in an honest and open manner, be aware of where blockages may occur and play your own part in breaking down barriers to the communication process.

# 2 Communicating skills

Communicating well – listening, questioning, expressing yourself at all times so that you are understood and your words acted upon – is an art and a skill. Like any other skill, it can be practised and refined until you move from unconscious incompetence – unwittingly putting your foot in it, or believing you have been heard and understood when this is not the case – through the stages to unconscious competence. These stages are as follows:

1. Unconscious incompetence – you are unaware that your lack of skill is leading to misunderstandings, misinterpretations, 'ruffled feathers', anxiety or frustration in the other person.
2. Conscious incompetence – you are aware that your communication skills are letting you down – you may be inadvertently tactless, reticent or aggressive, and leave the interaction knowing that you could have handled things better.
3. Conscious competence – through developing your people skills, you now know 'how to' but still have to rehearse and plan what you say, how you say it, how better to listen and question in order for everyone to leave the interaction feeling good about themselves.
4. Unconscious competence – with practice, excellent communication skills will become second nature. You will be recognized as a proficient and responsive communicator, and will be a role model for excellent interpersonal skills.

To arrive at unconscious competence, you first need to be aware of some of the elements discussed in Chapter 1. Every individual is just that – individual and unique. The person with whom you are communicating will bring his own beliefs, values and viewpoint to the discussion. He will decode your message in the light of these factors, the present context, and

11

against his experience of previous similar encounters. Remember also that most people like to feel good about themselves, and will care about the image they present and what others think of them. They bring complex emotions to the situation and have egos which can be threatened and dented. It is so easy for both sides to fail to interpret communication in the way it was intended.

In order to be an effective communicator, you need to be able to 'walk in the other person's shoes'. In an interaction which can be planned, it is useful to assess the situation from three different standpoints. First, assess it from your vantage point. Your internal dialogue will be punctuated by 'I' phrases. Then try to see the situation from the other person's point of view: 'If I were him I would want . . . I would be feeling . . .' This does not mean simply recognizing that they see things differently, but withholding your own views while you 'try on' their position. Understanding their point of view is not the same as agreeing with it, but greater awareness will benefit the communication from both sides. Finally, look at things as an outsider. Detach yourself from the emotions of the situation and take the objective position of a detached observer. From these three viewpoints you may well wish to revise your initial approach; you will become more enlightened and better prepared for a win/win interaction.

In conversation where forward planning is not possible, similar principles still apply. Concentrate on the other person and try to establish where they are coming from, understanding their point of view and the emotional force with which they believe it. As air space is passed from one to the other, each of you will be encoding and decoding, responding to what you hear and perceive. Be flexible. Know what you want to achieve, but be prepared to change tack to achieve it. Respect your own needs, and show sensitivity to the other person, recognizing changes in your own and the other's states and responding appropriately to these changes.

# Rapport

One of the essential elements of being a successful communicator is the ability to build and maintain rapport. Without rapport, very little meaningful communication will take place. Rapport is about empathetic communication, seeing the other person's point of view, getting on to their wavelength, and using your skill to demonstrate (and encourage the other to match) positive behaviour in order to create an atmosphere of trust and confidence.

Creating rapport is a skill which can be learnt – you don't even have to like the person concerned to develop a rapport with them. Just act as if you do! Use rapport as a bridge to better understanding. When dealing with strangers, the sooner you turn that person into someone you know, the easier the communication will be so begin at once to build these bridges. Rapport creates trust and gives both parties the confidence to participate fully in the interaction.

Unless you are a recluse, you are already experienced in creating rapport. Think of the people with whom you get on really well; those you find it easy to talk to and with whom silences, too, are comfortable. What is it about your joint behaviour, language patterns and so on that makes it an easy relationship? If you find it difficult to put your finger on what exactly it is that makes the relationship gel, observe two people who are obviously on the same wavelength. What do you notice? What do you hear? Communication flows when two people are in rapport because their bodies as well as their words tend to match each other. There is unconscious mirroring of movement, distribution of body weight, posture and gesture. There will be comparable use of eye contact and facial expression. The use of language and key words will be similar. The tone, volume, pace and rhythm of voice will correspond.

To explain this better let us consider an analogy – choral singing. Singers listen to each other and voices blend – there should be no prima donnas! Mirroring is like this; get in harmony with the other person. By mirroring (mirroring, not mimicking) you can create rapport with almost anyone you wish. Remember, when people are like each other, they like each other. You may find that even those you thought difficult, or who you did not much care for, can become allies and friends through rapport-building.

Before any interaction, whether meeting a colleague to discuss work, holding an interview or meeting someone new for the first time, creating rapport – finding the level on which you can both relate – is the first stepping-stone to successful communication.

Creating and building rapport is a vital communication skill. *Maintaining* rapport, however – building a relationship – is your choice. If your integrity is challenged, or you feel that there would be no mileage in bridging the gap between your values and beliefs and those of the other person, then you will disengage from this part of the transaction (in all probability, you will have automatically and subconsciously stopped mirroring the other person anyway).

# Listening

The ability accurately to receive information is as important, if not more important, than transmitting it. Listening is arguably the most significant of the communication skills – is crucial to maintaining rapport – yet is also the most neglected aspect of communication. There is a difference between hearing, which is an involuntary and passive process, and active listening. Hearing is merely the capacity to receive sound; active listening entails being selective and analytical of what you hear, and as accurately as possible, understanding the meaning of that sound. It involves hearing words, decoding vocal and non-verbal cues, and interpreting everything within the context of the communication.

Effective listening is a selfless process. You should concentrate as much as possible on the other person. In this way you will gain insight into what they are thinking and feeling, because words alone do not tell the whole picture. Frequently *how* someone communicates is more telling than what he actually says. Gestures, frequency of eye contact, voice tonality, pace of delivery and so on will give you clues to true meanings. General attitude may indicate that whatever words are being used, there is a hidden agenda there somewhere that you need to address. Alternatively, you may perceive someone totally at ease with his communication where words, vocal cues and non-verbal behaviour are all congruent. You can only define these things by conscious whole-body listening – attending with body, senses, thoughts and emotions.

By concentrating and focusing on the other person you will be less likely to fall into one of the poor listening traps:

- waiting for your chance to interrupt and have your say
- jumping to conclusions about the other person's meaning before hearing him out
- thinking about what you are going to say next
- getting side-tracked – 'that reminds me . . .'
- letting your own prejudices and feelings get in the way
- allowing external or internal 'noise' to distract you
- letting your own needs intrude.

Let's look briefly at each of these in turn. Too often conversation is comprised of interrupted monologues rather than interactive dialogue. It is about two people eagerly awaiting their chance to speak, with neither really listening to the other. Interruptions are frustrating for the transmitter; they show lack of respect. You should always stay focused on the other person, hearing him out, allowing him an equal share of air space. It is easy to 'be smart' – to listen for a few seconds, then assume that you have gathered his gist and need no longer actively listen. By jumping to conclusions and switching off, you may well miss the true import of what he is saying. (Incidently, if you are the victim of the constant interrupter, you should feel free *assertively* to say something like 'Please let me finish . . .' or, 'Sandra, you interrupted me; please let me finish explaining my idea'. Alternatively, after waiting for a pause in the other person's flow, you could say something like, 'I'd like to return to what I was just saying . . .').

Most of us are guilty of thinking about what we are going to say next, how we are going to respond to that last point or how we are going to frame our next argument, rather than giving our full attention to the speaker. Try to give more attention to what the speaker is saying and how he is saying it than to what you want to say and how you are going to put it across. To do this you need to practise concentrating. Be (and look) interested in the other person and what he has to say. Consider his perceptions, needs and pressures. Look for facts, evidence, examples, opinions. 'Read' his communication for full understanding. Close your mind to external and internal distractions.

Unless you are using all your mental powers to concentrate on, listen to and understand the other person, it is also easy to pick up words and phrases which have emotive connotations, and go off on a 'that reminds me' side-track. Before you know it you are thinking about something else entirely and will have lost the flow of the other's conversation. Whatever happens, don't take up this new line of thought with the other person, who will realize that you have switched off from what he was saying. This is demoralizing or annoying (depending on your frame of mind) and displays a total lack of respect for, and interest in, the other person. Get back on target as quickly as possible, if necessary interrupting with something like, 'I'm sorry Chris, but I didn't quite follow that last point; could you say it again?'

There will be times when a speaker's appearance, mannerisms, accent, or manner of speaking will just not sit right with you, and you will find it difficult to get beyond these external factors to listen actively to the message he is trying to convey. Similarly, it is impossible for us to like everyone we meet or with whom we have to deal; but none of these things should get in the way of effective communication. Be aware of your own prejudices; acknowledge and control them so that you can look beyond the annoyance and listen to the communication. You will carry around with you values, beliefs, ideas and attitudes which will be different from the other person's. Try to be non-judgemental in your listening. Be confident in your views so that you need not feel intimidated, offended or hurt by the other's opinions. You need not agree with what they are saying, but they have as much a right to their views as you have to yours.

There will be times when your own needs are too great for listening to be effective. You may be ill, tired, hungry or uptight, and find it hard to overcome these feelings. It then becomes increasingly difficult to listen objectively. One of the dangers inherent in this is reaching a hasty conclusion about the speaker or the content of his communication, then selectively hearing only that which substantiates that conclusion. At such times it is important to recognize the difficulties you are facing, and the reasons for these difficulties. Acknowledge them to yourself – then try harder to listen accurately. It takes discipline always to be an effective listener!

Attention is selective; there are umpteen reasons why we 'switch off' from listening. To practise concentrating, try this. Take a non-threatening situation like television news coverage or a consumer advice programme (where the other person is talking to you, but in the detached format of a television or radio programme) and record it. This type of reporting should be unbiased and factual, so you need not look for hidden meanings or emotional undertones. See how effective your listening is by trying to remember the salient points. Check your interpretation with the recording again, for accuracy/misinterpretation. Did you leave out, substitute or even add material to what was actually said? Be objective in your analysis to see whether you have altered meaning through your own prejudices. Did you tend to tune out anything which didn't fit your bias?

While stressing that listening is an active process, so far we have looked at concentrating on the other's words and non-verbal cues without considering response. Listening does not just take place between people – it takes place within people. As discussed in Chapter 1 there is a continuing process of encoding, transmitting, coping with barriers to communication, receiving and decoding taking place during all inter-actions. For successful communication to take place you should recognize that there is a difference between my view of me and your view of me, and between my view of you and your view of you. To understand the other person's viewpoint you need to be able to see things from his frame of reference – his view of himself and the situation. To do this you need to observe, listen and question (see questioning below).

As a people skill, why is listening so important? As we have seen, it is an essential ingredient in building and maintaining rapport. You are more likely to develop an effective working relationship if the other person feels that you have truly listened, understood, are interested in or curious about their point of view.

Relationships are improved when both respect and really listen to the other. As you observe and listen you will understand each other better. When you understand a person it is easier to work with them – even if you do not share their views. Understanding is not agreeing. You can understand fully and disagree completely. If you can convince the other person that you *understand*, yet disagree, you will find it easier to get them to listen to your viewpoint.

Being a good listener encourages the other person to talk. When they realize that you are listening in a non-threatening, non-judgemental manner, they will feel more free to 'open up'. With misunderstandings minimized by sensitive listening and questioning, people will find it easier to air ideas or contentious feelings. Good listening helps them feel affirmed and accepted, their views respected and understood.

Accurate listening improves not only your comprehension, but also the quality of what is said. The other person's confidence will grow. As you probe and encourage them to continue, they will realize that you are not just paying lip-service to listening, but really hearing and understanding them.

Behaviour is infectious. If you practise effective listening the other person may try to understand you better by listening more carefully to you. By listening and questioning well, you will usually inspire the other person to continue talking, adding detail to facts, so you will be able to elucidate as much information as possible.

You can help the other person take responsibility for problem-solving and decision-making through sensitive listening and questioning. It reduces defensiveness, so the other person feels more able to express his feelings and worries, and focus on his own behaviour – what he can do to sort things out. By talking through a problem with a sensitive listener, most of us can more easily work out possible solutions.

# Encouraging messages

There is a difference between listening attentively and actively, and listening passively and silently. Someone who listens merely because he has nothing to say can hardly be said to be a good communicator. Something more is needed to stop the other person feeling he is speaking into a vacuum. As the receiver of communication you need to let the other person know that he is being listened to and understood. Without interrupting his flow, you can give encouraging messages by your expression, by nodding your head slowly and occasionally, by making encouraging noises such as 'I see', 'uh-huh', 'Go on', 'Ah', 'Really?', 'Yes?'. In this way the speaker is reassured that you are interested, and want him to continue.

If you feel that the speaker has more to say, but needs encouragement to continue, try repeating his last words, but with a questioning intonation:

'There are advantages and disadvantages.'
'Advantages and disadvantages?'

You can see how this not only encourages the other person to say more, but will prompt *how* he responds depending on where you put emphasis on the words:

'*Advantages* and disadvantages?' (he will tell you more about the benefits).
'Advantages *and* disadvantages?' (he should give you a breakdown of the two).
'Advantages and *disadvantages*?' (suggests you want to know more about the negative aspects).

If you are merely trying to draw him out, repeat back his last words in a neutral tone.

You may wish to check your understanding of a point while the other person still has 'official' air space. Do this by reflecting back your understanding of what he's said; then allowing him to clarify, confirm and continue:

'My medical is coming up soon, and I don't know if I'll get through; my job depends on it.'
'You're worried about your medical.'
'Yes, it's crucial to my career plans that I get a clean bill of health.'

If you listen carefully, you will know whether the other person's communication is coming from fact or feelings. If you want to help him explore his feelings about the situation you could keep him on track by reflecting back in 'feelings' terms:

'You're feeling anxious because your medical is looming.'

If you want to turn the conversation from feelings to tangible facts, you could reflect back accordingly:

'Your medical is soon?'

If you didn't understand a point, or need clarification before responding, you might try something like 'John, you said that they expect too much ... who precisely expects too much? ...' 'what is "too much" in your terms?' or 'You felt that she undermined you ... how did she do that?' In other words, you play back the speaker's words, then follow up with an open question.

# Questioning

The two main divisions are closed and open questions.

## Closed questions

Closed questions can be answered with a 'yes', 'no' or one word response. They are useful when you want a direct answer to a direct question or in confirming facts: 'You started working for us in 1989, is that correct?' 'Yes'. Many managers – especially of the 'direct and control' era – use a lot of closed questions to block debate, push their opinions and get agreement with the minimum of discussion.

This type of question has limited value in general conversation, where you are seeking information on which to base further questions, or where you want to encourage the other person to speak, because a monosyllabic response is all that is required (although the more garrulous will often elaborate without further prompting). Closed questions should be used selectively and, where possible, followed up with an open question.

## Open questions

Open questions, however, are used to promote discussion. They are prefaced by (or include the words) 'who', 'what', 'where', when', 'how' and 'why', or are introduced by phrases such as 'In what way'; they demand a more detailed response. Open questions encourage the other person to speak freely. They can be used to give permission to talk – an indication that you are interested and prepared to listen.

In terms of problem-solving or in counselling another, the three key words are 'What', 'why' and 'how'. 'When', 'where' and 'who' are used more for establishing facts and for action-planning.

One word of warning about 'why' open questions: if you ask 'why?' and leave it as that, this can sometimes be seen as threatening – an implied criticism. Soften your 'why' type questions, cushioning them as in the following: 'That's interesting; why do you think it will fail?'

Other types of question include the following.

## Direct questions

An open question which demands a direct response: 'When did you discover the fault?'

## Marathon questions

This is where the question is long and convoluted, or where multiple questions are asked in a long stream, leaving the other person bewildered about which question to answer first. The dangers are that *you* will become confused, let alone the person who is supposed to respond! It also allows the other person to answer the question which suits them best, and this may not be the way you want the conversation to go. The maxim is 'one thought, one question'. If you have asked the wrong question, or phrased it poorly, let it go, then follow up with another more appropriate single-thought question. Even linked-thought questions, e.g. 'How would you resource the project; where would you go for funding?' would be better split into two separate questions.

## Statement questions

Some questions can be phrased as a statement. Intonation – a raising of the voice at the end of the statement – indicates to the other person that a reply is required. However, some people (television and radio interviewers seem adept at this!) deliver statements to which they require a response, but in such a way that the obtuse or reluctant receiver might well remain silent, or at best give a monosyllabic reply, e.g. 'The situation is deteriorating.' Response: either silence (waiting for a question to be asked), a bald 'Yes', or – if the receiver is feeling charitable – a fuller response such as 'Yes, the chances of finding a new supplier...'. If you find yourself often using statements rather than asking appropriate, obvious questions, you should be aware of the confusion this may cause. You should always be aiming for the clearest possible way of communicating.

## Probing questions

This type of question is intended to draw more information from the other person: 'Why was that?', 'What happened as result'. Probing questions should be used to clarify understanding of information already offered: 'So how could you get such an improvement?'

## Linking questions

Linking questions are useful for making smooth transitions from one topic to another: 'You mentioned graphics just now. What experience do you have of desktop publishing?'

## Reflective questions

If you reflect back the other person's last words with a questioning inflexion, it will often encourage him to say more – give further detail or information: 'that line would be more profitable?' If presented in summary form, it can be used to move the conversation on: 'So you are not happy with the overtime arrangements. What thoughts have you on how we might work "smarter" to cope with the backlog?'

## Imperative questions

Imperative questions are requests made in the form of an instruction: 'Tell me how you would . . .'.

## Summarizing questions

Whereas a summary of what has been said is not a question as such, there can be summarizing questions like the following:

> 'Let me make sure I've understood you; the key points are . . . is that right?'

## Leading questions

The answer required is indicated in the phrasing of a leading question. It shows an assumption or bias on the part of the questioner: 'Women make better secretaries, don't you agree?' Leading questions tend to be either intimidating or provocative and are best avoided.

## Loaded questions

'What do you think about the No Smoking rule?' is a loaded question. Whichever way the receiver jumps, the questioner may have opposite views. Of course, an assertive person would confidently give an honest opinion, respecting if not agreeing with the other's views, but sometimes, especially when status is involved, a loaded question might unsettle a subordinate, or put him on the defensive. As such, loaded questions should also be avoided.

# Words and phrases

You are probably familiar with the terms 'content and process' in management. The same terms can be applied to the communication process, the content being the literal meaning of the words used – the 'what' we say – and the process being the way in which the words are delivered – the 'how' we say it. Let's start by looking at the choice of words and phrases used.

The first sentence of this section is teetering on the brink of being a poor choice of words in that it could be seen as a potential put-down. What if, as a manager, you are unfamiliar with the terms 'content and process'? It could dent your confidence a little; you might feel 'I *should* know what it means – every other manager obviously does!' This kind of style should, therefore, be avoided. For example, saying 'As you know ...' when the other person might *not* know, or 'It goes without saying that ...' where it would take an assertive person to challenge you.

Sir John Betjeman compiled an amusing list of double-talk phrases which should be avoided: things like 'With all due respect' which the receiver will correctly interpret as you having no respect for his views – rather the opposite. Other typical examples of double-talk include:

'Correct me if I'm wrong', implying '*I'm* right; *you're* wrong and don't you dare to contradict me!'

'Well, you know best' – in other words '*I* know best, but go ahead and do it your way if it gives you pleasure!'

'You're entitled to your opinion' shows a disrespect for that opinion, and infers that the opinion is wrong.

'Interesting point – we'll come back to that later' shows that you haven't a clue about how to answer, and that you will try to avoid the issue altogether.

One preamble guaranteed to irritate me is 'I'm sorry, but I've got to say this', which usually flags up that the other person is not sorry at all, but is going to speak their mind usually riding roughshod over others' feelings.

Wherever possible, take responsibility for your own views and opinions rather than attributing them to some third party: 'I think it would be better done this way' rather than 'The directors would prefer it done this way'. The first takes ownership; the second is a cop-out implying that you have no control over your decisions – and if things go wrong or the other person disagrees, it's not your fault, it's the directors'.

Try to keep with 'I' rational statements, and avoid using 'you' blaming ones: 'I get angry when you continue to contradict me' rather than 'You always disagree with everything I say'.

Use tone of voice and intonation to your advantage. Make statements emphatic by finishing them with a downward tone; end questions with an upward lilt. Practise speaking with a lower, clearer voice. The richer and fuller your voice, the more powerful you will appear to be.

Be yourself. Don't try to impress by using long words and complicated sentence structures. Don't use jargon unless you're absolutely sure that the other person is on the same wavelength. Express yourself clearly in a direct, honest and spontaneous way, matching your vocabulary to the person receiving the communication. Think of how you would write a report for the Board of Directors, and the sort of language you would use to write a holiday postcard to a close friend. There will be (one would hope!) quite a difference in style. The same principle applies when speaking to people of different levels of ability intellect or social standing. Use language that the other will understand – that creates rapport by building a climate of trust and understanding – not which proves how smart or senior you are. However, one word of warning. An anecdote will help illustrate my point:

> I was training a group of school midday supervisors, and was astonished to hear that in one school the teaching staff insisted that the supervisors wear nylon overalls, not just in the dining-hall, but for the duration of the lunch-break. On investigating why these staff should be singled out in this way, I was told by a teacher, 'It's so that we know who they are – whether they are teachers, technicians, clerical staff etc'. 'Why do you need to know which staff are the midday supervisors?' I asked. 'So that we know how to talk to them' was the reply. Obviously, the supervisors were seen to be at the bottom of the pack in that school, and were treated and spoken to accordingly!

Language means different things to different people. If I were now to say 'I like to wind down after work by having a good meal' how would you interpret this? Probably through your own values – what you perceive to be 'a good meal'. Would this be dinner for two in a stylish restaurant? Eating with friends in a larger social setting? A relaxed pub meal? In fact, for me it is in thinking about, preparing and cooking food in a way that pleases me. Anticipation and attention to detail is a relaxant. When we hear words we give them meaning, but *our* meaning in the light of our experience and view of the world – not necessarily the speaker's meaning. Unless we listen and question we cannot be sure that what you say and what I interpret (and vice versa) are the same.

Because of this potential slippage between my meaning of the words I use, and your understanding of those words, try to choose 'lean' words when you communicate. 'Fat' words are those which have a multiplicity of meanings and interpretations. What does the word 'functional' mean to you ... or 'product' ... or 'happiness'? Most probably you have very different personal associations with these words, and this will influence your understanding. 'Lean' words are far more precise – less ambiguous. The potential for overlap of understanding is greater if you tighten up on your language. Spend some time with a thesaurus and you will see what I mean. Look up 'fat' words such as 'good' or 'nice' and see the options available to you which more accurately express your meaning.

# Communication styles

Have you ever wondered why it is that you can speak easily and freely to some people, but not others. What is it that sometimes makes conversation stilted and difficult? Below are two theories which will help you to recognize your own communication style, and recognize different communication styles in others so that you can build the necessary communication bridges for more effective interactions. The first is a concept central to Neuro Linguistic Programming (see Chapter 4). It requires careful observation and listening skills, and – I suggest – a lot of practice before you become proficient. The second is a more general observation about how important it is to be flexible in your own style of communicating so that you build rapport rather than create friction.

## Language reflecting sensory preferences

We take in information through the senses. We can all visualize objects and events, all recall sounds from our memory banks, all recapture feelings and emotions from past experience and apply them to current events. However, everyone has a preferred sense. For example, I am basically a visual person and 'see' things in my head rather than initially hearing, feeling, smelling etc. We decode information using our preferred sense. If I were to mention 'fish and chips' what happens in your mind? Do you visualize a plate of fish and chips, smell the typical 'chippy', remember with disgust or delight a recent meal? I see pictures in my head – have a visual bias; you may have internal discussions with yourself, or recall through sound.

These are preferences in thinking patterns and are reflected in the language we prefer to use. I may say things like 'I see what you mean' or 'Look at it this way', and subconsciously choose vocabulary that reflects my visual preference. Imagery I use will be visually based. You may have an auditory preferred sense; your language and your choice of vocabulary and phrasing will reflect this: 'I hear what you're saying' or 'Sounds good to me'. Often, the approach of people with whom you find it difficult to communicate will come from a different preferred thinking style and language. Recognize this, and match their preferred style, and you will begin to build rapport.

An excellent communicator will habitually use language which is rich in all the senses; it is compelling to listen to and reaches a wide audience. There is no point in talking if no one is listening, so it is important to have a wide range of verbal skills if you are to attract and hold attention, and have an impact on the interactions in which you engage. If you practise using language and imagery which appeal to *all* the senses, your people skills will be greatly enhanced.

## Language reflecting temperament

A different, and equally useful approach is to develop the ability to recognize different temperaments in other people, and (initially at least) to match or adapt to their preferred style of communicating. For example, you may have a colleague, boss or subordinate who lives his life in the fast lane. He is likely to talk quickly in short clipped sentences. In conversation he wants just the bare facts. He is intolerant of indecision. You know the type. If you try to slow him down or to involve him in long discussions, he will become impatient or even tetchy. To communicate effectively with him you will need to up your pace. Have facts at your fingertips. Be clear and concise in what you say, restricting detail. Don't be intimidated by him, or leave out necessary information just for the sake of brevity. Be confident and make your self-confidence evident by your clarity of expression and matching demeanour. Make your point clearly, then wait for him to contribute. If the situation demands it, give the information in writing a) to cover your back and b) so that he can peruse detail when convenient to him.

At the other end of the spectrum is the person who just goes on and on, wittering away, beginning with the general and taking an age to get to the specific point, giving every possible detail along the way. I don't suggest that you copy this style – you could spend your entire day in communicating with just this one person! You can help them keep to the point, however, by gently interrupting with questions which keep them on target. You need to be patient – if you get rattled this will not necessarily speed them up; it could embarrass, fluster or antagonize them. If you know in advance that this is the sort of person you will be dealing with, allow plenty of time to listen and probe. Be sensitive to their needs and feelings. If time is really limited, assertively and sensitively explain that time is short, and request an abridged version.

Then there is the perfectionist who is careful, a stickler for detail, is very precise, usually quiet and sometimes 'a loner' and uncommunicative. You need to slow down your pace, be patient, and prepared to give him all the facts and figures he needs. He may need time to consider what you have said before responding, so allow silences – don't jump in to fill the gap with further statements or questions which will only confuse.

These are just three generalizations of different communication styles. There are countless others. What you need to do first is recognize your own preferred style. This may be totally at odds with a person you are having difficulty communicating with – and will do a lot to explain why there seems to be a personality clash. Watch and listen. Recognize the opposing style and respond accordingly. Using this kind of sensitivity, you will be able to match or accommodate their style, putting them at ease and building rapport. Then if appropriate, and through your example, you can lead them to a more mutually acceptable communication level. Gradually you can begin to change your behaviour, and usually, the other person will follow.

In fact, this type of adaptive behaviour is familiar to everyone. Most of us speak and behave differently in different situations to different people anyway, modifying our style to suit the occasion or person. For example, would you use the same language, pace, tone and so on speaking to your partner or parent as you would to the local priest or your solicitor? You automatically fall into a style which puts you and the other person at their ease. In business where language is the currency of success or failure, it may well stand you in good stead to pay more attention to the other person's style and be flexible enough to match and accommodate what you see and hear. Remember that when people are like each other, they like each other.

Of course, the alternative is to keep your own behaviour and communication style the same, and hope that others will adapt to suit you. The chances of this are slight. If you are prepared to match and accommodate others' styles, you are bound to have more success.

# Non-verbal communication

I have used this phrase loosely to describe the whole gambit of messages not literally expressed by the words used. This includes kinesic communication, metacommunication and body language – in other words, actions, gestures, demeanour, hidden meanings and the kind of double-talk described above (e.g. 'It's in the post' meaning 'It's got buried in my in-tray, but I'll fish it out and deal with it now').

## Kinesic communication

This is where you communicate through your actions rather than words. For example, after waiting five minutes to speak with your boss who is talking on the phone, you fling your report down on his desk and march out of his office slamming the door behind you. Actions *do* speak louder than words, and in this instance, could land you in hot water!

Consider the following scenarios and the effects they are likely to have:

1. You are speaking on a personal matter to a colleague on the phone, and can hear by the poor quality of transmission that he has the handset balanced under his chin. You can hear shuffling papers and the occasional rattle of the keyboard as he enters data into his computer.
2. One of the directors has asked to see you and has arranged an interview for 11.00 a.m. It's now 11.30 a.m. and you are still waiting outside his office.
3. You arrive back at work just a few minutes late, but feel justified in having the occasional long lunch-break because of all the early starts and unpaid overtime you put in. A colleague looks pointedly at the wall clock, then to add insult to injury, checks with her wristwatch too.
4. You are visiting your doctor to get the results of some tests. She reads the laboratory notes, shaking her head and frowning. She then sighs, places the notes back in your records and turns to you smiling brightly saying, 'Well there's nothing to worry about there!'

There are two basic lessons to be learnt here. If you are on the receiving end of negative kinesic communication, be assertive enough to state how you feel and explain the effect the other's behaviour is having on you (using 'I' rational statements of course). Ask questions to open up communication, giving the other person a chance to explain. The other lesson is to be extremely careful about your own behaviour and actions. Realize the impact you can have on others without uttering a word. The literal meaning of kinaesthesia is 'sense of muscular effort in voluntary movement'. *Voluntary* movement. Kinesic communication is under our direct control and should be used to enhance people skills rather than the opposite. For example, a genuine smile of welcome, or a 'thumbs up' to share success, can often do far more for a relationship than mere words.

## Metacommunication

These are the unspoken, hidden messages that accompany words. I shall offer another anecdote to explain this concept:

A woman with a tiny infant came into an Adult Education centre. 'Which is the least demanding course you offer?' was her opening question to the receptionist. As this seemed rather an odd inquiry, the receptionist used her eyes, ears and questioning skills to ascertain that in fact the young woman had heard there was a creche facility at the college and was desperate for some time to herself away from the demands of her infant. She felt that by enrolling in an easy class, she could unwind, secure in the knowledge that her baby was in safe hands. It seemed the cheapest and least stressful solution to her problems.

None of this was evident from the words 'What is the least demanding course you offer'. This is a typical example of metacommunication where the meaning *accompanies* the message expressed in words.

The danger in not expressing yourself clearly and honestly is that the insensitive will not pick up your hidden message and merely take the words you utter at face value. Having the confidence to say exactly what you mean takes the burden of 'reading between the lines' from the other person. It also eliminates the chance to use manipulative behaviour, for example saying something like 'please try to come to this meeting' when you really mean 'You haven't attended the last two meetings. It's important that you attend this one; I would like you to be there'.

Every time you speak or act you will convey meanings and ideas to the receiver beyond the words expressed. That is inevitable. When developing your people skills it is important to minimize misunderstandings, and maximize the potential for effective communication, by being aware of the impact kinesic and metacommunications have on any interaction.

The subject of body language is vast, and we could devote pages to discussing it. Suffice it to say here that all the elements of communication must match – what you say, how you say it and your total demeanour – otherwise there is bound to be a degree of confusion on the part of the receiver. As has been shown, actions do speak louder than words, and it will be your body language which has the most impact in any interaction. In fact, statistics show that 55 per cent of the impact you will have on the other person comes from body language, eye contact, gesture, posture, facial expression, 38 per cent from tone of voice, leaving only 7 per cent impact from the actual words used. Every word has shades of meaning depending on intonation and the other factors involved, so these other factors must display congruence.

To show that you are interested and actively listening to the other person, a good degree of eye contact is important. You should lean slightly forward, towards the other person, with head held erect, or slightly to one side. Maintain an open body posture. Sit or stand still without fidgeting, pencil-tapping etc. As discussed briefly above, people who are communicating well and freely will be engaged in a kind of dance, each subconsciously mirroring the other's movements. Those in close rapport will also match tone of voice, volume, speech rhythms and pace of delivery – will even match each other's breathing patterns! By utilizing this phenomenon, i.e. mirroring, not mimicking, matching distribution of body weight and posture, effectiveness will improve.

The antithesis of this – consciously breaking away from mirroring – gives the other person the cue that the communication is at an end. By changing tonality or pace, or changing your body weight so that you begin to physically back away from the interaction, the other person will pick up the message that you are ready to close the dialogue.

Some final thoughts about encouraging and discouraging messages: always appear confident, relaxed and in control. Behaviour is infectious, and you will achieve more successful outcomes if you generate these positive feelings.

Be careful to meet the other person on as equal a footing as possible by creating the correct environment for win/win communication. Think about your environment because the formality or informality of the communication will be dictated, to an extent, by your surroundings. For example, two people trying to communicate alone in a high ceilinged, large room, will tend to do so in hushed tones.

For difficult interactions, consider carefully whether it would be better to meet on your territory, theirs or on neutral ground. If you are sitting, choose comfortable seats of the same height (someone sitting higher has a subtle dominance and advantage over the other). Don't put yourself or the other person facing a bright window as the glare is distracting. Avoid barriers; don't hide behind the comfort of your desk.

Don't invade the other's space. It is off-putting to have someone standing or sitting just that bit too close for social convention.

Remember that when another person is present, you can't *not* communicate with him. Some message is conveyed, even if you say nothing and keep absolutely still!

# 3 Assertiveness

Assertiveness training has been around for a long time now, so hopefully the confusion between assertive behaviour and aggressive behaviour – held by many sceptical about such training – is becoming a thing of the past. Assertiveness is now seen for what it is: an excellent aid to self-development and an important aspect of people skills. You cannot become assertive by reading words on a page, however. As with all interpersonal skills training, you need practice, and preferably the guidance and feedback of facilitators and fellow trainees. I recommend you attend training sessions. This chapter will give you some idea of what assertiveness training is about, but in itself, it will not make you assertive.

Assertion training has tended to be a 'how to' type of training, taking in elements such as how to handle criticism; how to give constructive feedback; how to say 'no' without feeling guilty. It instructs in how to choose appropriate words and phrases and to match these with congruent intonation, volume, facial expression and other aspects of non-verbal communication. It encourages building interpersonal relationships through active listening and questioning skills, and being direct and honest within a communication. It teaches respecting the other person's rights without neglecting your own. It allows for a choice of behaviour, assertiveness being one in a repertoire of options, but one which needs practice.

Until you are practised, and especially in difficult situations, assertive behaviour is not always the easy option. It is simpler, sometimes, to stand back and say nothing or to agree rather than make a scene (non-assertive/passive), or to 'lose your cool' (aggressive), but as will be shown later in this section, short-term fixes are seldom the best solutions – for either party.

Assertion is a self-generating process – the more assertive you become, the more your confidence and self-esteem will grow. However, unless you are a very good actor, you would be well advised to look to developing a positive self-image, because being assertive, especially initially and if your natural tendency has been to behave in a non-assertive way, requires you to counter negative feelings and doubts, and to halt that inner dialogue which tells you 'I can't' or 'I shouldn't'. It requires you to stay calm and relaxed even in the face of aggression, rudeness or anger. However appropriate your choice of words, without belief in yourself, it is easy for facial expression, tone of voice or body language to give you away.

So, this section will look at the various elements which make up basic assertiveness training; then apply these principles to the working situation. It will also look at the power of positive thought and relaxation as an aid to assertiveness. But first, a thought about why it is important to develop assertiveness skills.

## Why is it important to develop assertiveness skills?

The alternatives to assertive behaviour are aggression – basically where your own needs are put first – and non-assertive, passive behaviour – where you allow your wants, needs, ideas, opinions to be undermined. There is a long continuum between the two extremes, and variations on the themes are innumerable. We all use all three behaviour styles depending on the situation, and will continue, at times, to be more aggressive in our approach; at times, non-assertive if the situation calls for it. Behaviour is contagious. If you behave aggressively towards someone, he is likely to rise to the bait and become aggressive also. Far better to be a role model for assertive behaviour in the hope that the other person will emulate your style and work with, rather than against you. The more times you can choose to act assertively, the more you reduce the risk of conflict and misunderstandings. Assertive behaviour opens opportunities for constructive dialogue, healthy relationships and satisfactory outcomes. It communicates an impression of self-respect, and respect for the other person.

Assertiveness involves being honest and direct in your communication; listening to, understanding and respecting the other person's views even if you disagree with them. They have a right to their opinions, values and beliefs; the right to state their wants and needs; to be listened to and taken seriously – as do you.

Let's look briefly at the consequences of the three behaviour styles.

# Consequences of aggressive behaviour

There will be times when situations demand an aggressive response. In the short term it may appear that aggressive behaviour pays off. You can let off steam, and feel momentarily better for it. You might have 'got one over' the other chap, and feel smug and content. You could have made a sarcastic rejoinder, and patted yourself on the back for being so witty. You may have used (or abused?) your power and authority in a meeting, or 'won' your point through the force of your delivery. You may 'win' – get your own way in a disagreement.

But how about the long-term effects on yourself and other people? Your letting off steam might leave you feeling embarrassed or guilty; it could have damaged relationships. If you score points at the expense of another, that person may either not want to do business with you again, or look for ways to retaliate. Sarcasm may leave the other person feeling hurt, humiliated or put down. They may well feel anger towards you, or avoid communicating with you. Aggressiveness in business is often seen as a prerequisite to success, but people who feel they have been 'bulldozed' into acquiesence – at meetings or elsewhere – will be resentful. Some will wait to get their own back in overt or subtle ways. You may win the battle but lose the war, jeopardizing career opportunities and friends along the way. Sustained aggressive behaviour seldom pays off.

Physically, you suffer from aggressive behaviour. True, sometimes it's beneficial to express your anger, frustration or outrage rather than suppress your emotion, and it's beneficial to acknowledge and express strong feelings. Handled in an aggressive way, however, your blood pressure will rise and you may be susceptible to related illness such as headaches, indigestion, ulcers and other stress-related conditions.

As a manager, if you often adopt aggressive behaviour towards your staff, you could stifle initiative, breed resentment, and ultimately be the cause of absenteeism and high staff turnover rates. An organizational culture where managerial in-fighting is the order of the day is setting itself up to failure in today's climate of competition and change. Managers' energies should be utilized in meeting customer needs, creating an empowered environment, co-operating, using initiative to open up new markets – not scoring points at the expense of each others' interests.

# Consequences of non-assertive behaviour

As with aggressive behaviour, there will be times when you choose to be passive. For example, if a retired ex-member of staff, recently released from hospital after an operation, calls in unexpectedly, and you had hoped to spend the next hour on your report, it might be churlish to assertively state your priorities and send her away. You would probably choose to be assertive by stating your limits (see below) but non-assertive by taking time out to listen and talk. Generally, though, non-assertive behaviour does you no favours; neither ultimately will it win you friends or influence people. It communicates a feeling of inferiority. It can be damaging to relationships, and to your own self-esteem.

As with aggressive behaviour, you may feel good about the consequences in the short term. If a colleague asks you to change days off and although you don't want to because this will entail changing your social arrangements, you agree, you may well feel 'noble' about giving in. You might be pleased that you have given him satisfaction; grateful that you won't go home feeling guilty about refusing and so on. In the long-term, he might see you as 'an easy touch' and keep asking favours knowing you will find it hard to refuse. And what about your needs, and the needs of the people who were affected by your change of social arrangements? How will they feel about you? How will you feel about yourself, knowing that by avoiding one difficult situation, you have possibly created several others? You may well end up feeling sorry for yourself, blaming others for always putting on you, or becoming angry at yourself for your lack of 'backbone'.

Other aspects of non-assertion are the inability to take responsibility for your own life, finding it hard to stand up for yourself, being unable to use or capitalize on initiative, finding it hard to make decisions. Initially others may feel protective towards, or sorry for you, but this reaction can soon turn to annoyance and impatience. Persistent non-assertive behaviour can lead to lack of respect from others, and no respect for self. Negative self-image and lack of confidence escalate. Others may avoid contact rather than risk irritation through passive behaviour patterns.

For a manager, non-assertive behaviour can lead to lost opportunities. Rather than resolving conflict, it will be avoided. Important decisions will be deferred. This has a knock-on effect; problems and tensions could well escalate. If you cannot assert yourself with customers, suppliers, directors, other managers, colleagues and staff, you will ultimately lose their respect.

Passive behaviour can result in inner tensions, bringing similar physical symptoms to those caused by continuous aggressive behaviour. Paradoxically, it is common for someone habitually passive, and unable to react assertively to difficult situations, to suddenly be pushed too far and over-react with aggressive behaviour. Another paradox is that both aggressive behaviour and non-assertive behaviour often stem from the same source – low self-esteem. You find yourself in a difficult situation and the 'fight or flight' response comes into play. The tendency is to react aggressively, give in, or withdraw from the situation rather than respond assertively. This is why it's so important to develop a positive self-image and inner dialogue, and to practise assertive behaviour.

## Consequences of assertive behaviour

You may well be assertive much of the time, but no one is consistently assertive. Most people use all three behaviour styles throughout their lives. However, it will improve your communication skills if you can recognize the difference between the three, in yourself and others, so that you have a realistic choice of behaviour in any given circumstance, with any person. You can learn to be more assertive most of the time.

Being assertive means taking responsibility for your own behaviour, rather than letting others influence you. The benefit of assertive behaviour is that you are in control of your life. You will know your rights, beliefs and responsibilities, and respect the fact that everyone has similar rights. You will have a better idea of how to present your views while being sensitive to the needs and feelings of the other person. You will be equipped to deal with conflict. You will feel able to state your own opinions and emotions without feeling threatened because you will know how to recognize and respond to affirmations, criticisms or put-downs. You will be able to ask for what you want knowing that the other has a right to refuse, assured that even if you don't get what you want, at least the other person knows your views and where you stand on the issue. You can leave the interaction still feeling good about yourself. You will be able to refuse requests without feeling challenged or guilty. Your self-esteem and confidence will grow so that you can become more proactive in your life rather than waiting for events to force you into reactive or avoidance behaviours.

## The 'feel good' factor

Knowing yourself 'warts and all' is a significant part of effective assertiveness. You need to do some self-analysis to find out the things you like about yourself and don't want to change, the things you don't like about yourself but truly can't change, and the things you don't like about yourself that you could change – with a little help and guidance. You are aiming to reach a position where you value and feel good about yourself and can meet 'the world and his wife' with confidence that you will respect their needs without neglecting your own. In order to deal effectively with others, you must first accept that *you* are the most important person in your world. This is not self-centredness, but sense. From the aggressive standpoint, you will be able better to respect others if your own self-esteem is healthy; from the passive standpoint, you will recognize that you can have an equally high regard for yourself as you do for other people.

Often, negative self-images are created in childhood by what we were told by parents, teachers and other adults. The phenomenon of self-fulfilling prophecy is at work here. We feel or experience what we expect to feel or experience. If you are told that you are clumsy often enough, you will believe it to be true and consequently behave in a clumsy fashion. Similarly with feelings: some are instinctive and not under our conscious control; others are learnt and have been self-perpetuated through experience. A situation arises where you need to assert yourself. Your computer-type mind instantly rifles through its databank looking for similar situations and experiences. How did you respond then? Your feelings and emotions will also instantly come into play. Past feelings are likely to be replicated in the current situation. Chances are your previous experience and feelings will colour the way you respond to the present situation. If you get a similar outcome, this will reaffirm either your acceptable handling of the situation, entrench you in non-assertive behaviour ('I knew it would turn out this way') or escalate aggressive behaviour ('I knew he wouldn't agree, but at least I gave him a piece of my mind! Wait until next time . . . I'll show him a thing or two!). Experience reinforces and justifies what you believe, more and more.

Poor self-esteem is largely a problem of awareness. The human inclination is to become precisely that which we imagine ourselves to be. Recognizing this is vital for self-improvement. Assertiveness training will enable you to unravel unwanted, programmed behaviour patterns. Conditioned behaviours are learned, and what was learnt can be unlearnt and replaced with more appropriate behaviours.

## Barriers to assertive behaviour

Irrational fears, and inner dialogues which 'catastrophize', block effective assertiveness. If you let misgivings take hold of you, you will almost certainly operate in a non-assertive style. If you are forever held back by 'what if . . . ?' type thoughts, you will find it difficult to behave in a proactive way, to initiate, make decisions or express yourself clearly and directly.

Think of situations where you find it difficult to speak out. Some of the most common reasons are as follows:

- the need to be liked, e.g. 'she may think less of me if I speak out'
- fear of criticism

- fear of rejection
- fear of disapproval
- fear of an argument
- relationships might change; friendship might be threatened
- fear of making a fool of yourself: clamming up; blushing; getting emotional; not being able to think of the right words to express yourself; losing your cool etc.

# Internal dialogues

We all hold internal conversations with ourselves, all the time. To become more assertive, learn to recognize that inner voice which holds you back, or winds you up, and replace negative and unproductive thinking with constructive positive thoughts. Rather than catastrophizing, or justifying to yourself your non-assertive behaviour, rethink your inner dialogue with a 'can do' attitude. Typical examples of self-delusion are:

'I'll assert myself if . . .

1. I'm feeling on top of things'
2. I feel the other person can take it'
3. someone else doesn't speak up'
4. I'm pushed to my limits'
5. the time is right'
6. I'm sure of my ground'
7. it's on someone else's behalf'
8. I don't feel intimidated by the other person'
9. I can be sure of the outcome'
10. it won't cause a scene'
11. I'm sure my voice won't shake'
12. I can find the right words'.

Are any of these excuses for not being assertive familiar to you?
There are many, many more. Let's look at the possible consequences of not being assertive in each of these instances:

1. You will feel more 'on top of things' if you speak your mind in a clear, honest and assertive way, even if the outcome is not ideal for you. At least you will have made your views known, and the other person will know where they stand.
2. If you respect, and are sensitive to the feelings of the other person, your communication will come across as caring and empathetic. You

are responsible for how you communicate, and provided you've taken all reasonable care, you cannot accept responsibility for how the other person receives your communication.

3.  There will be many lost opportunities in your life if you wait for someone else to say what is in your mind.

4.  If you wait until you are pushed to your limits, your words and manner will probably be aggressive. Far better to tackle things when they are small in a constructive, assertive way.

5.  Sometimes it is important to choose the right moment to open a dialogue. For example, it would be foolhardy to decide to tell your partner that you don't want your in-laws staying for Christmas, when she has just come in, hot, tired and frustrated from an unproductive day's work. However, for the non-assertive, there is *never* a good time to broach a difficult situation. Sometimes you have got to take the bull by the horns.

6.  Yes, it is better to get your facts straight before launching into a dialogue, but sometimes you have to take risks. An assertive person will put his point across in a clear, succinct way, and actively listen to the other person. If the other's position turns out to be sound, he will be big enough to acknowledge this – in an assertive, not a grudging way.

7.  Most of us find it easy to stand up for someone else, but not so easy to be assertive in our own right. It is not being assertive, however, to continually solve other people's problems for them, to jump in where you're not needed, or to feel that you have to take responsibility for another person's life.

8.  When you feel intimidated by another person, whether because of his (perceived) greater knowledge, better education, social position, status, or because of his aggressive or bombastic manner, this is the very time when you most need to practise your assertive skills, because the human tendency will be to either go in 'all guns blazing' (attack is the best form of defence) or to be deferential and passive.

9.  However well you plan an interaction, you can never be sure of the outcome. However, with assertive handling, a win/win outcome is far more likely.

10.  Neither can you be sure of another person's reaction, and sometimes difficult situations, however assertively handled, can result in the other person getting angry, hurt, upset or moody. You can't hold yourself responsible for their reaction to your assertive request, refusal, feedback, self-affirmation etc. Remember that behaviour is

contagious. Keep calm and assertive, and hopefully scenes will be avoided and rational dialogue can take place.

11. Contemplating difficult interactions can be nerve-wracking. See Relaxation below on voice control.

12. With training and practice, you will be able to find the words and phrases; also delivery techniques for tactful and effective assertive communication.

If you know that you are going to have a difficult discussion with someone, plan ahead. Recognize and eliminate faulty internal dialogue beforehand. Get rid of all negative self-talk. Think through why you're thinking in this way and how rational your thinking really is. For example, you may feel that your assertion may start a row. Ask yourself if this is unavoidable. Probably not. If you phrase your opening in such and such a way, is it inevitable that an argument will ensue? Probably not. You may have an uncomfortable few minutes, but you can handle that. He may get angry or defensive, but you can cope and point out the effects of his behaviour in a constructive way without getting aggressive. You will listen carefully to his point of view without interrupting or getting defensive. You can assertively guide the conversation from conflict to a joint problem-solving exercise.

Become emotionally literate – in other words acknowledge the feelings associated with your negative self-talk. There's nothing wrong in feeling angry or embarrassed or hurt, and it's healthy to accept and express these feelings rather than bottle them up. Practise defining and stating your feelings, e.g. 'I feel very angry when . . .' or 'I am nervous about . . .' or 'I get anxious if . . .' . However, feelings associated with your self-talk may not be the most appropriate or productive for the particular situation, so as you change your inner dialogue, check your feelings too. You can learn new emotional responses by positive self-talk. Create a sound inner dialogue, and your confidence and ability to handle the situation, whatever is thrown at you, will increase.

If you are taken unawares by a situation where you suddenly find yourself taking a non-assertive stance, check your inner dialogue. Pause for a few seconds to slow things down and to recreate a sound self-image. Remember, with assertiveness skills at your disposal, you can handle anything. With practice, you can control unwanted feelings and not be fazed by others' aggressive or non-assertive behaviour.

Negative self-talk also gets in the way of positive action. Eliminate 'if only's', 'shoulds' and excuses 'why I can't' from your vocabulary. Look for positive alternatives. For example, instead of saying 'I really should phone Mary and arrange a meeting' replace this woolly thinking with either 'I will phone Mary today to arrange a meeting' or 'I'm too busy today, so I won't phone Mary to arrange a meeting'. You can then eliminate niggling pressures and guilts, and get on with your day.

# Relaxation

The very times when it is important to keep your cool or to be assured and confident are those when it is most difficult to be assertive: for example, the presentation which is causing you sleepless nights, or the time when you have to give bad news to one of your staff, or the encounter with a competitor's top negotiator. However well you prepare, choosing the right words and phrases, rehearsing timing, intonation, volume and tone, and so on, if your shaking voice or body language let's you down, you're sunk. Actions really do speak louder than words, and non-verbal communication is far more powerful than the spoken word.

Of course, developing a healthy inner dialogue sets you on course for successful communication. Being relaxed and in control will help even further. The remit of this book doesn't allow an in-depth look at meditation and relaxation techniques – there are plenty of books and courses on the subject and in any case, it's a subjective subject. What works for me may not work for you.

What I would like to share are just two simple ideas to effect relaxation. The first is a way to release tension in the body and is important because inner tension is visible in posture, in the set of the jaw and so on. Your tension will be conveyed to the other person/people and your effectiveness will suffer. Tense every muscle in the body, simultaneously. Clench toes, tighten calf and thigh muscles, clench buttocks, make tight fists. If the situation allows it, screw up your face as well, stretching and tightening all your muscles as much as you can. Hold just for a second or two, then let go, going completely limp. This is quick, simple, effective, and can be done at any time.

Another easy to do at any time technique is what Dorothy Sarnoff in her book *Never be Nervous Again* (Century Hutchinson, London, 1988) calls the Sarnoff Squeeze. With your forearms horizontal to the floor, press your hands tightly together while contracting the muscles between the ribs where they begin to splay (imagine you are rowing a boat against a strong current, pulling back, up and in). Breath out as you are contracting these muscles, through your teeth with a slight hiss. Relax and inhale gently. According to Ms Sarnoff, contracting these muscles prevents the body from manufacturing the tension- and fear-producing chemicals in your system and gives you additional physical energy. It reduces negative feelings like anger or stress and, because the diaphragm is involved in the contractions, aids projection and stops the quiver in the voice associated with nervousness or apprehension.

# Finding the right words (see also Chapter 1)

Don't try to be someone you're not – be yourself and use language which both suits the situation, and with which you are comfortable. Consider your audience – their education, social standing and status. Here are some simple rules you can follow in choosing assertive words and phrases:

- Choose words that are clear, direct, honest and which show respect for the other person.
- Use humour wisely; sarcasm can hurt or be taken as a put-down and, therefore, as aggressive behaviour.
- Don't patronize or talk down to people. This too can be seen as aggressive.
- Don't waffle; you will be seen as indecisive and non-assertive.
- Choose words which are constructive and positive, rather than destructive and negative.
- Avoid jargon or technical language unless you're sure the other person is on the same wavelength.
- Take responsibility for your opinions by using 'I' statements; so rather than saying 'It might be a good idea if we . . .' or 'My director feels that the price is too high' take ownership of your views; ' I think we should . . .' or 'I feel the price is too high'.
- Take ownership of your thoughts and feelings, e.g. 'I feel angry when he . . .' rather than 'he makes me angry when . . .'.
- Phrase in a positive way, e.g. 'Would you finish the photocopying after the meeting please' rather than 'Don't use the photocopier while this meeting is in progress'.
- Eliminate blaming 'you' statements from your vocabulary, e.g. 'You left the door unlocked again' replace with 'Please check that the door is locked before you leave; it was left unlocked again last night'. Talk about behaviour not personality.
- Don't generalize, e.g. 'You always leave the door unlocked'. It is unlikely that someone *always* is or does anything.
- Don't be judgemental, e.g. 'You are so careless' when a factual description of the behaviour you would like to change would be far more constructive.
- Be direct with your requests, e.g. 'Would you pass me form A592 please', rather than, 'I don't suppose you could get me a form A592 could you?'

- Don't address a group with an issue which just concerns one person, e.g. if timekeeping is a problem with just one of your team, don't say to the whole group that timekeeping must improve, hoping that the offender will take the point. He may not, and you could offend other team members. This is manipulative behaviour. The assertive approach is to talk privately with the poor timekeeper about the issue.

## Manner of delivery

Even if you choose all the right words, if the tone of your voice and intonation don't match the content, you will not be perceived as assertive. Your behaviour will dictate how the other person responds, so if your tone is too loud or abrasive you will appear aggressive, if you speak too softly or hesitatingly, you could appear passive – the other person gains control and will respond accordingly.

Try saying the following sentence, putting emphasis on a different word each time.

'Will you shut that door please?'

You will see how inflection totally changes meaning. It's hardly surprising that when asked to explain an interaction which has gone badly, people respond, 'Well I only said . . . !' They may have used those precise words, but *how* they said it makes all the difference.

## Non-verbal communication and body language (see also Chapter 1)

You can show that you are listening and interested in the other person by making encouraging noises – 'uh huh', 'mmm' etc. and by nodding, smiling and so on. Your facial expression, gestures and body language all form part of the integral whole which is communication. Because actions really do speak louder than words, and it will be your non-verbal communication which carries the greatest impact, it is important to use this element of the communication process to full and good effect.

A typically aggressive posture is standing tall – drawing yourself up to your full height, hands on hips, elbows out. Imagine the pointing or wagging finger, and you have a good impression of aggressive behaviour in full flight! Brows are drawn into a frown or scowl; smiles do not reach the eyes, which remain stony. Eye contact is likely to be too constant – to the point of staring. The jaw will be tense and possibly jutting. Anger is often shown by talking through gritted teeth. The face is often flushed as blood pressure rises.

Extreme passive behaviour, on the other hand, is characterized by withdrawn posture, slumped and curled in on itself. There will be 'crossing' gestures – protecting the body by tightly crossing arms or intertwined legs. Passive people tend not to look the other person in the eye or, paradoxically, gaze at the other person in meek subjection, hanging on their every word. There is likely to be nervous fidgeting and mannerisms, embarrassed smiles or a look of dejection. The face may become increasingly pale, or flushed with embarrassment.

Assertive behaviour is demonstrated by an open upright stance with hands hanging loosely at sides or in the lap. There will be little crossing of arms or legs unless in an obviously relaxed way. There is much palm-showing (indicating you have nothing to hide). Facial expression will be responsive, relaxed and appropriate to the situation, although a smile will never be far away. The overall impression is one of calm confidence with no excessive mannerisms or jerky movements. There will be regular eye contact to show involvement and interest. The other person's space will not be invaded (as is often the case with aggressive posturing).

Body language and non-verbal signals are usually decoded at a sub-conscious level and this is a very brief outline of a very complex subject – one which you do not need to study in depth in order to become more assertive. However, having some awareness is very important to assertiveness training, both in reading signals others are sending to you, and ensuring that all aspects of your communication are congruent.

Before leaving the subject of non-verbal communication, a word about image. You can do little about your height, the colour of your eyes or the size of your feet, but you can and should take care of things you can control concerning self-presentation. This includes things such as your appearance, and dressing appropriately for the event or situation. For example, if I want to maintain credibility as a trainer, I wouldn't stand in front of a group of managers dressed in T-shirt, jeans and trainers, but I might choose this style of dress if running a practical session on an outward-bound course. Presentation also includes elements such as colour choice. Do you think carefully of the impression you are going to create by wearing dull, pastel or bright colours? What about colour combinations? How do you feel wearing different shades? Which give you confidence; in which situations?

# Making requests

Bear with me if I seem to be stating the obvious, but before you make a request, first decide precisely what it is that you want, and from whom. Consult your inner voice and first ensure that you're inner dialogue is healthy and sound. If you feel good about yourself, you are more likely to achieve a win/win outcome. If you are still inwardly catastrophizing or feeling apprehensive you will not feel comfortable about asking for what you want, and will relinquish control to the other person. If you mentally get yourself into battle mode, you are likely to come over as aggressive and demanding – hardly the recipe for long-term success.

You also need to decide who to ask because often we express our needs to some third party in the hope that somehow they will transmit our request, accurately, to the person concerned. Daft isn't it, but I'm sure we've all been guilty of this non-assertive, manipulative ploy rather than confidently making a request, face-to-face, of the person who can do something about our wants or preferences.

So, take the bull by the horns and make your request in a clear, concise way, ensuring that elements of your communication – words, tone, pace, volume, etc – are synchronized: 'I would like you to type this out again' or 'I'd prefer a touring holiday this year'.

When you are confidently assertive, you no longer need to worry about rejection or what will happen if your request is refused. You have had the strength of character to make your needs known; others know where they stand with you. It will serve you well in future communications with them.

# Broken Record

As the name implies, this is a technique whereby you restate your case, over and over, until the other person gets the message. It can be used to good effect in making and refusing requests. The idea is not necessarily to use the same words, parrot-like, but to repeat your request or refusal, if necessary using different phrasing and word clusters, adding empathetic comments to 'cushion the effect', suggesting workable compromises if appropriate, respecting the other person's views, but never, never getting side-tracked from your own needs. It goes something like this:

Bill:   Jack, it will be OK for you to work the late shift on Saturday for me won't it?

Jack:   We're going to a party on Saturday night, Bill, so no, I won't be able to work Saturday night.

Bill: But I've already made arrangements for Saturday – you've always helped out in the past.

Jack: Yes, I usually help out if I can, but this Saturday I've arranged to go out, so no, I won't be able to work that shift.

Bill: Well you've really dropped me in it – what am I going to say to Elaine? She's so looking forward to Saturday.

Jack: I can understand that you're upset Bill, and if I could help I would, but I've made a commitment so no, I won't be able to work that shift for you.

You will notice that each time the refusal is made, the word 'no' is used, leaving Bill in no doubt about the strength of Jack's refusal. Jack doesn't use the word 'can't' which implies 'I would if I could, but ...' which could leave him open to persuasion. Jack could have gone on to suggest a workable compromise if he felt it could be offered without neglecting his own needs. For example, 'I've got to get to the party by 10.00 p.m. so we could split the shift; I could work the first three hours if that's any use'. If Bill can't find this acceptable, Jack would then go back to his Broken Record.

As with asking for what you want, listen carefully to your inner voice telling you what you truly want or don't want to do. You must learn to say 'yes' and 'no' to yourself too, act on these feelings, and become comfortable with them.

# Saying 'no' and setting limits

The persistent refusal as illustrated above, is a good way of saying 'no' and sticking to it. Most of us find it easy to say 'no' sometimes and with some people. For example, managers may be relatively guilt-free in refusing unreasonable staff requests, but find it almost impossible to say 'no' to their own bosses or directors. Assertiveness training gives you the skills to say 'no' to anyone, in any situation – if that is your honest choice at the time.

Again, the first step is to listen to that inner voice, or to use another anatomical expression, what is your gut reaction to the request made of you? Ask yourself, 'Do I really want to do this, or am I agreeing for some other reason, e.g. to please someone else, to avoid a scene, because I'll feel guilty if I don't?'

Then make your choice. As stated earlier, sometimes you may choose to be non-assertive and say yes when you would prefer to say 'no'. Ensure you make your choice for the right reasons. Having decided to say 'no', here are some tips about how to do this assertively:

- Only say 'sorry' if you genuinely are, and only say it once. Unnecessary 'sorries' and over-apologizing will only weaken your case.
- Say 'no' firmly and calmly. You don't have to say the 'no' word first, if you feel uncomfortable with this, but ensure that the word appears somewhere in your refusal: 'I'd prefer not to travel on a Sunday, so no, I won't be able to make the 9.00 a.m. start.'
- Keep your communication short and to the point. You can give an explanation for your refusal if appropriate, but don't over-justify or give too much detail.
- Don't make excuses. If you are going to give a reason for your refusal, make it a genuine one.
- If appropriate, add an empathetic statement such as 'Thanks for asking me Clare; I can see it's important to you, but I'm not prepared to ... so no ...'.
- If the requester is persistent, don't search around for better or alternative reasons why you have to refuse – more reasons won't strengthen your case; it will weaken it and give the other person more ammunition.
- Use language and phrasing with which you are comfortable, but do practice actually saying the word 'no'.
- Remember that actions speak louder than words. Check your eye contact, gestures, facial expressions and so on, so that every aspect of your communication is in harmony.

There will be occasions when it is possible to offer a workable compromise or where, having listened to the other person, you feel that you can negotiate towards a win/win solution. Your refusal might only be for this precise minute, e.g. 'No, I can't speak to you now as I'm due in a meeting, but I'll call you back in half an hour' or 'No I can't commit myself to that, but I would be prepared to halve what you suggest'. You may be willing to agree to a request, but not on the terms laid down by the other person: 'Yes, I could do that, but only if ...' or 'No, I can't type the whole manuscript, but if you don't mind my using a pool typist ...'.

There will also be times when you need to set limits: 'I'm not prepared to receive calls or visitors before 9.30 a.m.' Be responsible for what you want, and let others know precisely what your limits are. As with saying 'no' you need to be clear and concise, giving reasons as appropriate.

# Giving feedback

When management was largely about direction and control, managers felt the need constantly to be checking employees' work for accuracy, ensuring that standards were being met, and pressing for increased output. Often, this entailed a 'carrot and stick' approach where criticism of errors and working methods featured more than praise and encouragement for work well done. Happily, while elements such as accuracy and output are still important, today's managers are more concerned with creating an empowered workforce, where motivation, encouragement and praise are the order of the day. They are more aware that people work best in a supportive and positive environment. Criticism is looked on as constructive feedback where both parties can jointly look at problem areas and come up with solutions.

What is your opinion of praise? Do you welcome it, or find it embarrassing or patronizing? One survey found that the majority of people questioned were uncomfortable with praise, and I suggest it was because of past experience where 'you' statements were used. Consider the difference between these two statements:

> 'That's great; you are brilliant!'
> 'I'm delighted with the report; every aspect we discussed has been covered fully. Thanks a lot.'

Everyone likes to feel that they are valued and their efforts appreciated. Most will prefer to receive specific, detailed feedback to which they can relate. Gushing praise may give a short-term 'high' but doesn't tell the recipient why or how he's excelled. It could also leave him feeling vaguely uneasy.

People learn from success. Encouraging others by giving descriptive feedback on what they have done effectively, instils a pride which is self-generating. People will be motivated to work harder to replicate and improve on their success. It is an important people skill, therefore, to recognize that people thrive on positive feedback. If your staff do a good job, tell them, using clear descriptive phrases. Never take good work for granted. Don't be embarrassed to let them know how their efforts affect you, e.g. 'I'm really grateful that you put in those extra hours; we've met the delivery date with some to spare. Thanks.' or 'I'm excited about the new idea for ... let's give it a go'. If expressing gratitude, celebrating success or complimenting staff in this way is new to you or does not come naturally, be especially careful of body language. Maintain regular eye contact; don't let your temporary unease show. The positive results you get from giving positive feedback will soon make it second nature to you!

While it is important to build on strengths rather than continually address weaknesses and mistakes, it is sometimes necessary to criticize. First, some thoughts on your state of mind when contemplating giving criticism.

Positive thinking is the order of the day. There is no point in putting off the evil moment in the hope that the problem will go away. It most probably won't, and the longer you leave an issue which needs to be confronted, the more difficult it will be. Metaphorical molehills will become mountains in your mind, and the problem itself may well escalate over time.

Check your inner dialogue and dispel thoughts such as 'there's nothing I can do about it' or 'I've tried talking with him before – it's useless'. Rationalize this negativity and replace unhelpful self-talk with confidence-building, sound inner dialogue such as 'It will be difficult, but not impossible. I have the right to get him to accept responsibility' or 'I won't assume she is being deliberately uncooperative. I'll explain things again to her. Even if she does get indignant, I can handle it'.

Remember that you have the right to want people to improve; they have the right to be told in a clear, descriptive, non-judgemental way what is wrong with their performance or behaviour so that they can correct, adapt or change. You will need to listen and question well (see Chapter 1). It is up to you to phrase your criticism assertively so that behaviour, not personality is discussed, you don't put the other person, down or make them look small. This will involve some forward planning as to the 'where, when and how' you give the criticism. Here are a few tips about this forward planning:

- Choose somewhere quiet, private, and where you won't be disturbed.
- Remember to synchronize tonality, inflection, pace, volume, non-verbal communication and body language.
- Don't leap straight in with accusations or judgemental statements. Preface your criticism with something like, 'John, I'd like to talk to you about . . .' or 'Marie, I've noticed that . . . why is this?'
- Set a context. Explain how the other person's behaviour affects you, the organization, and himself. Be succinct – don't give masses of detail initially – let him respond.
- Don't blame; try to get the other person to recognize that a problem exists, then jointly look for a way forward.
- Use 'I' statements: 'I think . . .' or 'It seems to me that . . .' or 'I'm not happy about . . .'.
- Avoid phrases such as 'It has been brought to my attention', implying a third party involvement.
- Ascertain facts; seek information; listen well.
- Summarize and clarify to avoid misunderstandings.
- Don't confuse the issue by talking about too many problems; address the current issue only.

- Talk about behaviour – what he has done or not done – rather than what you think he *is*: 'there are five mistakes in this' rather than 'you're careless'.
- Be specific and objective.
- Get agreement to your criticism, then go on to ascertain why the problem has occurred and what needs to be done to put things back on the right course.
- Encourage the other person to suggest what can be done to bring about the required change.
- Throughout remain calm and firm; don't be tempted to meet resistance with aggression, or to back down.
- Close the interaction by summarizing what has been agreed about the changes the other person is to make and confirming time-scales, monitoring arrangements and so on.

If you follow these guidelines, paying particular attention to your own assertive style while recognizing the rights of the other person, the outcome should be a positive one.

# Receiving feedback

You may well become the most considerate and effective giver of criticism, but this does not shield you from receiving criticism from others who are less skilled. Often we have to parry aggressive outbursts, personal attacks and put-downs from colleagues and managers as well as people from our 'other life', outside work. Whereas, when giving criticism you usually have some time to plan your approach, these criticisms can come 'out of the blue' and unless your self-esteem and confidence are sound, can take you unawares, leaving you vulnerable and likely to over- or under-react.

Being able to handle criticism, in whatever guise it presents itself, is a major step towards being fully in control. Take a few seconds to get in touch with your internal self-talk and to evaluate the criticism. For example, through your assertiveness training you will have realized that there are certain sensitive areas peculiar to you, that if touched upon will ignite your anger or set up defensive mechanisms. Knock these unproductive feelings on the head! Recognize the criticism for what it is. Remember, it is the content of the criticism which has to be addressed, not how it is phrased or what you think is implied by your critic.

Is the criticism valid and justified? Is some of it justified, but surrounded by judgemental or generalized opinion? Is it unjustified? Is it a put-down, subtle or otherwise? Is it constructive criticism about which you should try to get more detail?

Yes, this is a lot to think about in the second or two you can allow yourself before responding, but seconds well spent nevertheless. If you are also comfortable with the fact that you cannot be responsible for the way the other person is reacting or feeling, you can deal with any criticism objectively and calmly.

You can buy yourself time, and clarify the criticism by reflecting back: 'I'm unprofessional in my dealing with clients? I'd find it helpful, Jane, if you could give me some instances when this occurred.' Alternatively, you could ask a question such as 'I see. What is it, precisely, about my manner which you consider unprofessional Jane?'

If the criticism is valid, say so – 'Yes, I have made a mess of that . . .'. Nobody's perfect and we all make mistakes from time to time. Apologize once and sincerely, and set about putting things right. If the criticism is justified, but phrased as a personal attack, you would address these two distinct issues. Separate yourself from the criticism – you are not your mistakes. Try to consider the content of the criticism rather than the way it was given: 'You're right; I could have handled that better Ken. However, I resent your saying that . . .'

If the criticism is unwarranted, say so with conviction, using 'I' statements: 'I don't accept that'. Even better if you can add a statement of self-affirmation, e.g. 'I don't accept that; I am very conscientious'.

Put-downs are not easy to recognize as they can be said as a joke, or as part of an otherwise innocuous conversation. It may be only on reflection that you think 'wait a minute, what did he mean by . . . ?' Although it's better to address the situation as it occurs, there is nothing to stop you from enquiring what was meant by the other person's comment, next time you meet them. If you ignore put-downs the other person will feel it is OK to continue to score points at your expense. You will also be unclear about the true meaning behind the put down. If you can respond assertively at the time – 'What makes you say that?' – so much the better. What you need to do is to show the other person that you recognize the remark for what it is, and that you are not prepared to let it pass unchallenged. This reduces the chances of you being a victim of put-downs at his hands in the future.

# Speaking up

I am referring here to speaking up when theoretically, you are not in the position of power, e.g. disagreeing with your boss, asking for information from senior management or stating your opinion to those higher than you in the organizational hierarchy. Of course, the same principles apply as dealing assertively with any situation, with any person, but often it is more difficult to be assertive with 'superiors'. This is risk-taking, but it is important assertively to express what you think, both for your own good and for the good of the organization. You have a right to have and express your own opinions and should not automatically defer to senior management just because of their status.

A bit of forward planning is invaluable if possible. Get your facts straight. Sort out facts from opinions and assumptions. You could lose credibility if you haven't done sufficient homework.

You also have the right to ask for information, and again it is in everyone's interests for you to know as much as possible about the organization, its ethos, its policies, its decision-making processes, how other departments function, and so on.

## Sorting facts from opinions and assumptions

For this you need good listening skills and the ability to identify areas which need further questioning and investigation in order to arrive at fact. For example, if someone says 'It will be more costly to employ temporary staff; it wouldn't be worth it' you need to establish: 'More costly than what, precisely? Against what criteria would it not be worth it?' Another example: 'They don't allow me the autonomy I need'; 'Who are "they"? Autonomy to do what, precisely? How don't they allow you?'

## Disagreeing

Your opinions are as valid as anyone else's, so provided you don't behave aggressively: 'That's a ridiculous statement!' or 'You're wrong', or in a non-assertive manner: 'Sorry to butt in . . . and I may be mistaken but . . . er . . . I don't think that's right', you can assertively express disagreement without it leading to conflict. Make 'I' statements, and assert your disagreement clearly and concisely: 'I disagree; in my experience . . . will work if . . .' Recognize the other person's point of view; listen and question carefully. If in the light of discussion, you feel that you can modify your views, be big enough to say so: 'Considering what you've just told me, yes, you're right; I agree that we should act now.'

## Dealing with another's anger

Don't respond aggressively, however tempting it might be! Meet aggression with aggression and the situation is likely to escalate, resulting in little more than bad feeling all round. Neither should you take it personally. Detach yourself from the emotional side of the interaction and listen carefully for the content of the communication. Keep quiet, until it is appropriate to begin to interact. Use this time to relax by whatever means suits you so that you can present a calm front. When the initial fire has died down somewhat, acknowledge the anger in the other person: 'I can see that you are very annoyed about this', and let the person respond. Begin to ask questions, showing by your tone of voice and body language that you are interested, listening, and wanting to help solve their problem. Ask for more information: use 'when, what, why' type open questions. Clarify understanding. Keep your voice calm, tone up and evenly paced. If you speak slightly more quietly and slowly than usual (without adopting a patronizing tone) this often has a calming effect. All this should help bring the discussion to a rational assertive level.

There will be times when the person you are dealing with is just plain rude, and however assertive you are, they will continue to bluster and attack. Again, don't take it seriously. If you can bring yourself to ignore the rudeness and get on with the business of sorting out the problem, all well and good. However, your rights are being abused, so you would be justified to end the interaction assertively with something like: 'Mr Jones, I'm not prepared to listen to bad language; if you continue to swear at me I shall hang up' or 'This is getting us nowhere Jenny; let's both sleep on it and meet again tomorrow'.

If there is a particular person with whom you always end up arguing, it might be appropriate to tackle your relationship as a separate issue. Initiate a conversation where you jointly discuss the reasons for your constant disagreements. Personality clashes are facts of life, but are not irreconcilable. You may be able jointly to find a way to recognize and deal with your problem.

## Dealing with non-assertive people

It is easy to stop listening for the content of what a non-assertive person says, and become influenced by their behaviour, tone of voice, body language and so on. In other words, you stop being assertive and react either with passive behaviour (giving in, taking on their problems for them, feeling guilty, protecting their feelings etc.) or with aggressive behaviour (becoming intolerant, getting annoyed or frustrated by the non-assertive behaviour). It is, in fact, as difficult to stay assertive in the face of non-assertive behaviour as it is when faced with aggression.

Non-assertive behaviour can be overt – helpless self pity, approval-seeking, and so on – or subtle. First, you have to be able to recognize the non-assertive behaviour for what it is. Look for speech patterns and non-verbal clues. Acknowledge your own feelings and initial reactions – do you feel sorry for the person; protective towards or irritated with him etc. Consider your self-talk. Ensure that your inner dialogue remains confident and assertive. If you know that a certain person has the ability to rub you up the wrong way by their self-deprecating manner, keep telling yourself that whatever happens you won't get irritated – you can handle it. Rather than saying something like 'For goodness sake, stop whinging all the time!' however tempting it might be to respond in this way, look beyond the moaning and talk about the issues at hand. Be a role model for assertive, positive behaviour. Always try to steer the conversation on to an assertive/assertive basis. Remember at all times to respect the other person's rights while not neglecting your own. All this done, and you will be ready assertively to respond to any guise of non-assertion presented to you.

One word of warning. It is often all too easy to ignore the non-assertive person – especially if their reticence means they do not impinge on your needs or feelings. As a manager, you need to consult and involve all your staff. If you don't, they will never reach their full potential and you and the organization may be losing out on useful ideas and opinions. You need to recognize the retiring, shy, nervous, reluctant members of your team and, through your own behaviour, encourage them to become more confident, self-assured and assertive.

# 4 Neuro Linguistic Programming

Neuro Linguistic Programming (NLP) is the rather intimidating title for an alternative and effective way of ordering your thoughts, feelings, behaviour and language. Some of the basic concepts of NLP have been around for decades, and fairly recently, in the 1970s, John Grinder and Richard Bandler coined the name of Neuro Linguistic Programming for this form of self-development which has applications in the fields of business, communication and education as well as psychotherapy. It has developed and matured over the years, gaining in reputation in the USA and Europe, and is currently enjoying favour in Britain. Some claim that NLP represents the shape of things to come in human resource management and development.

NLP is an evolving study and you will find many books on library shelves on its principles; also many books on management and communication skills which expound its theories without once mentioning the words Neuro Linguistic Programming or the initials NLP, such is its growing popularity. This chapter will give you a brief insight into NLP origins and theories, but I would suggest you look at an excellent book *NLP at Work* by Sue Knight (see Further reading) for a more in-depth, self-development guide and for a practical application of NLP in the business world. However, although the models of NLP can be presented in written form, it is a complex theory involving an awareness of your own and others' thought processes, so attending training sessions in the practice of NLP is recommended.

## The background: personal development

NLP is about responding effectively to other people and understanding and respecting their views, opinions and needs. The goal of NLP training is to give individuals more choice in their repertoire of response by reprogramming thoughts, feelings and attitudes. Belief systems that are unhelpful and entrenched can be changed so that they become more in line with the kind of reality you want to experience. NLP teaching is based on the fact that the unconscious mind is far more powerful than the conscious mind, and that everyone already has, within them, the resources to achieve excellence.

What you say and do influences the other person, and what they do influences you. NLP involves an examination of the entire system of feedback and response – both behaviourally and biologically – occurring in the interactions between a human being and himself, a human being and other human beings, and a human being and his environment. In business training, NLP can help with the following:

- the ability to learn; to be open to new ideas; to think laterally; to initiate as well as manage change
- to copy excellence – to understand what it is about successful, inspiring leaders that makes them 'tick', and to replicate this success for yourself
- to turn negative self-fulfilling prophecy into positive outcomes through the power of thought
- 'reading' others through subtle shifts in their behaviour, body language, eye movements, breathing rates, skin tone changes etc.
- influencing outcomes, by understanding and responding to the other person's value systems, time orientation and preferred communication style
- using language to create rapport
- encouraging understanding by recognizing slippages between perceptions, thoughts and language, and questioning for clarification
- 'matching' and 'pacing' so that you are on the same wavelength with the other person
- 'leading' – modelling good practice
- creating quality relationships
- developing flexibility in your life, and control over your thoughts, feelings and emotions
- learning how to best manage yourself in order to influence – not manipulate – and generate commitment in others
- recognizing the talents within – of self and others
- realizing that you already have within you all the resources that you will ever need to succeed
- beginning a process of continuous learning and improvement.

As humans we receive and transmit information through the five senses. We also have internal 'feelings'. Each sensory system is responsible for processing a set of characteristics about our immediate environment, and these characteristics will be unique to every individual. In NLP it is understood that these unique distinctions control our behaviour. However, nothing is 'fixed' for ever. With NLP, you can, as it were, extract from within an experience or feeling, have a good look at it, replace it with a more appropriate response, or one with which you are more comfortable, and return this new response to your own personal system of values and beliefs (see Anchoring below). This can be done alone with practice. However, as stated above, I would suggest that many of the techniques used in NLP need professional support and training.

In NLP 'behaviour' is not just external, observable behaviour like walking, but activity in any sphere – from eye movement to hearing, or internal visualization. Behaviour can be initiated either externally by the individual's immediate sensory environment, or internally by memory or imagination. It is an interesting phenomenon that your mind can be deceived time and time again – it cannot distinguish between what is imagined and what is real. If you were to step out into the road in front of a speeding car just managing to jump out of its way seconds before it might have mowed you down, you would probably experience the symptoms of mild clinical shock: you would go pale, possibly come out in a cold sweat; feel trembly and shaken; your stomach would churn at the thought of what might have been.

Recounting the tale later, similar symptoms may recur. Your mind triggers off a physical reaction; it cannot differentiate between real and imagined events. The way you react to imagined or remembered events can be altered from a negative to a positive experience through NLP. This is useful where you have had a bad experience with, say, giving a presentation. If you dwell on all the things that went wrong, the self-fulfilling prophecy syndrome will come into action. You'll be waiting for the same bad things to happen next time – and they probably will. However, if you can replace these 'bad' memories, with positive thought patterns, self-fulfilling prophecy will work for instead of against you. The presentation will be all the things you wanted it to be.

'Outcome' is a word you will find used a lot in NLP training. An outcome is a specific and positive result. An outcome is more finely honed than a goal. An outcome is stated in words that describe what you see, hear and feel. To continue with the example above, if you can recall a time when a presentation – or similar event – went well for you, NLP encourages you to recall the positive event; the successful outcome. What did it feel like? What did you see? What did you hear? Recalling these things makes you relive your success. With training and practice you can bring these positive vibes to bear any time you need to replicate the experience, turning potential failure into repeatable success.

# Why the title, Neuro Linguistic Programming?

The 'Neuro' part of the title refers to the concept that all behaviour results from sensory stimuli – sight, hearing, taste, smell, touch and feeling. Among other things, NLP requires the ability to get in touch with the senses and to be able to 'read' thought processes in others through eye movement, subtle changes in breathing and skin tone and through preferred language choice. It involves changing internal conflict, negative thought and behaviour patterns, to more positive states.

The word 'linguistic' recognizes that as humans we use language to formulate our thoughts, and to communicate to others our opinions, emotions and needs.

The 'programming' in the title explains how we organize our behaviour to produce results.

NLP is a complex theory based on the fact that every one of us is unique, yet composed of similar physiological, biological, emotional and spiritual parts which are intrinsically linked. Body and mind, conscious and subconscious, form a wholeness distinct to each individual. When the rules of interaction between the parts of the system are understood, the *effects* of different parts of the system on one another can be patterned, predicted and changed. A change in one aspect of our being necessitates change in other areas. The resulting behaviour change in ourselves brings about behaviour change in others with whom we communicate. In a very crude nutshell, this is why NLP is useful in therapy, counselling, business, education, communication and training in self-development.

You will already see, from this simplistic and inadequate explanation of a complex system, that NLP requires a substantial amount of knowledge, skill and application. As a form of self-development, or pursuit of 'personal excellence', it would be difficult to achieve without the help of an experienced tutor. I strongly suggest that if you wish to pursue NLP as an entire discipline, you attend seminars run by experienced exponents of this alternative approach to psychotherapy and self-development.

# Some models developed through NLP

NLP is complex. It is based on scientific knowledge of thought processes and the chemical reactions which take place in the brain. It applies this knowledge in a practical way to aid self-development, to improve relationships and to enrich communication. It enables individuals to manage their thinking processes. It addresses beliefs and values as well as behaviour. In fact, it would take a full textbook, plus, to do the theories justice. This section can only touch on some of the concepts; it is up to you whether you feel that NLP is a study worth pursuing as a self-development programme. However, some of the techniques can be 'lifted' and are useful people skills.

## Matching, mirroring, pacing and leading

You can assist the process of rapport and empathetic communication by altering the tone and tempo of your voice to be more in line with the other person. If he speaks quickly, up your pace slightly. If he has a soft voice, soften your own voice to match. Do not mimic tempo or tone, or copy accents, as this will quickly be perceived and taken as an insult by the other person. Aim to subtly emulate their style. On a subconscious level, this will flatter the other person, who will perceive you as 'on their wavelength'. Another technique of NLP is to recognize breathing patterns in yourself and others, and to match the other person's breathing rate to create rapport.

People in harmony with each other tend to mirror each other's posture, body weight distribution and body language. This happens unconsciously. In fact, it is a phenomenon that even inanimate objects prefer to match each other's movements. Presumably, the following has something to do with physics, gravity or whatever, but it is a fact that if you start up several pendulum clocks in the same room, at different times, ultimately they will synchronize their movements and all swing their pendulums in time. To build rapport, make a conscious slight adjustment in how you stand or sit, or how you hold your arms and hands so that you match the other person. Your change in demeanour has to be subtle – barely noticeable – if it is to be effective.

Crossover mirroring is an interesting variation on this theme. If you notice that the other person repeatedly uses a gesture or body movement, mirror the movement with a *different* repeated movement of your own. If he taps his foot a lot, every time he begins a sequence of tapping, rub your jaw or pull at your ear. Your movements, again, have to be minimal if they are to be effective. Believe it or not, this, too, will help establish rapport.

Pacing is about recognizing, acknowledging and respecting the state or feelings of others. If the other person is anxious, you do not match their anxiety, but pace them to show you understand and care about their position. If they are sad, use a sympathetic tone and manner. Mirror and match posture and tone of voice. Once you have paced them, you can then lead – gradually adjust your behaviour to a more positive and resourceful state. If you have built rapport, the other person will begin to pace you – follow your lead. They will have subconsciously accepted the fact that you have respected their position, and will follow your influence if that's the way they want to go.

## Eye-accessing cues

Below, under Representational systems we look at how we all perceive through our five senses, and how each of us favours one (possibly two) representational systems. We think via internalized pictures, sounds or feelings. Whether we are primarily visuals, auditories or kinesthetics will influence the language we use, the pace at which we speak, tonal quality, how we breath (visuals high in the chest; kinesthetics deep in the stomach) etc. People skilled in people-watching and trained in NLP techniques will be able to tell how the other person is thinking by the movements of his eyes while he is communicating. It should be pointed out that there are exceptions to the rule; you will need to observe each individual carefully and match his eye movements with other clues, such as choice of vocabulary, but generally, right-handed visual people will:

- look up and to their right for imagined images
- look up and to their left for remembered images
- look straight ahead in a defocused way for visual images, created or remembered. (Stand too close in front of a visual when they are defocused and you will have invaded their space; they will be unable to think clearly.)

Right-handed auditory people will keep their eyes level:

- to their right for constructed sounds
- to their left for remembered sounds.

Right-handed kinesthetic people will:

- look down and to their right for feelings and internal emotions
- look down and to their left for internal dialogue.

## Calibration

Calibration is claimed to be the key to successful communication. It is the term used for 'reading' other people – putting together the evidence from their eye movements, rate and type of breathing, changes in breathing rate, in skin tone and in facial musculature. Calibration is the ability to recognize how a person is feeling and responding to your communication by assessing his non-verbal signals. It will tell you when you have rapport, when you are on the right track to achieve your outcome, and alternatively when you are going off course and need to change tack to succeed with this individual. There are no hard and fast rules as every person is unique, so calibration is very much an observation skill which has to be practised with each individual and with each interaction.

# NLP and the use of language

## Representational systems

One of the tenets of NLP is that we are all the sum of our conditioning. In the biological sense, this means that as our brain cells developed, they sought sensory stimulation. At a crucial point in our development, if we were given objects to play with which were primarily made to stimulate our ears – rattles for instance – we would tend to prefer auditory information for learning and to develop language and behaviour patterns. Given picture-books we may well favour visual information.

In adulthood, individuals may still rely heavily either on auditory, kinesthetic (the feeling sense: tactile – external, or emotional – internal) or visual information. A primarily 'auditory' person may be able to 'see', but may not be able to 'observe'; a visual person may 'hear' but find it hard to 'listen'.

Of course, nothing is as cut and dried as this, and trying to fit individuals into neat boxes is always counter-productive. Everyone will react to the complete range of sensory stimuli, and will at times pay attention to one sense more than another, but according to NLP theory, everyone favours one perhaps two 'senses' regardless of what we are thinking about. You may prefer to trust pictures, sounds or feelings when considering information. This will be reflected in the language you use. For example, a visual person is likely to prefer using terms such as 'I see what you mean' whereas an auditory person would probably use a phrase similar to 'I hear what you say'.

Experiments have shown that people who favour the same sense find it far easier to communicate together. They 'see eye to eye', are 'in harmony' or 'feel comfortable in each others' company', depending on whether they are visuals, auditories or kinesthetics. It is easy to see the application to communication skills training. If you wish to create rapport with a person who doesn't share your preferred sense – for example if you are primarily an auditory person but can recognize that the person with whom you are communicating is a visual person – you can consciously alter the language you choose to match his preferred style. The skill comes in having a) the skill and experience to pick up the cues from the other's language and, then, b) having sufficient vocabulary to emulate his preferred style of communication. Here is another instance where appropriate training with a skilled NLP practitioner is so helpful.

Powerful communicators use language that is rich in its use of all the senses. Practitioners of NLP develop a very astute sense of language, the meaning of words and word clusters. Because each of us brings our own unique experience of the world to every situation, it is logical that the communicator's intention and the receiver's interpretation of the communication, can often differ. NLP advocates a precise use of language to aid mutual rapport and understanding.

In order to convey meaning we need to use words to express our thoughts. We gather information through the five senses and this information is processed by the brain. What we decide to do with this information constitutes the thinking process. Thinking turns our perceptions into words. As we think far faster than we can speak, there is a lot of complexity to our thought patterns – complexity which can be lost in translation into words and phrases. It's rather like doing copious research for an article or book, then having to reduce 50,000 words of notes to a maximum of 20,000. Something has to be left out, and it's all too easy to believe that the finished work is still as understandable to the reader as it is to the writer. Inevitably detail will be lost, but also thought processes might be lost which are crucial to understanding. Rather than taking the reader from A to Z, it is possible to make assumptions about prior knowledge and start at C or D, and leave out H, P and T – crucial to your argument. So it is with speech. *You* know what is going on in your head, and feel that you have accurately and precisely conveyed your meaning. It is very possible that the receiver of your communication has given different interpretation to your words; both of you may leave the conversation feeling that you understand and have been understood, but in fact neither may be the case.

## The Meta Model

John Grinder and Richard Bandler created the Meta Model to explain how language works. I am indebted to the work of Joseph O'Connor and John Seymour for their book *Introducing NLP* (see Further reading) for explaining so succinctly the linguistic categories précised below.

We have seen that during communication, the best we can hope for is an approximation of understanding. However, using as precise a system of vocabulary and grammar as possible lessens the gap between thought processes and the spoken word. In NLP, what is known as the Meta Model is used to aid this process. When we think, we do so in pictures, with feelings and other sensations as well as with language. To articulate our thoughts we need to internally summarize, deleting much detail, before voicing a simplified version. This inevitably requires some distortion and generalization of our thought processes. The Meta Model is a system of questions to help the speaker clearly articulate thoughts and feelings and to enable the listener to fill in the gaps, thus clarifying and minimizing disparity between hearing and understanding. The Meta Model does not ask 'why' questions; rather it asks questions which clarify meaning, and offers choices through opening the possibility of alternative outcomes. People using the Meta Model to elicit more information or clarify another's thoughts must constantly ask themselves 'What is the most useful question I can ask now?' and constantly must keep in mind the need for rapport, support and sensitivity.

## Unspecified nouns

When an individual habitually chooses to use passive statements such as 'a decision was reached' rather than specifying *who* made the decision and *what* decision specifically, or 'they should put a stop to it' rather than spelling out *who* should put a stop to *what*, this can be indicative of the speaker's state of mind. He may view the world as a place where things just happen; where no one wishes to take responsibility for events. To get a clear picture of this person's thought processes, the questions 'who, which or what specifically . . . ?' need to be asked.

## Unspecified verbs

This is where adverbs, which we need to hear if we are to understand fully, have been deleted from statements. For example
'You'll need first to preserve the timber' or 'He's injured himself'. To get the full picture requires you asking 'How' or What kind of . . . ?' or 'In what way . . . ?'

## Comparisons

Often people make statements using the words 'better', 'best' or 'worse' without giving a comparison – what exactly is it better than, for example. On a more subtle level, you may have internal dialogues with yourself on a 'I really made a pig's breakfast of that interview' type. To what or whom are you comparing your performance? Is this a realistic comparison?

## Judgements

If someone says 'I'm useless with machines' or 'I'm clumsy', you need to clarify 'In whose opinion?'; against whose criteria are you judging yourself?' Conditioning and self-fulfilling prophecy often go hand in hand. Another type of judgement is the 'As you realize, amalgamation is the only option' type statement, or 'It's obviously the only choice'. *You* may not realize anything of the kind; and to whom is it obvious? Speakers who make sweeping judgement statements shouldn't be allowed too get away with them! Judgement statements need to be clarified.

## Nominalizations

Nominalizations are what I choose to call verbal nouns; active concepts which are made static by making them nouns. There is nothing ambiguous about words which describe nouns such as a 'flower-pot' or a 'sandwich', but verbal nouns such as 'sensitivity' or 'intelligence' are open to a vast array of interpretations. There can be an ocean of difference between your understanding of 'aggression', 'respect' 'confidence' or 'reputation', and mine. Nominalizations are probably the biggest area of misunderstandings within communication. To clarify, return the noun to its verbal form and ask questions such as 'How is he being aggressive' or 'Reputed to do what, specifically?'

## Modal operators of necessity and possibility

These are explicit or implicit rules of conduct. Modal operators of necessity are the 'shoulds', 'ought to's' and 'musts' of our internal dialogue and need to be challenged by 'what would happen if you did?' type questions. When possible outcomes of what might happen if you *did* do something you feel you shouldn't, or reasons you *can't* do something, are honestly evaluated, more accurate decisions about behaviour choice can be reached.

Modal operators of possibility describe to the individual what he considers possible by words such as 'can' and 'cannot', 'possible' and 'impossible'. Of course, some statements of possibility are based in fact, such as 'I can't swim'. However, often an individual's limits are dictated by beliefs which may or may not be true, such as 'I just couldn't stand up and give a speech' or 'How can I refuse when she's been so good to me'. Questioning along the lines of 'What is it about giving a speech that makes it impossible for you?', 'What stops you refusing', or 'What would happen if you refused?' help define how amenable the individual is to changing or modifying behaviour.

## Generalizations

Generalizations are not always wrong. In the Julian calender, April always follows March; all reptiles are cold-blooded. These are factual statements. However, many generalizations are unhelpful in that they seemingly allow for no exceptions, e.g. 'the youth of today have no respect for property' or 'you are a bunch of hypocrites'. Statements containing the words 'always', 'never', 'everyone' 'all' etc. indicate generalizations. Sometimes the generalization is implied. However, in all instances the speaker needs to be invited to tighten up his statement, giving specific examples. This can be done most simply by reflecting the key word back as a question, 'Always?' 'Nothing?' or by challenging the detail behind the statement.

## Presuppositions

These are statements like 'Will you type this before you go out for my sandwiches' presupposing that the other person will be doing your lunch shopping. An astute response would be 'What makes you believe that . . . ?' Another example would be the accusatory 'Why don't you confide in me?' which presupposes that you do not share confidences. Again, an appropriate response would be 'What leads you to believe that I don't confide in you?'

## Cause and effect

While we are responsible for our language, behaviour and actions, we are *not* responsible for the effect these have on others. Statements such as 'You make me really angry when . . .' make the other person responsible for your emotional state. Their behaviour may have caused anger in you, but they were not responsible *per se* for how you react and feel. By looking at cause and effect, possibilities of how to cope with the situation may become more apparent. Another way of looking at it is to ask how and why, specifically, you become angry when certain behaviour is displayed. After all, you have no control over another's behaviour, but you do over how you react to that behaviour.

## Intuition

This can be a two-way communication block – assuming that you can mind-read, or expecting others to know, by instinct, how you feel or what you need. 'I could tell how he felt' is a typical example of the first phenomenon. How could you 'tell' without asking him? 'She should have realized that I would be annoyed' is an example of expecting others to intuitively know how you would react to a situation. In a counselling situation you might question the other person as to how, specifically, you know that ... or how should she have realized that ... to ascertain whether there is clear evidence to support the claim, or whether it is a questionable assumption on their part.

## Pointers

John Grinder has since refined the Meta Model to just five pointers:

1.  Nouns. In the English language many, if not most nouns have diverse meanings depending on context, and the experience and perceptions of the transmitter and receiver. Consider the noun 'product'. I know what I mean when I say the word, but what 'product' means to me, and what it means to you, the receiver, could be entirely different. To be as sure as possible that you and I share the same meaning, you should question accordingly: 'What product, specifically?'
2.  Verbs too have meanings which are idiosyncratic to the individual using them. You could say to me 'I'll edit Rashid's report'. I may think that you will proofread, check for grammar, accuracy and so on. You may mean that you will reduce it from 3,000 to 1,500 words. This does not imply that some people have a sloppy command of language (although some do!) but illustrates that meaning can differ from one person to the other, so needs to be checked. 'How' type questions need to be used to check for accurate understanding of verbs; 'How, exactly will you edit Rashid's report?'
3.  Rules. These are the 'should' or 'shouldn't', 'ought to' and 'cannot' type limitations that might or might not be reasonable, so need to be questioned. The sort of question to ask to verify or refute words and phrases that limit are 'What would happen if you didn't .. ?' or 'I'm curious; what might happen if you did .. ?'
4.  Generalizations, too, can be limiting. We generalize when we take the sum of one or two similar experiences, and wrongly conclude that any future comparable experience will produce the same results. Words such as 'never', 'every' and 'always' flag up generalizations. Seldom do these words give a true picture; there are usually more exceptions to the rule than generalizations would suggest. One way to question generalizations is to repeat the limiting word back to the other person with a rising inflection: 'Always?'

    Another typical generalization is the use of the pronoun 'they'. Who 'they' are is seldom specified, but 'they' are responsible for things that go wrong, things that have been omitted, for making the rules or for breaking them. 'They' are scapegoats, and in fairness to 'them' you should help identify who these people are! If you allow the other person to lay the blame on 'them' you are denying him the opportunity to take responsibility for his own life, his own solutions and decisions, and changing for the better.

5. Comparators are words such as 'faster', 'cheaper', 'more effective', 'better'. It is easy to accept blanket statements such as 'We have higher standards', yet you need to establish 'higher than whom?' before any credibility can be given to such a claim. Through questioning, individuals will learn to specify antecedants to give weight to, and provide evidence for, their claim.

# Anchoring

Techniques distinctive of NLP are anchoring and syntonic learning. I will not attempt to go into detail on this. Suffice to say that they are techniques which engage the senses of sight, hearing and touch to secure positive experiences in the consciousness. With apologies to exponents of NLP for this simplistic definition, you anchor a positive feeling, such as confidence, by mentally 'living' your desired state. When you are totally associated with this state – can see, hear and feel it most strongly – 'anchor' the feeling by, for example, touching forefinger and thumb together, touching your thigh or some other simple tactile expression, maintaining the touch while the feeling is at its most intense. This touch has now become the anchor for that feeling, so whenever you need to experience that feeling of confidence or whatever again, 'fire the anchor': press finger and thumb together, and the feeling of confidence will recur.

For another example of how syntonic learning and anchoring occur, let's consider the five pointers above. Associate the fingers and thumb of your left hand with the words 'noun' (forefinger), 'verb' (middle finger), 'should' (ring finger), 'all' (little finger), and 'comparison' (thumb); and the fingers and thumb of your right hand with the questions or pointers 'What specifically?' (forefinger), 'How specifically?' (middle finger), 'What would happen if?' (ring finger), 'All?' (little finger), and 'Than what, specifically?' (thumb). The technique involves lifting your left forefinger as you imaging the word 'noun' printed on it. Say the word 'noun' aloud. Repeat this three times. Now raise your right forefinger, imagining the question 'What?' printed on it and asking 'What, specifically?' out loud. Do this three times. Now repeat the process, lifting the left forefinger, thinking and saying the word 'noun' followed immediately this time by the right forefinger sequence. This should have fixed the sequence in your consciousness so that when you hear another person using a vague or unspecified noun, your forefingers will twitch prompting you to ask questions of clarification about that noun: e.g. 'What programme specifically?'.

You would need to repeat the process of fixing the pointer sequences in your consciousness by going through similar routines with the other fingers and thumbs of both hands. Once the sequences are secured in your neurology you will automatically recognize and react to unspecified verbs, limiting generalizations and so on.

You can learn to anchor positive experiences, recalling how you felt, what you saw and what you heard, then transferring these constructive feelings to a present or future situation. Through anchoring, you can even replace negative thoughts, doubts and worries or previous negative outcomes with how you would *like* to respond. These new anchored, positive feelings become reality for you. As stated several times above, it would benefit anyone considering using NLP for self-development or to improve managerial and communication skills to seek professional and expert guidance in NLP.

# Part II

# 5 Appraisal

In the past, appraisal interviews tended to be form filling exercises, where an employee's past year's performance was assessed and rated against prescribed criteria. Pay increases and promotion often depended on the outcome of the appraisal. Increasingly, organizations are realizing that performance appraisals should concentrate on staff development. There is a conflict of interests if appraisals also include discipline, pay and promotion issues. Rather than being formal judgement and reporting exercises, appraisals are now seen as ways to build on the past – recognizing achievements, acknowledging areas where extra training or support is needed, improving work performance and developing the potential of employees.

Appraisal interviews *are good things*. They exist to ensure that on a regular basis you can assess the quality of your staff, helping them to enhance what they're good at and to improve on weaker areas in order to develop as individuals and progress in their careers. The knock-on effect, of course, is greater job satisfaction for individuals, a more motivated workforce and better organizational effectiveness. Through appraisals you will be able to ensure that the abilities of employees are being fully utilized within the organization and thus make better use of the skills, talents and energies within the workforce. An effective organization-wide appraisal scheme will be able to identify skill shortages which require either training of existing employees, redeployment or recruitment.

Individuals can ascertain how well they are doing, report on achievements and discuss how they could build on these successes, find out about how they might strengthen weak areas, what training or support is available to them, and how they might better further their careers. It should also be an opportunity for you to foster the concept of teamwork and to ascertain how well you have functioned as their manager – whether you are 'there' enough to give information, support and encouragement – and how you can jointly improve working relationships. Effective appraisals involve joint collaboration in problem-solving, planning and learning.

So why do staff and managers alike tend to dread these events, or at best see them as annual chores? If everyone recognized that appraisals are for the benefit of all concerned – are positive opportunities to look to the future rather than dwell on the past – then more could be achieved from them on both sides.

Of course, the ball lies in your court regarding how appraisals are viewed by your staff. If you don't see the relevance of appraisals, or there is no obvious progress as a result of the interview, then your staff, too, will be disillusioned. If, however, you are a manager with excellent people skills, then formal appraisal interviews can be seen as a consolidation of an ongoing process of regular chats and discussions about work and performance – how the job is going, how things might be improved, how to overcome problems and what you, as manager, can do to help the individual and the job develop. You should be used to giving and receiving feedback and constructive criticism in a positive way, and giving praise for work well done. The formal interview should provide a written record of performance and recognition of the employee's efforts, with recommendations for future development. There should be jointly agreed action plans which should be supported, monitored and evaluated. Identified training and development needs should be acted upon.

## Appraisals: a waste of time in an already busy schedule?

Before discussing the nuts and bolts of running an appraisal interview, let's look more closely at some of the myths about, and misuses of these interviews which give appraisals a bad name.

Appraisals take time, effort and money. If senior management are not prepared to see appraisals as a crucial element of managers' work, allowing sufficient time and resources, then managers will resent this additional burden to their workload. There needs to be provision for adequate follow-up training and development opportunities, or appraisal interviews will be seen as lip-service exercises.

Even the word 'interview' can dredge up negative connotations for some people, and hamper the flow of honest communication. Some may have previous unhappy experiences of interviews, where they became tongue-tied at a selection interview, or chastised or humiliated at a disciplinary hearing for example. Although a formal procedure, appraisals should still be seen as joint *discussions* between two people who both want a positive outcome and a clear picture of the way forward. If necessary, give the appraisal interview another name, such as 'development review', better to reflect the tone of the meeting.

Some managers do not see the importance of holding appraisals, and have no incentive to carry them out effectively. As stated above, if an appraisal scheme is to work, it takes time, effort and resources. Appraisers need to plan and prepare; each appraisal is time-consuming, and each appraisee's performance will need to be monitored; there is inevitable follow-up work involved. It is the responsibility of senior management to ensure that appraisal is an integral and valued part of every manager's role.

In some organizations, the appraisal means little more than the manager 'going through the motions', ticking boxes on a preprinted sheet, 'scoring' each member of staff against personality or function issues. In others, the appraisal becomes an excuse for the manager judgementally to reflect on the past year's performance; little time is spent looking at how present efficiencies might be improved, or how the job could develop in the future.

Some managers have little idea of what appraisal interviews are truly about. They only appraise poor performers in the mistaken belief that appraisal interviews are an opportunity to tell under-achievers to 'pull their socks up'. Other members of their team don't need to be appraised because they believe the theory 'if it isn't broken, don't mend it'.

For appraisal to be effective, managers need to believe in and be committed to appraisal. They also need to be trained in appraisal skills. While there are numerous books on how to carry out appraisals on performance, and this section will give a brief grounding in the basics, appraisal is a highly skilled activity. You will need excellent interpersonal and leadership skills combined with elements of counselling and coaching. You will need to be able to analyse, diagnose, advise and direct.

Some companies invite the appraisee to do some forward planning for the interview realizing that this will help them 'own' outcomes of the meeting, whereas others don't even allow employees to see their managers' report on performance.

Appraisal interviews are not the place to discuss salary increases – pay reviews should be kept entirely separate. If an employee's increase or bonus appears to be dependent on undergoing a successful annual appraisal, he is not going to want to discuss weaknesses; neither will you get a true picture of achievements and general performance. For the same reason, promotions should not be discussed at this interview, but considered at a separate review.

Lastly, although you may need to criticize areas of an appraisee's work at the interview, it should be done in a constructive way, and not take up too much of the overall time. Appraisals shouldn't degenerate into disciplinary interviews. As you will see from the later section on discipline, a disciplinary interview follows entirely different procedures from appraisals.

If any of the above negativity rings bells, it would be well to begin to look into more productive procedures for your organization. Admittedly, it is far easier to be committed to positive, productive appraisals if you have backing and support from above, recognition at your own performance review that appraisal is a valued part of your own workload, and support and resources to follow up effectively with your staff. It may be that you have to take the lead in this, however. You don't have to wait for instruction from on high, or for other departments to break new ground. You will want to adopt a system whereby you and each member of your team meets formally every now and then (no, it doesn't *have* to be annually) to collaborate on positive ways forward. So how can you get the best from these meetings?

# Planning and preparation

Forward planning is the obvious starting-point. Do you know what you can offer each appraisee in terms of training and developmental experiences? What resources are at your disposal. Do you need to consult with the Personnel Department or your boss?

You should plan the appraisal discussion carefully. Don't think in terms of content – *what* has been done – rather on the process – *how* work has been achieved. Don't concentrate just on performance, but consider, too, working relationships, environment and other issues central to the world of work.

Be clear in your own mind what you want to achieve and what might happen when your mentally rehearsed monologues become an active interaction. Be prepared to be flexible so that the interview isn't rigidly restricted by your overall plan; the conversation has to flow if it is to be productive. Remember that although you are holding the reins, it is the employee's appraisal – his chance to establish how he is progressing in his job, and how he might develop potential.

If you are not the direct line manager of an appraisee, you need to speak with his supervisor to get his view of the employee's performance and potential for development. Does he know anything of the appraisee's long-term career objectives? Is there any new work coming into the department which will affect action plans that you need to know about? Are there projected targets and goals of which you should be aware? How will the supervisor measure performance and evaluate progress after the appraisal?

You may well be appraising several members of staff. Some may hold similar positions within the organization, but every person is different. Each will have different abilities; each will have different personalities and temperaments; each will be at a different stage of development. You cannot, therefore, have one overall plan of action which will suit everyone. You will need to set objectives, but these will need to be modified for each individual in your team. You need to ask yourself 'how is this person performing now; what are his strengths; where has he excelled; what skills does he need to develop; what is his potential for development; what should I be aiming to achieve with this person at this point in his career?'

Regarding this latter point, understand that the interview may highlight areas previously unknown to you which will have to be taken into account. At the end of the interview, your action plan will have to be clearly defined, and be challenging enough to motivate without being too immense to contemplate. Ideally you should set objectives which can be qualified and quantified so that you can measure progress. You should be looking at short-, medium- and long-term action plans for each staff members' development.

Ensure that both you and the appraisee have a copy of their job description to work to. Write yourself an agenda along these lines:

- the past year's work performance
- any changes in role or tasks
- the present situation
- planning for the next year
- training and development needs.

Include not only tasks and responsibilities, but also working relationships and how these might be improved. Set yourself a list of questions to ensure that you cover all aspects required of the appraisal. When you are happy with them, let the appraisee have a copy so that he can prepare in advance for the interview. In this way you have a shared understanding of the purpose and direction of the discussion. By encouraging the appraisee to contribute in this way, he has ownership of the appraisal, and hopefully a commitment to its objectives.

Use open questions such as:

'What are the key tasks and responsibilities of the job?'
'Is your Job Description still an accurate account of your key tasks and responsibilities?' 'If not, in what ways has your job changed?'

'What do you see as your main achievements over the last year?' 'Why?'
'What aspect of your work are you most satisfied with?' 'Why?'
'Were there any areas of work where you were less satisfied?' 'Which?'
'Why?'
'Which aspects of work have caused problems over the last year?' 'Why?'
'How can we make these areas of work less difficult for you?'
'What areas of your work might be developed further?' 'How?'
'Which colleagues/departments are directly affected by your work?' 'In
what way?'
'Which colleagues/departments directly affect your work?' 'In what way?'
'In what way might working relationships be improved – how can you help
them?' 'How might they help you more?'

Plan to hold the interview at a mutually convenient time, arranging
cover if necessary. Do not schedule anything important immediately after
the allotted time in case the appraisal takes longer than you intended –
neither of you will benefit from feeling rushed. Allow sufficient lead time
for you both to think about and plan the interview. Because this is to be a
joint discussion rather than a form-filling exercise, allow enough time
after each appraisal for you to record important data such as anything
agreed to meet job-related needs, career-related needs, training and
development, extra resources, and so on. Also who is to do what, by
when; how performance is to be monitored and evaluated, and by
whom.

If the appraisal is not to take place at your office, arrange a room for the
interviews. You need quiet, uninterrupted time for each appraisal. Ensure
that the layout is conducive to relaxed conversation – don't set up a
senior/subordinate scenario with barriers such as desks between you.
Arrange for tea or coffee if that seems appropriate – anything to aid a free
flow of conversation. Have note paper and pens/pencils available for
both yourself and the appraisee.

## The appraisal interview

Arrive at the interview room before the appraisee. Although the emphasis
is on discussion rather than interrogation, you will need to show authority and be in control. This is not easy to achieve if you arrive late and
flustered. You will need to have a clear head, relaxed body language and
calm modulated voice, so if the appraisal interview is likely to be difficult
for you – if you know the appraisee thinks appraisals are a waste of time
and is likely to be hostile, for example – take some time for deep
breathing or other relaxation exercise.

Put the employee at ease by engaging in some small talk while you
both get settled. Build and maintain rapport (see Chapter 2). Explain that

you will take the occasional note of points for action, and that he should feel free to jot down anything he wishes during the discussion. Define the purpose of the interview and the form it is going to take. Ask the appraisee if he is happy with that – if that's how he sees it – and take note of his responses. (By 'take note' I do not mean this literally! You should take as few notes as possible during the discussion, concentrating on maintaining rapport, actively listening, questioning, reflecting back, re-capping and summarizing).

Encourage the appraisee to 'open the batting' by giving his views of past performance and plans for the future. Hopefully he will have prepared beforehand by considering the questions on your crib sheets, so will be working to a similar agenda to yours. Listen well. Be flexible. If early on he brings up a topic which is way down on your own list for discussion, talk it through, then mentally rearrange your agenda, or bring the discussion back on course through careful linking statements. Pro-vided you cover all the areas you intend, ordering is not as important as the appraisee taking ownership of his own performance and develop-ment.

Use your preprepared list of questions as a general guide, but check facts and details with succinct closed questions, and probe and analyse using more open questions such as:

'Why do you think that happened?'
'With hindsight, how would you have done it differently?'
'How would you go about that?'
'In what way?'
'Tell me more about . . . '
'Why is that unhelpful, specifically?'
'Which did you find most challenging?'
'You seem doubtful about this; why?'
'Go on.'

Don't be afraid of silences. The temptation is to jump in and fill the embarrassing void, but everyone needs thinking time. Ten seconds is nothing when you are trying to grasp a point, relate it to your own situation and answer in an appropriate way. Ten seconds is a lifetime when you're sitting there waiting for a response to your question!

Avoid asking leading or multi-facetted questions which will only annoy or confuse, and cause a communication block.

At each stage in your agenda, remember that the initiative in the appraisal discussion should be with the appraisee. Give him the chance to give his views first, listen and question before commenting or offering your own opinion, then work towards a jointly agreed plan of action.

Close the interview by asking the appraisee what he felt to be the most constructive parts of the discussion. Briefly recap, jointly, on what was agreed, what job- or career-related needs have emerged, and how these will be met and evaluated. Thank the appraisee for giving his time and co-operation.

# So, what can go wrong?

1. Your attitude to appraisals. If you feel this is one more pressure you can do without, it will show. Appraisals are important to your staff, their well-being and development. They are also important to the organization, and if handled badly can have the opposite of the desired effect – to improve effectiveness within the organization by supporting, motivating and developing the potential of the work-force.

2. Your attitude to the appraisee. If we're honest we don't like everyone we meet or have to work with. Neither do we respond to all people in the same way. You will have to be objective in your appraisals, recognizing and working through prejudices, neither allowing the 'halo effect' nor the 'horns effect' to influence your judgement. You may have to justify why you have offered certain support or training to one member of staff and not another. If you can't give convincing reasons, based on the evidence of the appraisal, the employee is entitled to take out a formal grievance and this could ultimately lead to an industrial tribunal on the grounds of being denied career development opportunities.

3. Difficulty in giving constructive criticism. This can be for a variety of reasons, and in the appraisal situation you may well get employees who become hostile or defensive when weaknesses are discussed, or are over-confident and resentful at being offered training or development. You will have to use your assertive skills to give specific feedback on aspects of performance or behaviour which need to be worked on (see section titled Feedback in Chapter 3).

4. You may be unable to agree learning needs. Stay in assertive mode. Ask questions such as:

    'What is it about . . . specifically, that won't work?'

    'Why does attending a training course worry you?'

    'In what way do you see this as unreasonable?'

    In the final analysis, you can explain to them the consequences of not accepting your viewpoint, while promising to investigate alternative ways of overcoming your difficulties.

5. You may identify a learning need which the appraisee doesn't recognize. For example, you may feel that he would benefit from interpersonal skills development – his listening skills are appalling and he interrupts frequently. He feels he relates well to others and has different training priorities. Again, you need to keep your assertive skills in play, explaining why you feel it important, while recognizing his reservations.

6. You and the appraisee may have different perceptions of what organizational standards are appropriate. Don't make a hasty compromise which you might later regret. Question wisely to ascertain exactly where points of difference lie. If you can't arrive at a win/win solution, as with 4 above (and especially if you know you are right about company standards) state the consequences of not agreeing with your viewpoint.

# After the appraisal

Immediately after the appraisee has left your office, make a formal note of the key points of the discussion, areas of agreement (and any disagreement which needs to be followed up) and short- and long-term action plans. Don't rely on your memory, especially if you are seeing other employees for appraisals. Use the same positive language for your report as you did for the interview, acknowledging the joint nature of the discussion by using the word 'we' rather than 'I'. If your organization has a preprinted appraisal report form, of course this should be used.

Give a copy of your notes to the appraisee so that you can both agree that it is an accurate report of what was agreed and of the way forward.

Appraisal interviews are not stand-alone exercises. In the same way that planning and preparation are important, so is follow-up. You will need to inform anyone whose work is to be affected by the employee's appraisal to gain their support. The supervisor needs to know what action plans have been decided upon; your boss will need to know what training and development plans you have agreed. Be prepared to offer any support you can, and, while letting him get on with the job in hand in his own way, make time to periodically check on progress.

# EXERCISE

1. One of your supervisors has asked for guidance on how he should follow up with an employee after the appraisal. List at least six areas he should be considering.

_____

_____

_____

_____

_____

_____

2.  There is a definite personality clash between you and one of your junior managers. It is time for his appraisal and you can foresee all kinds of difficulties. What steps might you take to overcome these difficulties?

3.  In your opinion, what would be the best strategy if it becomes obvious that you have not allowed enough time for the appraisal interview:

    a)  Put your foot on the gas pedal and motor on swiftly through your agenda so that every point is covered.
    b)  Have a rethink about the most important issues and just cover these.
    c)  Agree to adjourn and fix another time and date to reconvene.

**Possible responses**

1.  He should:

    - get feedback from the employee about the appraisal itself
    - make time to talk frequently with the employee about progress
    - observe, monitor and evaluate
    - encourage and motivate
    - give praise for achievements
    - help with difficulties
    - help correct errors in a constructive way
    - adjust workload and/or time-scales if appropriate

- support training and development
- brief and debrief before and after development courses
- report progress to you.

2. Admit to yourself that unless you can put personalities to one side, the usefulness of any information gained from the appraisal interview will be suspect. Prepare carefully by studying his self-appraisal; identify where there are areas of potential conflict, and where agreement. Initially concentrate on the latter to build up a feeling of professionalism and trust. You will have to use all your interpersonal skills to choose positive language, phrasing and questioning which focuses on objective, job- and career-related issues. Discuss facts rather than feelings. Be open-minded and ready actively to listen to his point of view without being judgemental. You must be prepared to believe that the other person has valid opinions too. Be willing to hear him out rather than making assumptions from your own point of view.

   Reflect back, and summarize areas of agreement, and build on these rather than battle through areas of conflict. Ensure, at all times, that your tone of voice or body language doesn't give you away and show your hostility or annoyance.
   Where you cannot compromise, and he refuses to conform, as his manager you have the right to insist. Don't make idle threats, but make it clear that you intend to take the matter further. In their turn, they are also free to take the matter up with personnel or senior management. It might be appropriate to suggest you both take some time to think the issue through and talk about it again, but in the final analysis, you have the last word.

3. In an ideal world, the situation would not occur, because you would have a fair idea of how long each individual will need, and have scheduled accordingly, with some spare capacity. You will have kept the discussion moving and not be drawn off target or side-tracked. You would not have arranged for more than two appraisals in any one day; you would have arranged your work so that no time-bound meeting followed an appraisal interview.

   The best solution is c). Appraisee's will not feel valued if you start looking at your watch, forget about rapport and whistle through the last stages of the interview without giving each area due consideration. Neither is it appropriate to omit elements of the interview. Cover as many areas as you can as comprehensively as you can, and return to the others later.

# 6 Counselling

This will be a short section because although counselling has been mentioned several times in this book, I am not qualified to discuss counselling in the professional sense. I also feel very strongly that true counselling should be effected by individuals not only suitably trained and qualified, but emotionally competent; in other words, they should have high self-awareness, self-esteem and confidence so that their own emotions, feelings, attitudes and beliefs can be set aside. Sympathy can get in the way of empathy and relating too closely to another's problem can influence judgement. In my view, counsellors who are themselves emotionally competent can offer the best possible disinterested help to any individual or situation. They can be objective and truly 'professional', enabling the individual to help himself rather than create dependency.

Like most other skills, much can be learnt by reading about techniques, but there is no substitute for practical application, and I feel that counselling on a professional or voluntary basis should only be undertaken after training and supervised practice. In unskilled hands, 'counselling' can almost do more harm than good. The unqualified, or the amateur psychologist can – in all good faith – try to help another person, yet leave him feeling vulnerable and somehow incomplete. It is relatively easy to knock down someone's defences – walls which they have probably built over a considerable length of time. Without the comfort of the defences, a void can be left in the other person's life.

It is also relatively easy to get the other person to talk about himself and his problems, but what do you do with these issues once they are out on the table? You need the skills to enable the person to define and understand his problems, to take responsibility for his feelings, thoughts and actions, and develop and implement solutions. It takes a competent and highly skilled counsellor to help people rebuild self-esteem with positive strategies.

However, there is an important role for managers in recognizing staff with problems and creating an environment where they feel able to talk confidently about their situation. It is important to recognize your own limitations and to know when and to whom to refer individuals if necessary. Rather than 'counselling' I would prefer to call these 'helping' or 'enabling' skills for managers.

If you are the kind of manager who cares about his staff, you will know quite a bit about each member of your team such as the names of their partners and their children, whether they have parents living; something perhaps about their home life, interests and hobbies. Instinctively, you will be able to assess when things are not quite right with them. Even with members of your staff with whom you are not yet that familiar, by practising calibration techniques (see Chapter 4) you will be able to 'read' the other person for signs of anxiety or stress. Other indicators that all is not well are things like uncharacteristic mood swings, a lot of sick leave or absenteeism. It may be that you ascertain that the individual has problems during a formal interview such as an appraisal. You may have to 'counsel' during disciplinary or grievance interviews, when handling conflict, after a redundancy interview, or when organizational changes bring work-related stress to members of your team.

It is not your place to pry into matters which do not concern you, but neither should you turn your back on the situation hoping it will resolve itself without your intervention. What you need to do is to give the other person the opportunity to get his problems off his chest. Your role is not to offer solutions but to encourage the other person to develop strengths of his own and to work out his own plan of action. Hopefully, you will already have created a climate of respect and trust in the workplace, and will have a good rapport with your problem person. You need to create the opportunity and the environment for him to talk about his situation with you.

## Approaches to helping

There are four different approaches to helping the problem person. The first is to listen to their problem, then tell them what to do about it – impose a solution. With work-related problems, while this may be comforting to some passive individuals, it creates dependency and is the antithesis of empowerment. Less passive members of staff may well feel resentment at this directional approach and concede to your instructions grudgingly or in a half-hearted manner.

The second approach is to suggest solutions which suit you and/or the organization, but take little account of the individual's needs. In other words, he can adopt any number of approaches – suggested by you. Again, it creates dependency in passive members of staff (although they are probably less happy with being given a number of choices and will worry about opting for the right one).

There is a difference between enabling self-help and offering advice. The third approach is to discuss the person's problems, feelings, expectations and so on, then offer advice on how to solve the problem. I'm sure we've all been guilty of the 'If I were you . . .' type of comment. In some respects, this gives the individual a choice of whether or not to follow the advice, but where status is involved, some people may find it difficult not to follow a manager's advice, although they are not totally committed to the solution offered. If things do not work out favourably, they may react adversely at a later stage.

The fourth approach is counselling (with a small 'c') – using your helping and enabling skills to foster self-help. Whereas the first three approaches are more concerned with solving the problem than with the needs of the individual involved, enabling is about being primarily concerned with the person. You should facilitate a process whereby individuals can clearly define and explore their feelings about problems, examine solutions, make decisions, or if necessary, learn to live with the situation. We will look more closely at this fourth approach.

# Creating an appropriate climate

First and foremost you should be available to your staff – be there for them when they need you. Watch your non-verbal signals of non-availablity, e.g. a physical drawing back if a subject is broached about which you are personally sensitive, or have strong views. You will have modelled the sort of behaviour you require of your staff, so will have created a climate of support, integrity, respect and trust, where members of your team feel free to speak confidently (and if necessary in confidence) with each other and with you. Make time for the interview – as much as the individual needs – and don't be guilty of clock-watching.

If you have to initiate a meeting and need to use your helping skills on a specific issue, the usual rules apply: choose somewhere private and free from interruption. Choose a smallish room, preferably with easy chairs of similar height. Orientate the chairs for comfort, i.e. not facing windows, and at a suitable angle to each other so that you are not in confrontation mode, but can easily see the other's face so that you can 'read' expressions, musculature changes and so on, and can maintain good eye contact.

Put the other person at ease by setting a good example. Adopt an open and approachable posture, leaning slightly towards him (but not so far as to invade his space). Maintain rapport; be, and look interested in him and in what he has to say. Don't jump straight in with a 'What's bothering you?' type of interrogation, but ease him into the interview with a little non-threatening conversation. Use his name occasionally. It helps show that he is important and you care about his well-being. If you can create a climate of trust, where the other person feels free to talk about his problems, feelings, anxieties or expectations – where he is listened to and understood – then his own capacity for self-help will be enhanced.

# Skills of effective helping

The person with the problem is the only one who can accurately describe his situation, so your main contribution is in an active listening capacity. You will need to prompt, probe and question – with sensitivity – so that you fully understand. Your input is also about enabling the other person clearly to define his problem and explore his feelings about his situation. Until he is fully aware of all aspects of the problem, he will be thwarted in finding satisfactory solutions.

## Openers

It is often difficult to initiate a conversation which requires the other person to reveal something about themselves. They may well be anxious, or stressed; they could have had bad experiences when confiding problems in the past – felt rejected or let down. *You* may well feel anxious about the meeting because when you embark on a helping interview, you can never be absolutely sure of the outcome; solutions emerge from the enabling process.

It is well to talk about factual information first, then move on to your area of concern:

> 'You seem distracted (troubled/upset/agitated etc).'
> 'I feel that you're dissatisfied at the moment; I'd like to hear your viewpoint.'
> 'Why do you think this has arisen?'
> 'What do *you* feel is happening?'

You will need to move them from describing their problems to working actively for change.

# Genuineness

You must be seen to be sincere in your desire to help. Sometimes the boss/subordinate relationship can get in the way of openness, so it is up to you to create a warmth in the relationship by genuine and sensitive handling of the other person's thoughts and feelings.

# Listening

It is not sufficient to hear and understand; you must be able to communicate to the other person that he is understood. You will need to engage in whole-body listening – that is with your eyes as well as ears, emotions as well as intellect. You need to get into his shoes so that you can assess the situation from his, not your frame of reference. Although you need to remain objective, it is important that you recognize the strength of his feelings and use sensitivity and empathy in the way you handle the interview.

# Encouragement

You need to encourage the other person to talk and to guide him to explore his situation and his feelings about it in greater depth. This can be achieved by non-judgemental listening, i.e. holding back on giving your own opinion. You can 'give him permission' to continue and show that you are interested by your body language, by nods, smiles, 'ahs' and 'uh huhs', and phrases such as 'go on', 'I see', and 'that's interesting'.

# Reflecting

Another way to encourage the speaker to explore his problem in greater depth is to reflect his words back to him in paraphrased form. Don't depersonalize by saying something like: 'So the situation is made worse when Hank intervenes.' Ensure that the word 'you' or 'your' appears in the paraphrase: 'You feel the situation is worse when Hank intervenes.' Consider the following exchange:

'I just can't seem to concentrate, which is why the mistakes are happening. I'm worried about things at home.'
'Your work is suffering because your mind's on other things.'

You can steer the other person to talk about facts or feelings depending on how you reflect back his words. In the above example, the emphasis is on the work rather than his anxieties, and he is likely to respond in work terms. (He is also likely to see you as totally insensitive to his problems!)

If, however, you reflect back: 'You're really worried about problems you have at home', you will have given him permission to talk more about these to you, and he will feel encouraged to continue. It is an important skill a) to recognize 'feelings' words and phrases in the others communication and b) to paraphrase so that the conversation can be steered in an appropriate direction.

Don't overdo the reflecting back technique, especially if you use it in its simplest form – merely rephrasing what the other person has just said. Apparently, one counsellor's client, after about 10 minutes of this treatment asked 'Is there something wrong with the way I've been saying things the first time?'. However, if used subtly you will soon become skilled at encouraging the other to continue, in the direction you want the interview to go (and which is helpful to him). Reflecting back in summary form – 'So you feel that . . .' – will demonstrate that you understand or give the other person the opportunity to restate his position. By increasing your own vocabulary of 'feelings' words, you will be able to substitute within your paraphrasing better to clarify your and the other person's perception of their thoughts and emotions. You will be able to suggest alternative meanings better to explain their feelings and in so doing possibly uncover a deeper understanding of the situation.

## Questioning

The type of question you ask is significant. The interview should not be an interrogation, but the opportunity for the other person to be heard and understood. If you do too much of the speaking, this could be seen as controlling behaviour and lead to dependence; if you ask too many questions he may feel he is being pushed too hard, and get defensive. Better to ask a few open, probing questions to encourage him to speak freely.

Ask open questions which give the other person the opportunity to expand on what he is saying:

> 'What else?'
> 'Tell me more about . . .'

Use questioning to clarify understanding – for yourself and the other person:

> 'I can't get on with Raffi; he gets on my nerves.'
> 'What is about Raffi that annoys you, specifically?'

or

> 'Can you give me an example?'
> 'Tell me about a time when that happened.'

Ask questions to assess the other person's reactions to situations:

'How do you feel about that?'
'Do you have any thoughts about . . . ?'

Rather than bombarding him with questions, intersperse questioning with empathetic responses – reflecting back, summarizing etc.

## Space and silence

Allow sufficient time for the interview so that neither you nor the other person feels pressured. He will need space to think about and elaborate on his reponses. He will also need time to consider possible solutions and ways forward. Be comfortable with silences within the interview.

## Meaning

Because each of us brings a unique experience of the world to every situation, we tend to use and understand language differently (see Chapters 2 and 4). It is important to mutual understanding that you question 'fat' words such as 'good' which has a multiplicity of meanings in different contexts. Ask ' "Good" in what way, specifically?' Question too words such as 'can't' or 'always'. When the other person says he can't do something, ask what might happen if he *did* do whatever the thing is. If he says something always happens, question this by repeating the word back to him with a rising inflexion: 'Always?' Enable him to see the situation more clearly and in a positive rather than negative, destructive way. Similarly, try to get him to replace 'shoulds' with 'I will' or 'I won't' type assertions.

## Responsibility

Whereas you are both involved in solving the problem, and in the course of the interview you will uncover options for positive action, the individual concerned will need to decide on his own solutions and be responsible for their implementation. He will only be committed to doing something if he agrees with solutions which emerge from the interview – feels ownership of the problem and its solution.

Finally, whereas your role as manager is not just to 'heal' the individual, but to facilitate a situation where that person can perform better at work, neither is it your responsibility to take on problems which are outside the remit of the workplace, or are found to be too big to handle

alone. Know your limitations and when to refer to professional counsellors.

## EXERCISE

Ask a colleague or friend to help you with a role-play. Let him read
through this chapter – especially the section 'Skills of effective helping' –
so that he can offer you constructive feedback on your role as helper. (It
will not be easy to concentrate on playing a role and assessing your
performance, so, if possible, get a third person to act as observer so that
he too can offer feedback.) Ask your colleague or friend to think of a
problem he could discuss with you – real or imagined. Role-play the
interview, beginning from the moment you call him to your office, or he
approaches you asking if he could have a quiet word about a problem he
has.

Role-play until the interview has reached its natural conclusion, then
ask your colleagues to give their views of your performance, if necessary
using the 'Skills of effective helping' as a crib.

This next suggestion is only slightly tongue-in-cheek! If you are not yet
all exhausted by this exercise, you could try repeating it, this time you
being the person with the problem. Make the problem '*I have to counsel
staff in my work, and am finding it more difficult than I realized*'. Often by
reversing roles – putting yourself in the position of 'the other person' -
you learn more about techniques and pitfalls than you would by more
role-plays with you in the counsellor's seat.

# 7 Disciplinary interviews

We're not talking here of the informal 'tickings off' you may have to give to staff from time to time, but of part of a formal procedure which, in the worst scenario, could lead to dismissal (for the latter see Chapter 8). A disciplinary interview is basically an enquiry into the work or conduct of an employee in order to ascertain what further action needs to be taken. You could find that the employee would benefit from being given merely advice or extra support and training. On the downside, your investigation may result in anything from warning or reprimand to dismissal. It is important, therefore, that the seriousness of the situation be reflected in everything you say and do.

This is not to say that you do not offer the common courtesies due at any meeting – far from it. If the employee leaves the interview fully understanding the effects of his conduct or under-performance on the organization, to colleagues and himself, yet challenged and motivated to improve, you will have conducted a successful interview.

You need to prepare thoroughly, and create an environment suitable for holding a disciplinary interview. In terms of preparation, it will depend on whether you are instigating the formal procedure on your own behalf – as the result of behaviour which you have observed in one of your team – or whether one of your supervisors or line managers has already begun the disciplinary process by giving informal or formal initial warnings, and is now handing over the procedure to you. Let's presume it is the latter situation. The individual has already been spoken to by his immediate supervisor, and is now coming to you for a formal disciplinary hearing.

First you will need to get the facts from the supervisor – as he sees them. On what evidence and by whose judgement is the employee's work or conduct unsatisfactory? You will also need to remind yourself of your organization's code of practice concerning discipline, and check the boundaries of your own role in a procedure which could lead to eventual dismissal of the employee. In an ideal world, you will know the individual quite well without having to resort to checking his personal files. If you don't know the employee that well, you would be advised to check this out before the interview.

Arrange a date and time for the interview. Choose a suitable slot in the day to allow enough time for the interview without being pressured by other appointments, meal breaks and so on.

You will need to conduct the interview in a room suitable for the purpose. Two chairs in the corner of the workroom will not do. You need privacy; you need to arrange that you are not disturbed or interrupted. While not wanting to put the employee at an unfair disadvantage, consider the layout of the room. Might this be an occasion when a chair on the other side of the desk from you is appropriate? While considering the other person's needs, apprehensions and so on, *you* need to feel confident and in control. Decide on what feels right and comfortable for you.

There are not many people who enjoy giving negative feedback, or being the bearer of bad news. Although with practice you will be able to take such meetings in your stride, initially you may find disciplining staff potentially stressful, so also diarize time for yourself, before the interview, to get settled, organized and in control. You will not give the appearance of professional authority if you arrive for the interview late, flushed, harassed and disorganized. You need to be there, with notes to hand and your opening lines mentally rehearsed. If necessary, do one or two relaxation exercises before the employee arrives to reduce stress levels and help modulate your voice.

When the employee arrives for the interview you will need clearly to explain the complaint against him, and the basis of your information. Give him the opportunity to put his point of view. Don't just go through the motions of hearing what he has to say, but actively listen and question to ensure that the interview is fair and the employee has ample opportunity to state his case. The employee may be glad to have the opportunity to acknowledge that he has a problem and be receptive to offers of support and guidance. However, you may have to work at establishing joint understanding of the situation. He needs to be able to see that there is a discrepancy between the company's standards and his own conduct or performance.

If it becomes apparent that the supervisor's or junior manager's version of events is not as accurate as first appeared, promise to investigate further before proceeding. It may emerge that there were extenuating circumstances for the deterioration in work or unsatisfactory conduct, in which case the interview should continue on a counselling rather than disciplinary basis.

On the other hand if, after hearing the employee's version you consider the complaint against him to be justified, you should tell him so, but at the same time, make it as easy as possible for him to see his way to improved conduct or performance. Agree what he can do, with or without outside help, to put things right. It will be far easier for him to modify his behaviour than to alter his personality, so discuss the problem in measurable terms; do not criticize personality. Explain objectively why he is being formally reprimanded, giving examples of conduct, behaviour or poor performance, e.g.

> You failed to pass on an important telephone message on Monday; and again yesterday. John's report, which should have been duplicated and sent last Friday, was still in your in-tray this morning. This has resulted in ... so ...

Be clear about the standards of performance you expect. You must then explain what you intend to do about the situation: what you expect to be done differently, what improvements you expect to see, and by when. Tell the employee that this is a formal warning which will be recorded in writing. It will stay on his personal file for however long is appropriate. Make a follow-up date to discuss progress.

Does anyone else need to know about the outcome of the interview? Will the employee need support? Is anyone else's work likely to be affected? Who will have the job of monitoring progress, guiding and correcting on a day-to-day basis? Certainly, your boss and the employee's line manager need to be informed; possibly personnel if there is a chance that a final warning/dismissal is a possibility.

Keep the follow-up interview whether or not there has been an improvement. If there has, it's good to be able to offer a sincerely meant 'Well done'.

## EXERCISE

Consider the following scenarios. How would you deal with them?

1. Sally, one of your team, has been late for work three times this week. Yesterday you spoke briefly with her about it, letting her know that her late arrivals had not gone unnoticed, and that you want her timekeeping to improve. She's late again this morning, so you arrange to see her formally at 2.30 p.m.

2. As part of the weekly meeting with your boss, he tells you that he had called at one of your retail outlets and was appalled to see that a sales

assistant had ignored a black male customer on three occasions, serving other customers ahead of him. 'Do something about it; I will not tolerate racism within this organization' he says.

**Possible responses**

1.  We will assume that you have arranged for the interview to take place somewhere private and have agreed for Sally's duties to be covered, and for someone to field visitors and telephone calls so that you will not be interrupted. We will assume also that you are prepared and have done your deep-breathing relaxation exercises if necessary!

    First, you will need to state your case, objectively, giving the dates and times she was late. When she has agreed these facts, give her the opportunity to explain her poor timekeeping. Her response will dictate the pattern the interview will take, so we will have to offer hypothetical reasons for her being late.

    What if she says, 'I'm so sorry, but I've this temporary problem at home. I should have told you about it before, but I hoped I could make other arrangements. My mother usually takes the children to school, but she's been taken into hospital. As you know, I've no one else to help out. The school gates aren't opened until 8.30 for security reasons, and I can't leave them on the street outside – it takes me at least 45 minutes to get from the school to here ... I'm so sorry ... it won't be for long I promise ...' etc.

    In this instance, it would be very unreasonable to continue with the 'big stick' approach. Sally needs a bit of understanding and support at this time, although in the final analysis she has a contract to fulfil. No doubt you could come to some arrangement for her to make up the time. While Sally does not need additional stress at this time, she should be made aware that this has to be a temporary arrangement, however.

    On the other hand, if Sally's reason is something like, 'the buses have been so unreliable this week' or 'sorry, I overslept – been burning the ol' midnight oil a bit of late!' these are not reasons, but excuses.

    Ideally you should attempt to get Sally to identify for herself the standards expected of her, where she is falling short of these standards, and the knock-on effect for other staff members. Obviously you do this by careful questioning. If necessary you will have to tell her the standards you expect, and why. For example, if Sally's job involves opening post, staff members will get their correspondence later than usual; if she has telephone duties, someone else has to take her calls until she arrives; if another member of staff has to cover for her in any way, their work suffers. If the time is not made up at lunch time or after work, she is effectively stealing time from her employer. In the final analysis, she is not fulfilling the terms of her contract.

Be specific about what improvement you want, and the time-scale involved. For example, Sally must be at her desk ready for work by 9.00 a.m. each morning, and the situation reviewed after a month; or Sally must report to you personally each morning before commencing her duties. The situation will formally be reviewed after a month.

2.  Do not act formally on hearsay. You didn't see the alleged 'offence'. Check out the details with the sales assistant. There may well have been mitigating circumstances. What if you jump in with both feet, call a disciplinary hearing and accuse him of racism and he says 'I knew he was there; I said he could wait in the warm while his wife and child went to the "Ladies" ' or 'I'd already served him; he was waiting for his taxi'. You would end up with egg on your face and a lot of apologizing to do!

Get the facts. Many organizations have equal opportunities policies, and infringement of company rules in this aspect will not be tolerated, so if, after hearing the sales assistant's side of the story you feel that there is cause for complaint, leave him in no doubt that this is a formal warning and a further offence of this nature could lead to dismissal.

# 8  Dismissals

It's all too easy to say that a good manager will have not let a situation get to the point where a problem member of staff has to be dismissed. One would hope that being closely involved with your team, perceptive of team spirit (or lack of it) and maintaining good communication with your staff, should have enabled you to iron out any difficulties before they became major issues. This is not always the case. Whereas prevention may well be better than cure, there may be occasions when dismissal is the only answer.

It is not in the remit of this book to go into lengthy details about the rules, regulations and legislation concerning dismissal. If you work for a large organization, your Personnel Department will liaise with unions and oversee the dismissal process. Your concern, as manager, is more likely to be with identifying the problem, communicating with the person concerned, issuing informal and formal warnings, and keeping meticulous records of all communication and meetings; or it could be that your key role is in overseeing your supervisors as they carry out these tasks. More of this later. For the minute, let's look at some of the reasons staff can be dismissed:

1. A new recruit has given false information on application for a position for which he subsequently shows a lack of aptitude. Checking credentials proves that he untruthfully claimed to have certain qualifications or experience.
2. Someone fails to match up to minimum standards after a stipulated probationary period.
3. Assault/drinking/drugs.
4. If it can be proved that someone has taken a lot of time off work with no good cause, or has extended sick leave.
5. Dishonesty – stealing etc. at the workplace.

6.   Insubordination or failure to respond to authority.
7.   Organizational inefficiency.
8.   Incapability.
9.   End of temporary contract.
10.  Where rules necessary to maintain standards have been broken.

Taking these one by one:

1.   This was an error which occurred at selection. It is sometimes the
     case that a person might claim certain qualifications obtained at
     school many years ago; it is unlikely that an employer would need to
     follow this up a) because it was so long ago and the qualifications
     were minor or b) because subsequent qualifications and experience
     are far more relevant to the position applied for. Dishonest though
     this may be in principle, it is unlikely to be a real issue.
        More serious is the false claim of acquired skills, levels of compe-
     tence etc. A recent television programme exposed the leniency of one
     national organization in checking applicants' eligibility to register as
     a member of that professional association. If a newly recruited
     member of staff can be shown to have falsely claimed skills, compe-
     tencies or qualifications *required for the performance of that position* he
     can be dismissed.

2.   Again, this is a selection problem. It should have been established, at
     interview, that the person had an inherent aptitude for the work
     applied for. If, as sometimes happens, a person is skilled at being
     interviewed, and deceives his interviewers into believing his compe-
     tence, but then is found to be incapable of performing the work,
     *despite training and ongoing help with learning the necessary functions,*
     technically he can be dismissed. In practice, it is sometimes a 'face-
     saver' to offer alternative employment within the company on
     extended probation.

3.   If a member of staff displays violence to his employer, colleagues or
     clients, he can be summarily dismissed – that is fired without notice.
     However, you need to collect all the facts of the situation. For
     example, if there was a fight, were there mitigating circumstances?
     Were both parties equally to blame? Will both be similarly dis-
     ciplined? It should go without saying that you need not go through
     the oral and written warning procedures (explained more fully later)
     if, for example, your supervisor stabs you in the arm!

Drinking and/or drug-taking which renders the employee unfit to fulfil his duties and/or jeopardizes safety, are also situations which can lead to dismissal. Again, all the facts must be considered, and the employer's decision to dismiss must be based on reasonable grounds.

4. Absenteeism – especially of the 'long-weekend' syndrome – can lead to an employee's dismissal, but only supported by well-documented evidence of recurring absence. Sickness, whether genuine or of the '(suspect) bad back' variety, is difficult. A person who is genuinely long-term sick poses a moral as well as logistical and financial problem for the organization, but if it can be proved that sufficient communication and reasonable care has been taken, ultimately the decision may have to be to remove this employee from the books, and would be considered grounds for fair dismissal.

5. Again, this is a case for summary dismissal – that is dismissal without notice or money in lieu of notice. Should the fired employee subsequently claim that he was unfairly dismissed, you, or your organization, must be able to show that you had investigated fully, giving the employee ample opportunity to explain, and then had sufficient grounds/proof of dishonesty to warrant instant termination of the employee's contract.

6. There is sometimes a problem with an employee who, though capable of doing his job, is reluctant to give of his best. When this involves refusal to obey reasonable instructions, it can be interpreted as not meeting the terms of his contract. Here again, the manager will have to demonstrate that he has fully investigated the misconduct, and given the employee every opportunity to improve his behaviour or poor performance; but in the final analysis, the insubordinate, habitually careless, or demotivated employee can be dismissed.

7. This is a term which refers to an employee who is a disruptive force in your team, or has a disruptive affect on the organization as a whole. Each case must be looked at on its own merits, but technically, if disruption of staff relations can be proved, it is a fair reason for dismissal.

8. Employers are entitled to dismiss any person who is, or becomes, unable to meet the demands of the job. This could be under the

banner of poor performance in which case the individual should be questioned as to why they are underachieving, and their explanation fully checked. If training, in some form, is a solution, this should be provided where possible, and the individual given sufficient time to improve his performance. There are some instances – where technology has moved a job into a different area of expertise, for example – when a person is literally incapable of effectively performing the new work. If this situation occurs, and if no suitable alternative work is available, technically the person can be dismissed. However, all alternative means of keeping the person on the books should have been exhausted, and if the main cause of incapacity is because the nature of the job has changed, redundancy rather than dismissal should be considered.

9.   Obviously, if someone is hired on a temporary basis, and the fixed term contract comes to an end, the person's rights to be employed with you cease. It is important that the individual is fully aware that his contract is temporary before he commences work.

10.   This includes situations where an individual disregards rules or instructions jeopardizing his own or others' safety. Continual absence or poor timekeeping can also adversely affect organizational standards.

This is not an exhaustive list; there are many other grounds for dismissal. However, they will generally fall into one of two categories: grounds for summary dismissal, or dismissal with notice/money in lieu of notice. It will be fairly clear which offences warrant instant (summary) dismissal without notice, but the employer must be clear that the seriousness of the misconduct warrants such dismissal. Regarding dismissal with notice, there is legislation and clear rules dictating how much notice (or payment in lieu) should be given. The Advisory, Conciliation and Arbitration Service (ACAS) has produced a code of practice on procedures. Their publication, *Discipline at Work*, is available from ACAS Reader Ltd, PO Box 16, Earl Shilton, Leicester, LE9 8ZZ and has a checklist for handling disciplinary matters.

Generally, you will need to be sure of who within your organization have the powers to dismiss employees, and where your role begins and ends with regard to this. You will need to know your own organization's disciplinary procedure. In any event, as stated above, you will need to consult with the Personnel Department, senior management, or seek advice before embarking on the dismissal process if you are to avoid damage limitation at best; or being taken to an industrial tribunal for unfair dismissal at worst.

Assuming for the moment that you are in a line management position, let's take a closer look at your involvement with the initial stages of the process. It is likely to be you who identifies the problem member of staff; it is certainly up to you to put the disciplinary wheels in motion. (If your supervisor or junior manager is likely to be dealing with these initial stages, your role, of course, is to train and support him accordingly.)

With relatively minor offences (and potentially dismissible ones), first you will need to speak, informally, with the individual to gather all the facts and to get their perspective on the situation. You will need to have this interview somewhere quiet, where you will not be interrupted. If the situation allows, choose your time so that you will not be rushed, and the individual can give you his full attention. Consider the environment and atmosphere you wish to create. For example, would your office, their place of work or neutral territory be most suitable? Do you want the armchair, chatty approach to this meeting, or should you consider a more formal room setting? What affect is each likely to have on the individual with whom you're dealing?

Ensure that your body language reflects a) the seriousness, and b) your confidence and command of the situation. Come straight to the point. Explain the circumstances as you see them. Remember to concentrate on facts, not opinions; behaviour not personality. Give him the opportunity to explain. Question well to clarify the situation, e.g. 'What precisely happened?' 'How did . . . arise?' 'What do you mean by . . . ?' and actively listen to ascertain relevant facts. Reflect back and summarize to ensure mutual understanding.

If the matter can be cleared up, and/or an informal warning and arrangements for improvements can be made at this stage, so be it. The matter can remain confidential, until review, between the supervisor/ manager and member of staff. If, however, you decide at this stage that a formal oral warning is called for, ensure that the individual knows that though oral, this warning is the first stage in the disciplinary procedure. Don't finish the interview until you are confident that you have understood, been understood, and that the individual knows what will happen, initially, as the result of the meeting.

If appropriate, interview other members of staff/witnesses of the misconduct; collect statements and documentary evidence. If a formal oral warning has been given, inform your boss so that details can be officially recorded. *Always* diarize what was said, to whom and when.

Decide where you go from here. If, after your initial meeting, an unofficial warning has been sufficient initial action in the circumstances, how will you go about monitoring the individual's performance? When will you talk about progress informally and/or formally? (The latter should have been discussed at the initial meeting, of course.) Would counselling, or additional training be appropriate?

What if formal disciplinary action is required? Consider whether suspension is called for while investigations are pursued. Will the suspension be with or without pay? How long might the investigations last? Obviously, the individual must quickly be informed of the decision.

If there is to be a formal, disciplinary interview, ensure that the individual is fully aware of why he is being called, and that he may bring along a friend or representative. It would be useful if a second member of management is also present. At the interview itself, start the formal proceedings by introducing all in attendance. Explain that notes will be taken of the interview. Succinctly explain the reasons for the interview, and check that the individual understands the nature of the complaint, and his rights within the procedure (the right of appeal at each stage of the formal procedure, for example). Ask the individual to explain his case; question fully, reflect back, summarize etc. to ensure all evidence is 'on the table' and again, that you understand and have been understood. If any new facts emerge, decide whether further investigation is required. If it is, adjourn the meeting and reconvene when investigations are completed. *Record everything.*

If there is no adjournment, next explain what corrections to behaviour or performance are expected, and by when. If a written warning is to be given, explain how long this will remain on the employee's records. Assert the consequences of failing to improve. The written warning should include details of the nature of the offence, the consequences of failure to improve or of further offences, and confirmation of which stage in the disciplinary procedure this letter represents.

As manager, you will need closely to monitor the individual's behaviour or performance – helping, counselling, and encouraging improvement. Keep communication channels open; discuss progress regularly.

If it still comes to a final warning (which will be in writing) make clear that the consequences of non-improvement or further offences could result in dismissal.

## EXERCISE

Consider the following scenarios. What would be your initial action to rectify the situation?

1. Ann is a clerical assistant responsible for processing sales staff expenses claims. On several afternoons you have noticed the smell of alcohol on her breath, but have assumed that she had had a lunch-

time drink; her work hasn't suffered. This morning, however, she seems pre-occupied and unhappy. Although it is just 9.30 a.m., you notice the smell of alcohol on her breath.

2. Jack works on a motor engine production line as part of a team. His work involves welding. Because of health and safety regulations, it is against company policy to drink alcohol during working hours. It is the start of Jack's shift, and you notice the smell of alcohol on his breath.

3. For some time you have suspected that a cashier has been cheating your company by letting her friends have goods free or at a reduced price. Today you catch her red-handed; you personally observe her pretending to pass items over the bar code scan – in fact, just sliding them along the counter to her friend.

4. Barry interviewed well; he seemed the ideal candidate for manager of a new resource centre and was duly appointed. Unfortunately his performance has been poor; he seems totally unsuited to the job and unable to cope with its demands. On investigation, it is discovered that claims he made on his application form were invented and previous posts quoted, with similar responsibilities, non-existent.

5. Karen has been off sick for several months, and although she is still entitled to sick pay from your company, your boss is concerned that the organization can no longer afford to pay Karen, and for cover for her post (which is crucial to the smooth-running of the company).

**Possible responses**

1. From the scant evidence of this scenario, you can deduce a few things. Unless your company has clear, written policies on drinking alcohol or being under its influence while at work, this is not a case for summary dismissal; not even, perhaps, for a formal warning. It would appear rather that this member of staff might need help and counselling. An informal meeting is called for and it should go without saying that it should be handled with sensitivity. You should try to create an atmosphere where Ann feels able to 'open up' to you should she wish to. Your role is not that of counsellor, but of a facilitator to help create an awareness in Ann that she may need professional help. If she is in agreement, you can then go on to arrange for a referral to a trained counsellor, welfare officer or doctor.

   If Ann refuses to admit there is a problem, an informal warning may then be appropriate.

2.   Jack's situation, however, is slightly different. While it is difficult to assess how much anyone has drunk, and how their performance is impaired as a result, where there are company rules, and where health and safety are involved, being under the influence of alcohol while on duty can be a dismissable offence. In an instance such as the one recorded in the scenario, Jack should be sent home (suspended) until a disciplinary interview can be arranged. The suspension would usually be with pay. The interview should follow the lines shown above with a formal written warning, because if it comes to dismissal, and should Jack take his case to an industrial tribunal, you will need to prove that you had reasonable grounds for the termination of employment.

3.   The cashier has been caught in the act, but you need a witness, so ask a colleague to check the goods in the friend's possession with the till receipt. Don't do this in front of other customers or sales staff, but ask the friend to accompany you and the colleague somewhere private. If there is a discrepancy of just one item, and the cashier makes an excuse such as 'It missed the scanner light and I was busy chatting so didn't hear the bleep', there is little you can do there and then. You are quite entitled to call her for a subsequent interview, state the case as you see it, and issue a warning. If, however, it can be shown that you have specific evidence of dishonesty (such as several items passed through without being scanned and therefore paid for*) your company could instantly dismiss the cashier without notice.

   *The *organization* would be within its rights to summarily dismiss. Make sure you know who, within your company, has the authority actually to dismiss staff.

4.   The options are to suspend Barry pending full enquiries so that sufficient evidence is gained to warrant dismissal. If it is possible to redeploy Barry within the organization in a position more suited to his ability, this would be an alternative solution. Theoretically, however, he has acted unlawfully in giving false information at the time of recruitment and can be dismissed on these grounds. Even with senior posts where it is customary for CVs plus letters of application to be used rather than completing a customized application form, it is well to consider having some documentation on file where the individual has to sign to the effect that information given at the time of selection is true. With this signature, proven false declarations aid the dismissal process and reduce the risk of industrial tribunals. Of course, as with all cases of dismissal, the employer needs to be able to show reasonable grounds for terminating a contract.

In terms of your role in this process, you would have to make it clear to Barry why he is being suspended, whether this is to be with or without pay, the process of investigation which will now be under way, and when he is likely to hear of the company's decision. This meeting should be recorded, and Barry given written confirmation of the above. It should go without saying that your manner should be professional, your communication succinct and unambiguous leaving Barry in no doubt about the seriousness of the situation and the possible outcome.

5.  Dismissing staff because of sickness is always a difficult issue. However justified the dismissal, remaining staff's morale can suffer, and the reputation of the company can be adversely affected unless the situation is handled fairly, with tact and sensitivity. However, the fact remains that an organization cannot afford to have absent staff on its books for too long, and ultimately something has to be done to sever ties with the long-term sick employee.

Incidently, in the scenario it states that Karen is still entitled to sick leave. Expiration of sick leave entitlement is not necessarily synonymous with a suitable date for termination of employment. Some larger organizations can perhaps 'carry' absent staff for longer than small companies who need 'all hands on deck' to keep afloat.

In this instance, Karen can be dismissed, because technically she is unable to fulfil the terms of her contract, but you will have to be careful to follow adequate and appropriate procedures. First you need to talk with Karen and this may mean a home visit if she is too sick to come to your place of work. You need a fuller picture of the situation than a medical certificate can provide in order to establish whether she might be fit for less demanding work (should any be available) in the company. This is best done through a doctor, of course, so with Karen's consent, her GP could be consulted. Karen has legislative rights in this matter and should be informed of these at this stage. She has the right to refuse consent; she is entitled to see her GP's report before it is submitted to the company; she has the right to refuse this report being given to her employer; she also has the right to amend the report if she feels it is unfair or untrue in any way. The GP is bound to include these observations and comments in the report.

Of course, if the organization has its own doctor, he can be called upon to examine and talk with Karen, and to give a medical opinion. Wherever possible, if Karen can return to work in some capacity, whether to a suitably modified position or alternative work albeit at a lower grade, this should be preferable to dismissal. However, Karen needs to be informed of her situation, and that her case is now proceeding formally towards ultimate termination of contract unless an alternative solution can be found.

## Grievances and constructive dismissal

It would be wrong to leave a chapter on dismissals without some mention of the fact that employees also have grounds to take their employers to task. If your company has a discipline procedure, it will also have a grievance procedure whereby staff can formally complain about unfair treatment.

If an individual can prove that his employer made his working conditions so intolerable that he was forced to resign, he can claim compensation on the grounds of constructive dismissal.

# 9  Empowerment

The employment culture has changed drastically – and continues to do so – as organizations become flatter, hierarchal structures disappear, and job security in return for loyalty and an acceptable days work, becomes a thing of the past. Gone are the halcyon days of a job for life. Whereas previously there were obvious career paths within organizations, and climbing the promotional ladder was seen as a matter of course, today there are few incentives to offer staff. Organizations have fewer resources; they have to provide more, of better quality, for less if they are to compete and survive in the market-place. Even in the public sector, 'in-house' jobs are on the decline as more and more services are being provided by outside agencies – and competition is rife.

So, if organizations cannot offer promotion, extra pay or resources to staff as they did in the past, what motivates them to continue giving their best to the company? Interestingly, when managers and employees have separately been given lists of factors which motivate staff, and asked to prioritize these factors, what managers think employees want – money and promotion – do not rate highly on employee's lists. In fact, recognition and appreciation for work well done, personal development, a sense of belonging, and 'ownership' of their work are often rated far higher by employees.

A solution to the problem of meeting organizational needs – where heightened competition and increased demands for better quality and service have to be constantly addressed, as do employees' needs for more involvement, job satisfaction, learning opportunities, and 'life-training' – lies in a complete rethinking of traditional management practices. Managers need to abandon their role as controllers, decision-makers and problem-solvers, and hand over responsibility – and authority – to employees. Middle management's role becomes one of facilitation, encouragement, enablement, motivation and support to their teams.

Employees – individually, in work groups or teams – take responsibility for setting their own agendas, organizing their workload, taking the initiative, being responsible, and accountable, for results. The emphasis is not just on a job well done, but one that can be replicated and improved on. They take control over their own work environment, and for the quality of their working life. This is what motivates them. *This is empowerment.* It is essentially a new collaborative approach to organizational effectiveness. Instead of managers thinking 'How am I going to organize this work?' they will now ask their staff, 'How can we achieve this together?'

This involves fundamental changes which will affect every person in the organization, and many people feel threatened by change; some will actively resist it. So how do you make it work? What is involved for you as a manager? One thing is certain, empowerment requires the best of your people skills. It is essential that you are an excellent role model for your staff, that you have good communication and assertiveness skills, that you can lead from behind, yet be up front with support and encouragement. In a nutshell, you need to be able to create the environment and conditions whereby your people can excel. Many of these skills have been described in other sections of the book. See the chapters on assertiveness, communicating skills, NLP, influencing, motivation and team-building. This chapter will concentrate on your own changing role, and on how to begin and lead the empowerment process.

Empowerment has to begin with the manager. I make no apology for frequently using the third person, referring to 'the manager' in this section, because you may very well already be an empowering manager, and merely need to enhance the skills of this new role. New managers – empowerers – will need to be open to new ideas and willing to explore new possibilities.

However, many managers will find difficulty in relinquishing power, control and authority to employees, and will find it difficult to see their function in an entirely different light. There are areas of management, such as interpreting company policy, supervising quality and resources, where you will still have tight control. There will be other areas where control and responsibility for action can be devolved down through the organization. A good example of this is the handling of customer complaints by shop assistants. In the past, front-line staff could do little more than apologize for faulty goods or service. Formal complaints had to passed on to a manager or customer services department. But who knows best how to handle the complaint? Who has had direct contact with the customer? Who is handling and selling the products? (Arguably, who can best assess customer needs?) The answer is the front-line staff. Empowered shop assistants will be able to make decisions about how best to handle a complaint without *having* to refer to a manager or distanced department. They will have the skills to placate the dissatisfied customer and the confidence to know what redress is called for. They will know procedures for replacements, refunds and/or compensation and the authority to offer what they consider appropriate. They will know that should they need the support of management, it will be there for them. They will be aware that responsibility for their decision rests with them – for good or bad.

The overall effect on the employee is that he will have 'ownership' of his work, and the satisfaction of seeing a job through. He will feel more in control; hence more motivated. He is not just doing a job – completing allocated tasks – but achieving results, helping the whole organization to work better. He will appreciate the value of teamwork where there is co-operation and collaboration between team members and leaders, and between work groups and teams.

The implications for the manager is that he will need to train, coach and support staff, enabling and encouraging them to use their creativity and initiative. As facilitator rather than director of effective work, he must take a back seat in the planning and implementation of work, but be there for staff should they need him. First, however, he must get into the state of mind to make all of this happen. He must have faith in himself in order to have the confidence to let go, and have faith in others so that abilities, talents, skills, responsibility, authority and control are shared.

Where does an organization begin in a process which has to be all-encompassing if it is to succeed – because empowerment means a total change in the way of working. First there is a need to establish where the organization is now, then plan and manage the stages of devolvement. Remember that just as you will decide where and to whom you will delegate responsibilities and authority, senior management will also be looking to middle managers to take over accountabilities. There will need to be wide-scale learning and training opportunities, and support for everyone involved – true team spirit!

# EXERCISE

It would be useful to consider the first of these stages – deciding where you are right now – to assess the sorts of issues empowerment encompasses. List the people skills you would need to use/develop to cover each area.

*Personal*

Empowered employees know where they stand and what is expected of them. Individually, or as part of a team, they have control over their work, and responsibility traditionally given to managers. They have good company/product knowledge and are confident with systems and procedures. They understand the company culture and ethos. They know where the company is going and are committed to helping it get there. They trust the company and its managers.

———————————————————————

———————————————————————

———————————————————————

*Morale*

Empowered individuals are trusted, and respected for who they are, irrespective of lifestyle and values. They are enthusiastic about their work, and enjoy working for the organization. They feel they have a positive contribution to make to the success of the enterprise. Relationships and personal life are important aspects of the world of work. Change is managed well. Work is challenging, but not pressurized.

———————————————————————

———————————————————————

———————————————————————

*Decision-making and objective-setting*

Empowered people feel a sense of ownership for work goals and targets they have established. They have authority to make decisions regarding their work, or share in the decision-making process. They are responsible for the results of their work. Customer complaints are resolved at local level.

_____

_____

_____

## Teamwork

Empowered individuals share, and help each other. They work well together. They recognize interdependence and realize that goals are better achieved with mutual support. Team members are encouraged openly to express ideas, feelings, opinions and disagreements. People work together to solve problems. They make an effort to understand each others' point of view. Individuals care about each other and are prepared to help each other out. There is a good working relationship between work groups/teams.

_____

_____

_____

## Involvement

Empowered people are consulted on a regular basis. Questions are welcomed. Individuals are encouraged to grow, and develop new skills. There is no tight control over procedures; individuals are encouraged to enhance the process and task elements of their job.

They work towards continuous improvements.

_____

_____

_____

*Communication*

Empowered individuals and teams communicate well. People are kept up to date with company policy. They know what's going on in the organization. Communication lines are open horizontally and vertically; information is passed quickly and clearly. Individuals practise open and honest communication. They actively seek others' views, opinions and suggestions. They try to understand each others' points of view. They see areas of disagreement as opportunities to exchange views, and work constructively to resolve misunderstandings.

---

---

---

*The organization*

Empowered individuals/teams get the resources they need to do a good job. Organizational structure aids individual/team effectiveness. People are rewarded for work well done. Rather than being small cogs in big wheels, individuals feel they are a valued part of a large, cooperative, successful team. They trust what the company says.

---

---

---

**Possible responses**

Responses are going to cover the whole range of communication and interpersonal skills. To take up a few issues: managers of an empowered workforce will need to:

- abandon the notion that managers keep processes and people under tight control
- facilitate – be able to create an environment and provide the resources for teams to excel

- provide direction and clarify objectives
- enable – give them the confidence to perform to maximum potential
- focus on staff development
- ensure that every employee has good company and product know-ledge, knows the value of his work, and where he fits in
- enthuse teams so that they believe in themselves and their abilities
- practise excellent change management skills
- initiate enquiry about how tasks are achieved
- help teams to concentrate on process rather than content
- assist teams to enhance the content and context of the work
- delegate – devolve responsibility and authority as far as possible down the organizational structure. Ensure that the employee has the experience, skills and, if necessary, extra training or coaching to achieve – then stand back
- be there to support, but not to direct
- allow teams to take control over the planning and implementation of their work
- relinquish the concept that managers need to control
- be a role model
- demonstrate personal commitment
- trust the team
- recognize that employees who have the best understanding of a given situation are likely to be the most appropriate people to make decisions regarding that situation, so delegate power accordingly
- foster a learning environment
- make learning opportunities and training accessible
- brief and debrief well; support training
- tolerate temporary lowered effectiveness during learning curves
- collaborate with teams. Empowerment is a different way of working *together* continually to improve performance
- share vision, but allow structure, procedures and systems to evolve within the team. Inspire, enthuse and energize staff
- encourage mutual support – within and between teams – in order to achieve organizational cohesion, improved performance and higher levels of productivity
- instil commitment. The bottom line is survival. If jobs are to be kept, a commitment to the organization and its success against competition is paramount
- maximize previously untapped skills and talents. Allow employees to perform to capacity
- enable individuals and groups to do their own problem-solving. Coach teams in the principles of effective problem-solving if necessary – then leave them to get on with it

- set challenges
- seek out new ideas
- welcome experimentation and risk-taking; be tolerant of mistakes along the way
- abolish blame. When things go wrong, discourage apportioning blame, but encourage joint problem-solving
- teach teams to *understand* problems; don't just fix them
- keep up to date with global trends, the competition and company policies
- interpret, and disseminate information to employees
- maintain clear, open communication channels, up, down, across and between teams and departments
- promote honest, open interactions
- request and encourage constructive feedback
- help teams recognize that conflict can be healthy if seen as an opportunity for new ideas and creativity
- mediate, only when hostility cannot be resolved between individuals or by the team
- fight for adequate resources for employees to do the best possible job
- control quality and resources
- weed out structures, procedures and 'red tape' which hamper pro-activity
- listen
- have time; be there for them
- care for, and about people
- be honest, sincere and trustworthy
- keep commitments and expect others to do so in return
- inspire trust and respect
- acknowledge achievements
- recognize effort and accomplishments
- praise work well done
- publicize and celebrate success.

You will be able to ascertain, from this list, where you are right now as a manager, and how far along the empowerment road your organization has progressed. If you are new to empowerment, the list will give you some idea of your role in the empowered organization. Empowerers need to be able to develop a climate for team excellence; they must help employees to develop and grow as individuals and team members. They will be a communication link between policy-makers and employees, and the link connecting teams, integrating effort. If you are to be an empowerer, you will need commitment and energy. You will need to trust yourself and others. By relinquishing power and control in the old managerial sense, you are in fact gaining a powerful and motivated workforce, enabled and prepared to do what needs to be done rather than what they are required to do.

## New leadership

Empowerering managers need to be open to new ideas, new ways of doing things and have an openness to learning. They should learn from competitors, ask advice, practise lateral thinking. They should look to expand their own skills and abilities; in short, be a role model for their team.

One of the key elements of the new manager's role is to encourage learning. To be fully effective, teams need to look not just at the content – *what* has to be done – but at the process – *how* best to do a job. They should be more concerned with doing the right thing than in doing things right. They need to be innovative and creative; they need to experiment and test to see not only how to get a job done, but be able to do it again more productively.

## Change management

This is not the time or place to tackle the huge issue of the management of change, but let's just look at some of the issues involved if you are just setting out on the empowerment process in your organization.

First you need to recognize that resistance to any change is a natural human reaction. There is a multiplicity of reasons, some of which will be easier to tackle than others, but it is a fact of life that while some individuals relish challenge and thrive on change, there will be those who want to maintain the *status quo*, and others (hopefully only a few) who will actively resist change – unless or until they can be convinced of the benefits. The key is sensitive management. Recognize anxieties and uncertainties – yours and theirs. Confront and deal with them. Know your allies and those who will offer the most resistance.

Fully understand why there is going to be a radical change in management practice and explain this to your team. Talk through the principles of empowerment, demonstrating your commitment to it and stressing the benefits to employees: they will be working in a more flexible way, being able to take responsibility for setting their own agendas, and defining the quality of their working lives. They will have far more control over their world of work. Talk about the changes empowerment is going to make to everyone in the organization.

Communicate, consult, communicate. Involve everyone in forward planning. This is time consuming, but remember, it takes more time to get more commitment. Find out more about resistance. Question and actively listen. What are the resisting forces? Where do they come from? Why are they there? Nudge, rather than drive change through. When those who most strongly resist change see the successes of the new system, they will not want to feel isolated from colleagues, and hopefully will want to be a fully participating part of your winning team!

## Empowered teams

Empowerment is about teams of people working together to do the best possible job for the organization. In an empowered workplace, decision making will gradually pass from the manager to the team. There will be five stages in this process:

1. You decide and ask for feedback and opinions.
2. You ask for input from the team; then make a decision, asking for comments.
3. You discuss the issues fully with the team. There is active participation from everyone. You decide, checking that everyone goes along with the decision.
4. You collaborate. Everyone is involved, working on the issue until a consensus is reached. Everyone takes responsibility for the decision. You share the glory or the criticism.
5. They decide. They take control.

Empowered teamwork is about sharing – sharing vision, goals, information, ideals and ideas. It's about honest, open communication. It's about mutual respect; expecting the best from your colleagues.

The role of the manager, in setting a positive example, is crucial to the effectiveness of an empowered team.

# 10 Induction

I'm assuming that you are working for an organization which has a personnel or human resources department, and that they will look after administrative details for the new recruit. This section will give some guidelines on how you, as manager, receive a new member on to your staff. It will offer suggestions on how to make him feel a welcome and valued member of your team, and to maximize his effectiveness in your department and with the organization.

I would like to start with a true account of what happened recently to a friend of mine who applied for a position with a small market research company. The post was administrative manager and field co-ordinator of the market research teams. She was recruited and interviewed by the boss/director. He seemed very efficient and friendly, and although the job was a departure from her usual line of work, she felt that the position would be a challenge she would like to take on. She was therefore delighted when he telephoned to say that she had been successful, and to arrange a starting date.

She should have been warned by the fact that no letter confirming her appointment or contract of employment arrived in the post, but she turned up for work on the appointed day, assuming that administrative details would be taken care of then. On arriving, she was met with blank stares from the other employees in the office (who would all be junior, in position, to her). 'The boss is away on business this week', she was told.

For the sake of brevity, I won't give details of the dreadful week she spent, trying to ascertain what her job entailed (the previous occupant of the post had long since departed, leaving mountains of work which meant very little to my friend, who tried nevertheless to deal with the backlog). No one befriended her; she had to find her own way about the building; make assumptions about meal breaks and so on. The atmosphere in the office was unfriendly and tense, and it appeared that everyone was expected to work through their lunch-hours and stay late to cope with the volume of work – although commitment over and above the call of duty was not reflected in the salaries offered.

My friend thought she would weather it out, and confront the boss with her concerns on his return. On the Friday of the first week he telephoned to say that he would be in the office, fleetingly, on Monday to collect some important papers, then would be overseas on business for a few days. He hoped she was settling in alright, and would see her about her contract etc. later the following week. Having no contract on which to renege, she departed on the Friday never to return.

Hopefully you have never experienced such a dreadful initiation, but probably, like me, you have some unhappy memories of first days, shut in an office with a pile of manuals to read while waiting for appointments with personnel, or having been shown to your office or workstation, being left there to guess who your fellow workers are, what their role is in relation to you, when you are to see the boss, where the toilet is etc.

A manager with good people skills will not be guilty of any of the above, of course. You may have been involved in the selection process, so will have some knowledge of your new member of staff. If you were not involved at that stage, you will be aware of the time and date of the recruit's arrival and will have made appropriate arrangements for their welcome and induction. These arrangements should follow the outline suggested below.

1.  Check with the Personnel Department the exact date and time of the new person's arrival on the premises.
2.  Inform reception that your new member of staff (let's call him Ben) will arrive at, say, 9.00 a.m. Make arrangements for his first few minutes with the company, e.g. that he should be welcomed, and asked to wait in reception while the receptionist calls you. You will then come (immediately) to reception to collect him yourself. Either this or inform reception to which floor and room Ben is to be sent, ensuring that he is given adequate directions. You will know what is best because you alone know the calibre of reception staff you have.
3.  Check with the Personnel Department regarding their role in the induction process. Will they be talking with Ben about anything other than pay and conditions? Agree a time that they will see him on that first morning or over his first few days. Will Ben be invited to join an organization induction training programme, and if so, when will that be? Will he be required to see a medical officer and if so, when?
4.  Delegate someone on your team to take Ben under their wing for the first few days. Explain what you expect of them, e.g. that you will hand Ben over to them at approximately 11.00 a.m. on the first

morning, and that they should show him where he is to work, explain the telephone systems and how to use other equipment, where he is to find stationery and supplies etc. He should ensure that Ben knows where the toilets and rest rooms are, where he should park his car, arrangements for lunch and refreshment breaks, in other words, domestic arrangements to make Ben feel secure and beginning to belong. Brief this person fully so that they are able to answer questions and/or provide Ben with written information – organizational charts showing the names and positions of employees, information on fire drills etc.

5. Ensure that Ben's workstation is ready and waiting for him, and that no one has swapped their old rickety chair with the one at his desk, or 'borrowed' his stapler or work manuals.
6. Ensure that you have allocated time in your diary for an hour or so at the start and end of the first day to meet with your new recruit.
7. Think about your own role on Ben's first day. What information does he need to know? What can you do to see that he has settled in? What task can you set that he can accomplish on that first day? (This doesn't mean, 'what chore can I give him?'; rather 'what simple, yet meaningful piece of work can I allocate?').
8. Write up your plans for Ben's induction over the first week, month and year. Fully integrating a new member of staff so that they are motivated and effective team members and employees can take up to a year!

Let's look more closely at the last three points listed. When you collect Ben from reception it is crucial that you set the tone for the rest of his working life with your organization. You must model the behaviour you expect from Ben and all your team. If you arrive late and flustered at reception, making it obvious that Ben is an added burden to your already stressed and overloaded working day, think of the impression this will have on him and on his morale. Don't keep him waiting (or if you have to because of unforseen circumstances, ensure that you let reception know so that they can explain the delay, offer him a coffee and magazine to read etc.). Greet him in an open and friendly manner. Use his name to make him feel recognized and an important addition to your team. As you walk him to your office, put him at his ease and create rapport by initiating neutral conversation. Ask easy-to-answer, ritual-type questions, for example about his journey, method of travel, remarking about his car, the book he is carrying – anything to break the ice.

When you get to your office, maintain the rapport. You will already have arranged the seating so that you have no positional power through barriers like desks, or chairs of unequal height. You will need to move the conversation on to the business in hand – integrating him into your department. Explain your plan for him for this, his first day. For example, it might be that the first hour you will show him around the department and other related sections, introducing him to key people and explaining their role in relation to Ben's position. You will then hand him over to John who will show him his workstation and explain where everything he needs is located. That should take him to lunch time.

You will have had to decide beforehand whether you will take Ben to lunch, or whether John or other team members should be responsible for showing Ben local eating places or the staff restaurant. *Someone* must be responsible for seeing that Ben is not alone during the lunch-hour on his first day with your company.

After lunch, it would be well for Ben to get down to some work to give some real purpose to what might otherwise be an overwhelming and potentially confusing day. If there is an overlap – if the person who is moving from Ben's job is still in the department – this could be a 'sitting by Nellie' session. If this is not the case, you, or someone to whom you can delegate the task, should show Ben a simple aspect of his new job that he can master quickly so that he can go home at the end of his first day feeling that he has achieved something.

At the end of the day you will have put aside some time for a meeting with Ben to check how his first day has gone and answer any questions he might have. At this point you should set Ben's agenda for the next day.

During the first few days of Ben's employment with you, you need to decide what he *needs* to know in terms of: organizational goals; departmental functions; job duties and responsibilities; procedures, policies, rules and regulations, and what can be left for subsequent weeks, so that he will not be overwhelmed with information. You might involve him in planning his induction and training programme. Be available to him during his first week, and set some time aside at the end of the week to review progress and answer any questions he may have. Give him the opportunity to express concerns and discuss these fully with him.

The process of integrating Ben into your section does not end with the first day or first week. It is an ongoing process for as long as it takes, and it is your responsibility, as his manager, regularly to meet with him to monitor progress. You will need to:

- offer help and assistance
- listen to his needs
- ensure that you are utilizing his capabilities to the full
- provide coaching and arrange training as necessary
- encourage him to think for himself, and as quickly as possible to become a self-sufficient member of your section.

If you are heading an empowered team, or if Ben is to become part of an existing team (in the strictest definition of teams) his integration will involve all other team members (see Chapter 18). You will need to build the team again from square one, as if it were a completely new set of people, because otherwise Ben will find it extremely difficult to fit in, or effectively fill the gap left by the person he replaced. Remaining team members will want Ben to be a carbon copy of the other person, and not 'rock the boat'. Ben will bring with him his own personality, values, opinions, and needs; skills, knowledge and attributes. He will not be able fully to achieve if he is constantly trying to walk in the shoes of the previous incumbent.

# EXERCISE

Your new member of staff will need to know about the organization, policies, rules and regulations, the department, his own role, responsibilities and duties, processes and procedures. He will also need to know practical things such as car parking facilities, how to operate the photocopier and who to call when it goes wrong, what software the computer holds, and so on.

Imagine that a new recruit is starting in your section next week. Your personnel or human resources department will explain things such as pay and conditions. Draw up a checklist of what a person completely new to your organization would need to know in order to be integrated into your section, under the following headings:

*The organization*

*Policies*

*Rules and regulations*

*Your department*

*His role, responsibilities and duties*

*Processes and procedures*

*Practical details*

**Possible responses**

This cannot be a prescriptive list because every organization is unique; each department will be different, and the new recruit's position and role will define areas for inclusion, but here are just a few general observations which will indicate the sort of areas you should be looking at with any new team member.

Under *The organization* you will probably have things like the hierarchical structure – an organizational chart showing who everyone is from the Chief Executive down, and how departments interrelate. You might include mission statements, or organizational goals, annual reports, national/international operational activities.

Under *Policies* you may have things like Health and Safety, or Equal Opportunities, appraisal systems.

Under *Rules and regulations* you might have hours of work, time sheets, lunch and refreshment breaks, fire drills, reporting of hazards and accidents, security, smoking.

Under *Your department* you could have 'who's who' and 'who does what', organization structure, relationship of jobs within the department, inter-departmental functions, current goals and targets, teamwork, meetings and team briefings.

Under *His role, responsibilities and duties* could be things like job description, person specification, performance standards, overtime, reports.

Under *Processes and procedures* would be things like record keeping, statistics, pro-formas for completion, requisitioning supplies, equipment maintenance and repair procedures.

Under *Practical details* would be things like car parking facilities, lockers, location of fire alarms and first aid boxes, permitted smoking areas.

# 11 Influencing

At first I was reluctant to include a section on influencing in a book on people skills where the emphasis has been on respect for the other person's rights and needs while not neglecting your own. Somehow the very word 'influencing' implies manipulation – through persuasion, getting the other person to think *your* way; to do what *you* want. This sort of influencing can certainly lead to short-term success, but at what cost to your own integrity, to the relationship and to future interactions?

However, after giving it some thought, provided the influencing is done through altruism, e.g. influencing another's behaviour for their own good if, say, their poor self-image is holding them back, or otherwise for the good of the individual, the team or the organization rather than for self-interest, then influencing is a valid skill to learn and perfect.

In fact, we all influence, all of the time; hopefully with integrity and for the purpose of arriving at win/win transactions. The act of building rapport with someone – getting on to their wavelength, speaking their language, building bridges between differences so that you can communicate freely, is influencing. Doing your utmost to understand the other's point of view (while not necessarily agreeing) puts you in a position of power because you then have both sides of the story – theirs as well as yours – so you are more likely to affect mutually satisfactory outcomes. If you did not put yourself out to do these things, there would be more discord and fewer areas for rational discussion; but what are you doing when you create rapport if it is not trying to influence the outcome of your communication? The quality of the rapport you create will influence the communication.

Let's look at one or two examples of where influencing skills would be productive for both parties.

# Influencing interviews

Very often people who have to attend interviews become very 'uptight' and nervous. Even with people you have never previously met – at recruitment interview for example – you will be able to read the signs of anxiety and stress from the applicant's level of breathing, skin tone (flushing or tell-tale red blotches around the throat), pace and delivery of speech, mannerisms and body language, tightness of muscles around the mouth and jaw and so on. Much of this is intuitive, but with practice you will be able readily to identify the subtleties of tension in others. With people you already know – at appraisal interview for example – the tell-tale signs will be even more obvious. You can either ignore the signs saying to yourself 'that's their problem' or you can use your people skills to put them at their ease, help them to relax and open up. The latter course of action is in everyone's interest, and will influence the outcome of the interview.

You will, in fact, be influencing the other person to modify their behaviour so that they can feel more comfortable and give of their best. You do this by modelling the behaviour you want them to display: open, calm and friendly. You don't even have to like the other person to create an empathetic atmosphere between you for the duration of the communication.

There is enormous value in remembering and using the person's name. He will feel valued and important. It will help create an atmosphere of receptivity and openness. A short diversion is called for at this point. If you have difficulty remembering a person's name when first introduced, a simple trick is to ensure that you repeat it to him as soon as possible. This should help fix the name in your consciousness. So, if you are introduced to John Brown, say at once something like 'It's nice to meet you John.' Continue to use his name occasionally during conversation, and close the meeting, using his name again: 'Bye John; see you at the monthly conference.'

By using a person's name, he will get a little glow of inner warmth towards you; he will be more receptive to what you have to say. You have acquired an influencing skill. In the interview situation, build rapport by using small talk, feeding from free information he gives you and showing an interest in what he has to say. Consciously influence his behaviour by matching and pacing (see Chapters 2 and 4). This does not mean mirroring his nervousness of course, but using a communication style similar to his own and leading him towards the behaviour you require by modelling that behaviour. Keep good eye contact; smile and encourage until you can see by his non-verbal as well as verbal communication that he has begun to relax and settle down. Don't switch off the rapport as you get down to business, but maintain the atmosphere you have created so that you can both leave the interaction feeling good about yourselves and your outcomes.

Influencing is not the same as directing or manipulating. Directing and manipulating behaviours persuade a person to do something, even against their wishes or against their own best interests. Even with discipline interviews, you can use influencing skills to enable the other person to agree that there is a problem to be addressed. You do this by maintaining rapport (even though it is a discipline interview, common courtesies need to be maintained, and you will have more success if you remain open and responsive rather than closed or accusing). By careful questioning you will be able to see the situation through his eyes, and help him clarify his view of the situation. He can be persuaded to come up with his own solutions about how better to improve his performance.

# Influencing meetings

## Chairing meetings

If you are a team leader or a manager who chairs meetings, you can influence the meeting so that it is productive and effective, even before it takes place. Initially, you must be clear in your own mind about the purpose of the meeting: what you need to achieve – your outcome. Know in your own mind how you will know when that outcome is achieved. So many organizations still have meetings for the sake of meetings, with no clear outcomes in mind. More by luck than judgement, they may well produce some powerful results, but they can also be time-wasters for many of the people attending.

Which brings me to the second guideline for influencing effective meetings: choice of membership. If you are leading an empowered team, whether it is an ongoing work team or a special project, limited duration team, you can do a lot to ensure that you have a balanced team profile – a group of people whose knowledge, skills, abilities and attributes complement each other (see Chapter 18). Meetings will go more smoothly if people know why they are there, what role they are filling, and the contribution they can make.

If you are a manager who has to hold *ad hoc* meetings, ensure that the people who attend the meeting have something to contribute to at least two-thirds of the items on the agenda. It is time-wasting for the individual to sit through irrelevant items. It can also be disruptive if vociferous individuals have their say on items that don't really concern them.

Choose your meeting room and seating arrangements with care. This can make a subtle difference to the outcome of debates. Think about the people attending and how seating orientation can affect how people inter-relate. Face-to-face arrangements can be confrontational, for example.

Sometimes it is helpful to have a flip chart to write up the purpose of the meeting and the outcome you wish to agree with members. Having this 'in black and white' often makes it easier for members to keep on target and not go off on irrelevant side-tracks.

Now to the meeting itself. Another good influencing technique is to arrive early so that you can greet each member personally as they arrive. This achieves several things. You can make small talk, and build rapport on an individual basis. If you are receptive to them from the outset, they are more likely to be in a positive frame of mind and receptive to your and others' views during the meeting. By carefully observing and listen-ing, you can pick up incongruences which might indicate that they are anxious about the meeting, have other (perhaps more pressing) engage-ments on their mind, have personal problems, have hidden agendas that they want to discuss and so on. This not only gives you prior warning of how they might perform during the meeting and how you can respond, but can give you the opportunity to address difficulties prior to the meeting itself. For example, if a member really does have more pressing engagements, his mind will not be on the business in hand, so it might be better for him to be excused attendance on that day. Ascertain his views on crucial items so that you can present them on his behalf, or if necessary, postpone that item until he can be truly present in mind as well as body. If someone has a concern or hidden agenda, far better to know about it beforehand so that you can address it on a one-to-one basis initially. Remember that group dynamics can do strange things to people. 'In packs' individuals act in different ways than they do alone.

I will stress yet again that influencing does not mean manipulating people and situations – deceiving individuals so that you can get your own way or your own decisions implemented. Even if you can subtly persuade someone to do something which is in your favour but against their wishes, ultimately they will realize what has happened and be resentful. You will lose your credibility as an 'honest broker' and lose their respect and trust. At best they will be reluctant to communicate with you on matters that count, and cautious about committing themselves to anything you are involved in. At worst they will want to get back at you for manipulating them to do things against their best interests. Relation-ships always suffer.

However, you can use influencing skills to ensure that meetings run smoothly, keep on target, and achieve agreed outcomes. By asking pertinent questions to clarify others' comments you help ensure that everyone at the meeting is 'talking the same language'. Don't allow woolly statements to influence proceedings. For example if someone says 'They'll never agree to that', ask 'Who, exactly won't agree?' 'What, precisely, from this proposal won't they agree with?' 'How might we reword the proposal so that it will be more acceptable?' and so on.

Summarize decisions reached, using 'lean' words that have tight meanings. Use a variety of vocabulary and phrasing that will appeal to all present (see Chapter 2).

Watch members closely to check for dissent, hidden agenda and so on. It will be obvious to a practised 'people watcher' when someone is not totally happy with proceedings. Their facial expression and muscle tone changes, and body language and non-verbal behaviour gives away feelings of unease. It will be up to you to decide whether to challenge the person, there and then, about their feelings: e.g. 'You look anxious Martin; is there a problem?' or just to note them so that you can address them at a later date. Remember, though, that discontent can influence a meeting too.

You can influence the effectiveness of a meeting by confirming that all members agree to the required outcome of the meeting, and then ensuring that only discussion relevant to the business in hand is entertained. If a person's contribution appears to be diverting from the main issue, or if someone has a hidden agenda, question the relevancy of their contribution. Some people tend to talk first in general terms before moving to the specific. They need a little more air space to get their point across. If this is the case, be patient, yet guide them towards the relevant specific point. If the contribution is not pertinent, or has no bearing on the agreed outcome, question its relevance. If necessary, assert that it is not within the remit of the current meeting to pursue the matter. You could agree to discuss the matter at another meeting if this seems appropriate. Because you will at all times be maintaining a good rapport with team members, remember not to criticize any person or rubbish their contribution. If it is the information they are giving, or the departure from the agreed outcome that is questionable, talk about the information, or question the relevance of diversions, without attacking the individual. If you model good practice in this way, other members of the meeting will hopefully emulate your style.

Finally, you will need to summarize decisions made, sum up, and confirm next steps so that everyone leaves the meeting feeling that the outcome of that meeting was achieved. They will know what is expected of them from whom and by when; they will know when the group is to meet again and have an approximate idea of the content of the next meeting. You will not only have influenced the successful outcome of a meeting by carefully defining content and overseeing process, but will hopefully have influenced individuals who will have begun to learn from you how to run a successful meeting.

Of course, meetings cannot be so tightly structured that there is no room for humour, short diversions – or for creativity.

In Chapter 18 brainstorming is advocated as a 'fun' way to ensure contributions from everyone and to make the most of all the brains at the meeting. Leading meetings is a finely tuned skill; you need to create a balance between formality and informality, structure and freedom. By creating and maintaining rapport, encouraging relevant contributions and modelling good practice, you can influence the process of meetings so that they are effective, an efficient use of people's time, and enjoyable and productive parts of their working day.

## Attending meetings

So far we have talked about you, as manager or team leader, running a meeting. Can you influence meetings that you attend as an ordinary member? The answer is 'yes'.

First let's look at the environment. Unless places have been appointed around the meeting table – there is a card with your name on it stating where you should sit – always try to place yourself as near to the Chair as possible. There is an historical precedence for this. In medieval times, when guests sat down to eat, those with the greatest status sat nearest to the host. The condiments were the dividing line and anyone 'worth his salt' sat above the condiments in the pecking order. Lesser mortals sat below the salt at table. At meetings, people sitting nearest the Chair are still perceived as of greater status than those furthest away. Also, because the Chair is directing proceedings, the main thrust of the discussion usually takes place near the Chair so even if you do not contribute frequently, you will still be seen to be in the thick of things and your contributions – if sound – will carry weight.

If the Chair is proficient at his job, you are fortunate. If he is not, there is nothing to stop you using some of the influencing skills mentioned above. For example, if a contribution is woolly, or you are uncertain of the contributor's precise meaning, question until you are satisfied that you and other members of the meeting are clear about the content. You could try contributions such as: 'I'm interested in what you say about weekly briefings. Who would be briefing whom, exactly?' or 'I'm curious; what would happen if we *didn't* go ahead as planned?' You will probably be addressing other people's uncertainties by your questioning, and members will soon become aware of the need to tighten up their thinking in their pursuit of effective outcomes.

You might also question the relevancy of some contributions if the discussion seems to be straying from the point. Do this assertively and firmly, without apology, yet with respect for the contributor. Question the content of his contribution; do not criticize him personally. Say something like: 'I feel that Jack's objection has more to do with finance, and should be discussed at the sub-committee meeting. The objective of this meeting is to ... '.

If the discussion is going round in circles and getting nowhere, again you can assertively influence the process by asking something like: 'What exactly are we trying to achieve here?' Bring the meeting back to looking at objectives and outcomes. One suggestion, which seems a bit risky but apparently works, is to employ 'pattern interruption'. This involves doing something physical like suddenly getting up and going to look out of the window. Unless they are so preoccupied with their diversions or splinter group discussions, most people will be stopped in their tracks – be surprised or feel uneasy about your unexpected behaviour. In this state they will be more prepared to listen to your next statement, which should be an open and assertive suggestion about how to further the desired outcome of the meeting. Return to your seat – or occupy a different one if you want to make more of an impact – and say something like: 'If the objective of this meeting is to ... perhaps we could look at ...' Skilfully done, this will bring them back to the central issue.

# Influencing negotiations

Negotiating is one area where it really does pay to be interested in psychology, or to have studied the principles developed through the NLP process. Rather than concentrating on your own interests – what you want from the situation, what you would be prepared to give (or how little you need give to gain the biggest advantage) – learn as much as you can about the other person and what he needs from the transaction. Question and listen well. Learn to 'read' the other person by observing closely to see what advances and what retards progress. You will be able to 'feel' this by subtle, non-verbal reactions to your communication. There could be a tightening of the tiny muscles around the mouth or a perceptible brightening of the eyes to give you clues whether or not you are 'on target'. If you pursue this path of analysing people's thought processes, you will need to be aware of the following:

## The other person's favoured communication style

The benefits of recognizing, then matching the other person's favoured style has been covered in several sections of this book. To reiterate briefly with a few examples: if the person with whom you are negotiating is a person of few words – he gives and wants information in succinct, short sentences – then do not go on at length or give detail unless he asks for it. Be concise and to the point, speaking clearly but with pace, and you are more likely quickly to gain rapport. Rapport leads to trust and effective communication. Similarly, if the person with whom you are negotiating has a more slow and ponderous style, don't rush him or overpower him with information. Allow plenty of time to listen. Match his pace, and again, you will influence the transaction favourably.

Learn to recognize and speak the other person's language. If you become skilled in recognizing the preferred representational system of the other person (whether they are primarily visuals, auditories, kinesthetics or cerebrals – see Chapters 2 and 4) you will be able to choose vocabulary to which they best respond. If you practise and use enriched vocabulary, appealing to all the senses, this too is influential in establishing rapport and gaining the other's trust and respect. When you have established the other person's preferred system – whether they opt to trust pictures, sounds or feelings in their communication – you can further influence the negotiation by how you present your information. A visual person will be impressed by visual aids such as charts, photographs, brochures, slides and so on. An auditory person will need to be convinced by listening to information – don't initially give them the brochure to look at but read them the facts you want to get across.

Mirroring (not mimicking) the other person's pace of speech, tone of voice, volume and so on also leads to empathetic communication. For example, some regional accents favour slow speech – other regions typically talk faster than most others. Some have a greater intonation range; other regions have a flatter tonal quality. Don't try to imitate another's accent, but do change your own speech pattern – subtly – to get in step with the other person. By changing your rhythm you are joining the dance of rapport. This is especially useful in telephone conversations where you can't see the other person for non-verbal cues. The first stage of influencing a successful outcome is to get onto the same wavelength as the person with whom you are negotiating. Remember, this is a skill you can utilize to your mutual advantage, and you don't have to like the person (or their style of communicating) to achieve your ends.

## The other person's position

If you know the person well with whom you are negotiating, this set of guidelines will be somewhat easier to address. If you do not know him, now is the time to find out as much as you can. Turn a stranger into a friend and you are on the road to a win/win solution in the negotiation process.

You will need to find out not only his outcomes – what he wants from the negotiation – but what lies behind the outcomes – *why* he wants what he does. By careful questioning, observation and perceptive listening you should be able to get some ideas of his values. By probing to discover why he wants what he does, often other outcomes emerge. This gives you both a wider range of options on which to negotiate, increasing the chances of a win/win conclusion.

Another useful ploy is to ask him several times what specifically he wants and why. This repetition has to be done with a fine degree of skill and subtlety, of course, or the other person will just consider you particularly obtuse! However, if you can get him to *redefine* his ideal outcome, he will use different vocabulary and phrasing which will enable you to get a more precise picture of his needs and how they might dovetail with yours. Inevitably there is a slippage between words used as understood by the transmitter, and as received by the listener. By clarifying certain words and phrases through careful questioning, other outcomes or options for mutual gain may well come to light.

## The other person's values

We all have different belief systems and values. For example, I may care about what other people think of me and want to be liked; you may not give a hoot for others' opinions. I may be more concerned about excellence and attention to detail, and deadlines do not feature highly; you may feel that getting jobs out on time is a priority and that sometimes 'good enough' is good enough. If through questioning and getting to know the other person you can discover his hierarchy of values, you will be in a strong position to negotiate a deal which meets his needs in this area and which dovetails with your own. Let me give you an example of how this works in practice.

A friend of mine who is in social work spends much of her time doing outreach work. She enjoys being out and about, not being confined to the nine to five regime of the office. Recently she has had to do a lot more paperwork and this has coincided with a reorganization of departments in the area meaning more people working at her office base. Whereas once she had an office to herself, she was faced with the possibility of spending much more time in the office, writing complicated reports and bids for funding, in the clamour of crowded accommodation.

Her boss, already stressed by the additional pressures on him, and unhappy himself with the new arrangements, would not have taken kindly to her bursting into his office complaining of her cramped conditions, the noise levels making it impossible to concentrate, and her newly 'clipped wings' (being restricted in her home visits by the additional paperwork). She decided that it would suit her if her boss would agree to her working from home, thus freeing up office space and not restricting her to the nine to five regime.

She knew her boss well, and what would enthuse him and what would make him dig in his heels. She influenced the negotiation by appealing to the former – his personal values. She acknowledged the difficulty of his position and the problems inherent in making the new system work. She also acknowledged his concern about the morale of his staff, the acceptability of their working conditions and so on. This was a real priority for him, as was the quality of the work produced by his team, and the care they offered the clients. The next move, therefore, was to point out the negative effect working in such conditions was likely to have on her performance. (It is always a good idea to give the reasons first before making the request.) 'I'm concerned that I will neither be able to give my best to the clients, nor produce the results you want', she said. She then made her request to use her office at home as base so that she had the time and conditions to provide the top quality reports and bids he required, and could fit her client visits around the paperwork better to meet the needs of the clients, and without the constraints of office hours.

The negotiation went well. She was able to present her case in a way that met his value system. She had to make a few concessions such as agreeing to a regular weekly meeting at base to report on progress, and a bit more paperwork to account for how she spent her time, but the transaction was concluded with both parties getting what they wanted – in fact, both benefiting from the negotiation.

Often, casual small talk will give you the basis you need to assess a person's values. Questions such as 'Why did you decide to work for Brannagh's?' or 'What made you choose ... ?' are the sort of openers on which you can build to provide you with information about how to present your case.

## Time

Yet another means of influencing the outcome of a negotiation is to assess how the other person processes time, then focus your discussion around that perspective. Some people tend to live in the past. They dwell on what happened yesterday, last month or last year. Whether you have had concurrence or disagreements in the past, they remember details of the interaction, and their feelings about your past relationship will influence their current thinking. You will need to remind them of, and build on, past successes. You can influence their opinion of you/your organization by providing evidence of your previous success rate, past performances and anything already achieved which supports your position.

Other people live for the present. What's past is past; it is only the here and now that counts. The good news is that every transaction is treated as new, and judged on its own merits. The bad news is that you can't rest on your laurels, but need to prove yourself and present your case as if this was your first encounter. Past performance tends not to impress them. They are interested in conditions which exist now.

The third group are 'future' people. They are more focused on questions such as 'what will happen if . . . ? They plan for the future, and to influence them in a negotiation you will need to keep this perspective in mind. They thrive on forecasts and projected improvements but will be concerned about future implications of proposals, and will need to be convinced of how a negotiated agreement will affect the future situation in a positive way.

If you know the person with whom you are negotiating, you will already have a good idea of their time orientation. When dealing with a stranger – a client or supplier – your time spent on small talk and building rapport, by using all the skills mentioned in this book, should give you insight into how the other person perceives time. It is then up to you to influence the interaction accordingly.

Finally, let's take a quick look at a technique which veers closely to manipulative behaviour, so use it with integrity. Chapter 4 on NLP briefly describes the principles of 'anchoring' and syntonic learning. Put very simply, you can 'fix' behaviour by using a physical action. The repetition of that physical action replicates the desired behaviour pattern. Every time the person with whom you are negotiating displays behaviour which you want to further progress, make a subtle physical gesture, such as lightly rubbing your forearm, or putting a hand to your ear. As he displays positive behaviour, 'reward' it with exactly the same gesture. The subconscious of the other person will pick up the message you are conveying – 'I like the way you are responding now, and would like that behaviour repeated please'. After you have established this sequence, if the negotiation starts going off course, you can use the gesture – rub your forearm or whatever – and the other person will revert to the behaviour which you want to lead you to positive outcomes.

# EXERCISE

Pam has recently been appointed to an administrative post in the mental health service. Tom has done business before with her predecessor, but this is his first meeting with Pam. She meets him at reception. On their way to her office, Tom initiates small talk.

Consider the following dialogue. What can you learn from Pam's responses that Tom could use to influence the interaction?

Tom: It's good to meet you at last; how long have you been in the post now?

Pam: Nearly three months. I'm sorry I haven't been in touch before, but I've been settling in – trying to get a handle on the job.

Tom: Have you always worked in mental health?

Pam: No, I read engineering at university, believe it or not, and worked in industry for a number of years.

Tom: That's quite a change. Why did you move to this type of work?

Pam: My job was very exacting – which I liked – but I felt isolated from human contact; I like people around me.

Tom: So you have face-to-face contact with the public now do you?

Pam: With the public, the clients – and my work team of course. I'm really enjoying that aspect of my job. We work really well together. We support each other, and it's good to share and solve problems.

Tom: I have the feeling you are really enthusiastic about your work!

Pam: I didn't think it would be possible, but I look forward to coming into work each day now to see what challenge waits for us. Yes, the future's looking good.

Tom: So you think you'll stay in mental health work?

Pam: Yes. It was a bit of a culture shock at first, but the prospects are good. It's challenging work and every day is different. It's great working with such a motivated team to help the less fortunate.

**Possible responses**

Pam likes challenging and exacting work yet her main concern is with people rather than things; she is people rather than task oriented. This would tell a skilled negotiator how best to approach this person to influence a successful outcome, i.e. always keep in mind the effect proposals would have on other people concerned in any agreements reached – her team and clients.

Pam is primarily a kinesthetic individual. Feelings are important to her. This is demonstrated by the language she uses. Phrases like 'in touch', 'get a handle on' and 'culture shock' are typical choices of kinesthetics. Already Tom has picked this up and is beginning to use phrases such as

'I have the feeling' which Pam will readily relate to. She will prefer to trust feelings when considering information or making decisions.

Tom's questions demand Pam makes reference to her past and to her current situation. However, her responses show a concern for the future. An awareness of Pam's perception of time should give Tom clues about how to present information and thus help him influence the outcome of the negotiation.

# 12 Motivation

Motivation is not only central to good managerial practice, but it impinges on virtually every aspect of organizational effectiveness. Currently we are living in a time of rapid change. The world of work has been transformed: world markets have opened up, competition is rife, and the public are increasingly demanding better quality and service from organizations. Technological potential is expanding and growing almost faster than the average person can keep up.

To meet these demands, organizations are having to rethink strategies. Gone are the days when productivity and profit are central to their thinking. Whereas these elements are still, of course, crucial to survival, it is the customer-focused organization which will have the edge over competitors – not just meeting customer needs, but anticipating and exceeding them. Such organizations will prune dead wood and strip layers of middle management. Empowerment is the order of the day, where employees each take responsibility and authority for an expanded days work. Middle managers have a new role – one of facilitating, enabling and encouraging. Every employee has to rethink his future, become more flexible, and understand that to survive he must reconsider his way of working.

In today's empowered workplace, motivation is a prime managerial task, and often a perplexing one. There are many different theories and approaches, lots of questions and very few simple answers. It requires self-confidence, good leadership and team-building skills, excellent role modelling and people skills.

## What is motivation?

*Collins Dictionary of Business* gives the following definition: (essentially, motivation is) 'the force or process which impels people to behave in the way they do. In a work setting, motivation can be viewed as that which determines whether workers expend the degree of effort necessary to achieve required task objectives' or as John Adair in his book *The Action-Centred Leader* (Industrial Society, 1989) puts it: (motivation is) 'getting people to do willingly and well those things which have to be done'.

If you pick up any book on management, motivation is sure to feature. Over the decades there have been many theories about what motivates people at work. Most writers include at least a passing reference to the theories of social scientists, but after that, the handling of this complex subject differs greatly. This section will begin with the assumption that motivation has to begin with an understanding of human nature, behaviour and personality – i.e. in order to motivate people you must first see them as individuals with unique needs and drives. To this end we will look initially at various theories about personality and behaviour in the context of management. No section on motivation would be complete without reference to Maslow and other theorists, so this will be touched on briefly before looking at practical measures to energize and motivate staff.

## Personality and behaviour

Personality and motivation are closely related topics. If you want to understand human behaviour in the organizational context, it is important to know what makes people tick, and something about individuals' similarities and differences. No two people are alike; even the same person will behave differently at different times and given different circumstances. In order to motivate your team it is essential to recognize this. The workforce is made up of people each with their own drives and needs. To get the best from people, wherever possible these individual drives and needs should be met within the context of organizational objectives.

## Research into personality

One of the best-known researchers into personality was Sigmund Freud. One of his theories claimed that the eventual goal of all behaviour is obtaining pleasure and avoiding pain. Looked at in its broadest context, there is a lesson here regarding motivation at work, as we would all prefer to enjoy our time working (this includes social contact as well as the content of the work itself, and earning enough to enjoy leisure hours). If 'pain' is interpreted as dreading Monday mornings, disliking our working conditions, and poor or non-existent working relationships, then this is something, like physical pain, which we avoid. Part of the role of today's manager is, therefore, to create an environment which is cheerful, relaxed yet challenging, and enabling rather than controlled.

According to Freud, human personality is determined by previous experience. If we found that by behaving in a certain way, this behaviour was rewarded, we tend to reinforce this learning by repeating the behaviour patterns. Here, too, is a lesson for today's manager. You will need also to help individuals not only repeat approved behaviour (or achievement/success), but seek constantly to improve on past performance.

Similarly, we reinforce ways of resolving conflict by building on past experience. This behaviour is often controlled and directed by unconscious processes which are beyond direct observation. Because of this it is hard to prove the theory empirically, although no doubt you can recognize these patterns in your own behaviour. However, remember that every person and situation is different. You cannot repeat past successes in conflict handling, and expect the same formula to work every time for you. *Build* on past experience; don't be dictated by it.

A simple if not very subtle example of this theory can be observed in the temper tantrums of a child. If a child, by screaming, yelling and stamping on the ground, eventually gets a parent to capitulate and give in to its demands (even if it is to avoid a scene, or 'anything for a quiet life') then the child has 'won'; this behaviour has been rewarded. The behaviour pattern is reinforced – the child has got its way and knows what to do in the future when mum says 'no' to one of its requests. This is not the place to speculate how this learned behaviour in a child might manifest itself in its adult working life!

# Other personality theories

Other theorists have argued that underlying personality traits – dispositions to behave in certain ways – explain human behaviour. Terms such as shy, outgoing, or tense are used to describe personality traits. There are emotional traits such as cheerfulness, despondency and fearfulness; and character traits such as skilful, determined, industrious, tolerant, practical and cautious. However, the behaviour noted by a trait name is not necessarily identical in everyone in whom it appears. For example, if you were to take the list from after 'skilful' above, as the personality traits of one person, and substitute the word 'inflexible' for 'tolerant', the personality of the two individuals bearing these traits could be quite different. A person who is determined, industrious and *inflexible* is quite different from an individual who is determined, industrious and *tolerant*. In staff management terms, different stimuli are needed to motivate different personality types.

To motivate effectively, it is important to assess the other person's outlook. Personal Construct Theory is an interesting theory in this context. It argues that personalities are determined by how, through experience, we interpret the world around us; how we classify another person; how we understand our environment, and so on. Each person has a unique view of the world; each uses and develops different 'constructs' to understand and evaluate situations and interactions. The extent to which we share our constructs with others determines the extent we can achieve mutual understanding. (NLP practitioners advocate emulating others' constructs to create initial rapport.)

We share our constructs by talking to people, communicating our ideas, feelings and beliefs. By their nature, personal construct systems develop and change as the result of experience. (For self-development purposes, there are NLP techniques whereby you can change unhelpful or negative personal constructs to more beneficial and productive ones. See Chapter 4.) Construct theory has a variety of applications in management, largely because to understand things from the other person's perspective is crucial to motivation, team-building and other aspects of leadership.

## Behaviour, personality and motivation

Human behaviour is a vast and complicated subject. It can be influenced by a number of variables. Basically it can be described as the total response of an individual to various motivating forces, because we behave as we do in response to a force which has motivated us to act. For example, the force/stimulus might be a hunger pang. This is the motivating force which drives us to act, in this case from both ends of the Freudian spectrum: avoidance of pain (the hunger pang) and pursuit of pleasure (gratification through food). We go in search of a chocolate bar or a square meal (motivation leading to behaviour) thus satisfying the motivating forces.

Behaviour is conditioned by the need to satisfy various motivating forces – forces which vary considerably not only from individual to individual, but also within each person at different times. A basic awareness of behaviour and personality theory – why people behave as they do – is valuable for effective motivation and sound management practice.

# Motivation theories

Research has produced many theories regarding motivation. It all really started with an American called Abraham Maslow (1908–70), who identified what is now known as the 'needs' theory. Maslow argued that individuals have intrinsic needs which they are compelled to seek to satisfy. He divided human needs into five categories – a 'hierarchy of needs'. Once the needs of a lower level are met, the individual strives to satisfy a higher need. The most basic needs are physiological/physical – survival needs. In Maslow's terms these are air, food, water, sleep. In a proactive organization this could be interpreted as an employee's need for gainful employment, to have an effective and supportive manager, and the resources for the job. Physiological needs exert a tremendous influence over behaviour, especially at work, and especially in times of high unemployment, because the fundamental purpose of gainful employment is to provide the means of satisfying basic needs such as food and shelter. The next level in Maslow's hierarchy of needs is safety. Maslow uses the analogy of a sick child to demonstrate this aspect of his theory. He observes that when a small child is ill, pain makes the world a different, unstable and frightening place. It is no longer safe. For a while after the illness, the child may experience unreasonable anxiety, nightmares and a need for protection and reassurance. The child will need undisrupted routine or rhythm in order to feel safe and function well. (Can you see another analogy – with members of the workforce who need reassurance and the 'safety' of routine when faced with the 'pain' of change and insecurity?)

For most adults, the safety need is concerned with security, self-preservation, the need to protect one's position and, to an extent, to provide for the future. In a forward-looking organization, at this level employees will need to be involved in interesting work, be able to think for themselves and see the end result of their work.

Social needs are next in the hierarchy. Maslow, in his essay *A Theory of Human Motivation* (in *Human Relations in Management*, edited by S.G. Hunergager and I.L. Heckmann, see Further Reading p. 224) calls these 'the love needs'. He states:

> If both the physiological and safety needs are fairly well gratified, there will emerge the love and affection and belongingness needs. . . . Now the person will . . . hunger for affectionate relationships with people in general, namely for a place in his group, and he will strive with great intensity to achieve his goal.

In the management context, hopefully most of the workforce are satisfied with their physiological and safety needs so initially they will be striving for this next tier in the hierarchy, namely to feel part of the organization – part of the team. There are very few people who can genuinely say that they don't get satisfaction from giving and receiving friendship. If you observe people, from the smallest child to the oldest citizen, you will see the pleasure which is derived from being accepted by a group, and conversely the wretchedness that can result from being excluded. Poor performers are sometimes those who don't fit in with others in their work group or team. They may be more or less efficient than the rest; much older or younger than the average age of the team; they may be more or less intelligent/skilled/experienced; they may have different social or cultural backgrounds. Obviously, this is not the sole cause of poor performance, but as a manager you should be aware of the dangers of trying to fit square pegs into round holes.

As a manager you should, of course, avoid time-wasting by your staff, but don't underestimate the importance of a degree of social contact and its impact on motivation. Surveys have shown that whereas money as a motivator comes fairly low down on most people's lists, social contact and good relationships at work figure very highly. A congenial social atmosphere is a factor of great importance in the choice and retention of jobs. In today's organizations, this social tier in the hierarchy is addressed by informing and listening to employees, and developing good working relationships and team spirit.

The fourth tier in Maslow's hierarchy concerns esteem needs. He separates these into two categories. The first is 'the desire for strength, for achievement, for adequacy, for confidence in the face of the world and for independence and freedom'. The second is 'the desire for reputation or prestige ... recognition, attention, importance and appreciation'. (Maslow, 'A Theory of Human Motivation' in Hunergager and Heckmann, *Human Relations in Management*.)

Maslow goes on to claim that:

> Satisfaction of the self-esteem needs leads to feelings of self-confidence, worth, strength, capability and adequacy, of being useful and necessary in the world ... thwarting of these needs produces feelings of inferiority, of weakness and of helplessness. These feelings in turn give rise to either basic discouragement or else compensatory ... trends. (Maslow in Hunergager and Heckmann, *Human Relations in Management*.)

These needs, often called 'ego' needs, are concerned with an individual's view of himself. Their influence on human behaviour is very important in the context of management, as the above quotation from Maslow implies. In the past, as motivating forces, these needs were often difficult to satisfy in the workforce. Managers could achieve prestige by the acquisition of symbols of status, such as company car (and the make and cost of this car in relation to other managers' vehicles). This is the sort of thing by which satisfaction of esteem or ego needs are met.

As the above quotation implies, the blocking of esteem needs can be a demotivator, and behaviourial problems can result – 'if I can't have ABC I won't do XYZ' or 'if I can't have ABC I'll do XYZ instead'. Satisfying esteem needs, however, can be as simple as giving status by changing title. For example, a 'pest control operative' may take more pride in his job than a 'rodent exterminator' or 'rat catcher' would. 'Midday supervisor' is a far more appropriate title for the role that 'dinner ladies' used to perform in schools. With title comes status, and the respect due to the people concerned. A 'refuse collector', just by the value attached to the title, has more status than a 'dustman' or 'binman'. (Neither are these titles sexist.)

Research has shown that membership of and acceptance into groups, whether work groups or larger organizational groups, influences the manner in which individuals work. The feeling of belongingness identified by Maslow, and the desire for social approval, are reinforced by the feeling of security group membership brings. Of course, in an empowered organization, esteem, and the final tier in Maslow's scheme – self-actualization needs – are within the scope of every employee. (See Chapter 9.)

According to Maslow, when all physiological needs are satisfied, that is, food, shelter and rest are assured; when individuals feel safe and secure; when they are accepted by others and are giving and receiving affection; when self-confidence is at a maximum through proving independence, having the esteem of others, and being in the position to acquire desired outcomes; then the prime motivator will be the desire to fulfil one's potential, whatever form that might take. In Maslow's words:

> A musician must make music, an artist must paint, a poet must write, if he is to be ultimately happy. What a man *can* be he *must* be. This need we call self-actualization. (Maslow in Hunergager and Heckmann.)

Maslow goes on to qualify this by accepting that every individual will have a different level and form of self-actualization, which does not necessarily have to be creative. The important thing is that everyone, by nature, is only truly content when allowed to go as far as they possibly can to make the fullest use of their capabilities. In the context of the work environment, in the past specialists and top management were probably the only people to be fully developed in this way. In an empowered organization it is possible for every member of staff to be challenged and to reach their full potential.

Maslow contends that individuals tend to satisfy their needs in a rising order of precedence. In order for a higher level need to be met, lower needs must first be satisfied. Satisfaction at a lower level means that satisfying the need at the next level becomes the prime motivator. For example, if you get a substantial salary increase, your basic needs are presumably taken care of quite adequately. It is likely that worrying about how to pay the food bills, whether you have immediate job security and so on, pale into relative insignificance. Assuming you have the respect and friendship of colleagues at work, it is likely that motivators at this stage will be at the esteem level of needs, i.e. what your new office will be like; whether you have a 'status' desk or carpet, or a company car. Once a level of need is satisfied, it is no longer a motivator (although that need may return later – with redundancy for example).

There has been criticism of Maslow's work, largely because of its rigidity, but Maslow himself acknowledges this, recognizing that there are some people, for example, for whom esteem and prestige are more important than belonging and affection. There will be others whose need to be creative exceeds their need for personal comfort. There is also the multiplicity factor of motivation. As an example, sex is a basic physio-logical drive (a survival need – the base-line in the hierarchy). However, it may be used to satisfy the esteem or ego needs – to make a conquest, to dominate, to feel powerful or to win affection.

Maslow's theories still have a relevance for managers today. In simplis-tic terms, job security (which provides the cash to satisfy basic needs) and safe working conditions need to be ensured before individuals can fully address themselves to higher level needs. Maslow emphasizes the pos-itive side of human nature, however. He contends that despite the requirements for the satisfaction of lower needs, people generally strive to achieve their potential, and gain personal satisfaction from using their abilities and attributes to the full. This idea is taken up by empowered organizations in that they recognize that it is in their best interests to see that jobs are designed so that lower level needs are met, and employees are motivated by their own needs for personal achievement and recogni-tion (esteem) and self-development and realization of potential (self-actualization).

Other theorists include Clayton Alderfer who revised Maslow's theory to three categories of need with less emphasis on hierarchical ordering. He proposed that the less a high level need is satisfied, the more import-ant a lower level need becomes. A demand for more pay may in fact indi-cate that there is a desire for the work itself to be made more interesting, for example, or an individual who fails to get expected promotion may then display a greater wish for social interaction. This is an important theory in today's economic climate, when big salary increases cannot be afforded, and when promotion is no longer automatic with seniority. Managers need to look for other ways to motivate their staff through job satisfaction and giving each individual the chance to grow and excel.

Frederick Herzberg's Two Factor Theory of Motivation needs a mention. Rather than define motivation in terms of human needs, Herzberg looked at various job factors and how they relate to needs. He divides the factors of the work environment into two categories; basic needs like adequate pay, good working conditions, fringe benefits etc. which, if not satisfied, lead to unhappiness, but whose satisfaction does not in itself bring happiness, and higher order needs like achievement, recognition and responsibility which, when satisfied, lead to contentment. He called the first category hygiene factors, and the second, motivators.

Herzberg recognized that the terms 'satisfied' and 'dissatisfied' are not opposites. He states:

> The opposite of job satisfaction would not be job dissatisfaction, but rather no job satisfaction; and similarly the opposite of job dissatisfaction is no job dissatisfaction – not job satisfaction. (Herzberg, F. 'The Motivation Hygiene Concept and Problems of Manpower', in *Human Relations in Management*, edited by S.G. Hunergager and I.L. Heckmann, see Further Reading p. 224.)

This is not just a play on words. Give it a minute's thought and you will see the subtleties and their importance to the understanding of motivation of work.

Herzberg's most important breakthrough was in his assertion that work itself is a potential motivator. His research showed that the elements which gave most job satisfaction had little to do with money and status; far more to do with achievement and responsibility within the job. The importance of this theory in a work environment is that managers should ensure that both hygiene factors (pay, working conditions etc., roughly equating with Maslow's levels 1 and 2) and motivator factors (need for personal fulfilment – Maslow levels 4 and 5) are satisfied if employees are to be both contented and motivated.

One last theory which needs mention: Douglas McGregor's Theory X and Theory Y. He identified a distinction between managers who believe in Theory X and those who believe in Theory Y. Theory X managers believe that employees are naturally indolent, working as little as possible, lacking in ambition, disliking responsibility and preferring to be led, inherently self-centred and indifferent to organizational needs. They feel that employees need to be prodded and pushed in order to achieve their best, and that the only incentives to do better lie in pay awards and other external factors. He noticed that management adopting this style usually assumed one of two approaches: 'hard' (disguised coercion or threat – the carrot and stick approach – close supervision, tight controls) or 'soft' (satisfying people's demands to achieve harmony in order to make them governable).

The problems with either of these approaches hardly need to be spelt out today. The hard approach is counter-productive. 'Force breeds counter-forces; restriction of output, antagonism, militant unionism, subtle but effective sabotage of management objectives' (McGregor, D.M. 'The Human Side of Enterprise' in *Human Relations in Management*, edited by S.G. Hunergager and I.L. Heckmann, see Further Reading p. 224.) The soft approach also breeds difficulties for management, because managers are seen as 'soft touches'. Employees continually expect more, but give less and less. Even a compromise between these two extremes is unsuccessful, because basically Theory X management has got its priorities wrong. To quote McGregor:

> The philosophy of management by direction and control – regardless of whether it is hard or soft – is inadequate to motivate because the human needs on which this approach relies are today unimportant motivators of behaviour. Direction and control are essentially useless in motivating people whose important needs are social and egoistic. (McGregor in Hunergager and Heckmann.)

McGregor's Theory Y is 'based on more adequate assumptions about human nature and human motivation'. He believes that most people want to do a good day's work, but need an appropriate environment in which to do it. He says:

> The motivation, the potential for development, the capacity for assuming responsibility, the readiness to direct behaviour toward organizational goals are all present in people. Management does not put them there. It is the responsibility of management to make it possible for people to recognize and develop these human characteristics for themselves ... The essential task of management is to arrange organizational conditions and methods of operation so that people can achieve their own goals best by directing their own efforts towards organizational objectives. (McGregor in Hunergager and Heckmann.)

Although this was written decades ago, McGregor was spelling out some of the basics for empowering a workforce. His Theory Y gave scope to satisfy Maslow's higher needs, in particular, esteem and self-actualization needs.

## EXERCISE

Below is a list of criteria which may or may not be important to motivate employees to do their best work. In the first column on the left, tick the ten criteria you think best represent the motivating forces of the average employee. (It may help you to think of your own staff in evaluating these criteria.)

1. __ __ Challenging goals

2. __ __ Relationships with colleagues

3. __ __ Not having to work too hard

4. __ __ Efficient management

5. __ __ Being treated with respect

6. __ __ Good pension scheme

7. __ __ Clear company policy

8. __ __ To see the end result of their work

9. __ __ Opportunity to use own initiative

10. __ __ To be kept well informed

11. __ __ Career prospects

12. __ __ To think for themselves

13. __ __ High pay

14. __ __ Interesting work

15. __ __ Opportunities for development/training

16. __ __ To be recognized for their efforts

17. __ __ Good working conditions

18. __ __ To be challenged in their work

19. __ __ To be listened to

20. __ __ Fringe benefits

21. __ __ Having a supportive boss ☐ ☐

22. __ __ Free to organize own work & time ☐ ☐

23. __ __ Involvement in decision making ☐ ☐

24. __ __ Responsibility and authority to see
            a job through ☐ ☐

25. __ __ Knowing what is expected of them ☐ ☐

Now, in the second column on the left-hand side, rank the ten criteria you have chosen in order of importance.

When you have done this, repeat the exercise using the boxes to the right of the page, this time selecting the ten areas which motivate you at work, then ranking them in order of importance.

### Possible response

There are no right and wrong answers as such, but before giving you the ten qualities which research has shown to be consistently important for employee motivation, consider these questions:

- Did you select different, similar or the same criteria for subordinates and yourself?
- Would you expect the selections to be different? if so, why?
- What assumptions did you make about factors which motivate other people?
- On what evidence have you based the criteria chosen for employees? Were they guesses from observations of your staff? Were they impressions about the workforce in general? Are they objective impressions arrived at because of previous discussions with your staff about their needs?

Of course, I don't know what your responses were, but you will have guessed from the questions posed that invariably we make assumptions about other people's motives and needs without consulting them or discussing the issues which affect them.

Whatever your own responses were, research has shown that managers' views of employee needs differ greatly both from what really motivates staff, and from their own priorities in terms of job satisfaction and motivation. One study produced the following top ten:

1.  (4)  Working for an efficient boss
2.  (12)  To be allowed to think for themselves

3.   (8)   To see the end result of their work
4.   (14)  Interesting work
5.   (10)  To be kept well informed
6.   (19)  To be listened to
7.   (5)   Being treated with respect
8.   (16)  To be recognized in their efforts
9.   (1)   Challenging goals
10.  (15)  Opportunities for development/training.

Whereas there will be little difference in general terms (most people want recognition for good work, a sense of achievement and so on), each individual's needs will be different, and a good manager will establish what these needs are and try to accommodate them if the best is to be obtained from the team. You may wish to use the 25 criteria listed as a starting-point for discussion with your own staff. I stress *starting-point* because this is by no means an exhaustive list; there will be personal factors which motivate individuals not listed here.

# Motivating people at work

This long section began by drawing your attention to personality and trait theories. In a nutshell – no two people are alike; neither will they react in exactly the same way to a given situation. Everyone has a unique view of the world based on conditioning, learning and experience. Individuals will react differently at different times to different situations. What can be taken in your stride today may seem a mountainous problem tomorrow because you are more tired, going down with the flu', or some other situation has affected your emotions or attitude.

Whereas some generalities can be made about how to motivate people at work, the starting-point has to be communication with individuals in your team. You need to know your people, and this can only be achieved by talking with them, questioning, actively listening, and observing. This will help you to design work to suit individuals – for example, if you have a garrulous employee who is distracting the rest of the team by constantly wandering from his workstation for short chats, see whether a more front-line job where he has customer contact or communication with other departments might better suit his abilities and attributes. If you know that an employee gets annoyed by a 'that will do' attitude, and is a stickler for detail, arrange their job accordingly so that they can get personal job satisfaction, and you know that you can rely on the work being accurate and thorough.

'But you haven't seen who I've got to work with' I hear you say – and true, while most people want to be happy in their employment, to give an honest day's work and to do a good job for their organization, there will always be the difficult employee. The answer again lies in communication. How will you know what the problem is if you don't ask? Here are some tips:

- Treat them as professionals and experts in their own sphere of work, and don't patronize.
- Praise aspects of their work which is well done.
- Question to find out how they see their situation.
- Listen carefully and show that you are listening by eye contact, nods and non-verbal gestures.
- Try to get into their world; to see things from their point of view.
- Discuss facts – don't be judgemental or criticize personality.
- Read between the lines – listen with your eyes as well as ears to ascertain hidden agendas.
- Do something with the information you receive – give your views, say what will happen, monitor/report on progress.

Underperformance can be for a number of reasons. Long-term unemployed who have recently found work may be stuck at the basic levels of Maslow's hierarchy, and as long as they have any job and the working conditions are satisfactory, they are not concerned with esteem, prestige, or self-actualization; they are probably frightened at the prospect of responsibility and authority for their section of work. Encouragement and possibly coaching is required to improve job performance, energize and motivate them to work towards their full potential.

Then there are those who lack confidence – they *can't* do the work for some reason – who need more training and support to do an effective job. Ensure that you are giving enough information to these people. Are they getting the right resources to do a good job? Have they sufficient relevant experience? Check that they really know how to do what is expected of them. Do they know where their work fits in the organizational structure? Are they seeing the end results of their work?

You might have employees who overestimate their ability, and are therefore thwarted because they are trying to achieve beyond their means (or they may be pushing themselves because of external pressure to do so). Until such people recognize their limitations, performance, morale and motivation will suffer. While you are striving to enable every individual to reach their potential, you also need to recognize that employees who cannot recognize their limitations for themselves, need counselling and guidance from you. They need to feel OK about themselves, for themselves, and not pressurized into being something or someone they are not.

Employees will find it difficult to maintain commitment and motivation if the jobs they are doing seem pointless or are boring. Job enrichment, job enlargement, job rotation or changing the work flow are possible solutions to these problems, and of course, explaining where their work fits into the larger structure. Involving every member of staff more fully by empowering them in their work is a solution currently fashionable. Staff take ownership of their work; invariably individual output and productivity increases and morale rises.

The most difficult employee is the one who isn't motivated because he doesn't want to be. He is likely to be a time-waster, and a deflator of morale. If you have communicated well – questioned and listened and taken an active interest in needs and ambitions – still to no avail, divert your energies to enabling the rest of the team to excel. Don't 'send him to Coventry'; keep him informed. As was stated earlier, most people want to belong, and your difficult employee should soon see the benefits to be gained from pulling together in a committed team against the deprivation of being an outsider.

Leading by example is a crucial aspect of motivation. If you can share your enthusiasm for organizational goals and visions with your team, you are on the way to energizing them. Make your work environment a happy and mutually supportive place. Keep well informed, and share information with your team. Act with vigour and purpose, and your team will do the same. Be a role model. Keep your work area or office tidy; be organized with your time as well as paperwork. Show your competence; employee confidence will grow with an efficient leader at the helm. Be prepared to learn, to be innovative, to try something new, to make changes, to take risks. Involve your staff as much as possible in planning, change management, problem-solving and decision-making.

Communicate. Teach teams to think for themselves by brainstorming ideas. On an individual basis, ask staff probing questions to enable them to think more laterally, and make decisions – questions such as:

> 'In what other ways could you tackle that?'
> 'If you did . . . what is likely to happen?'
> 'What would have to be different for this to work for you?'
> 'Is this the result we want, or could we aim for . . . ?'
> 'What is it about . . . specifically, that makes it difficult for you?'
> 'How might you change things so that . . . can happen?'

Recognize achievement. Celebrate success. (Nothing acts more as a demotivator than being taken for granted.) Care for your people. People-centred leadership is by far the most effective way of getting the most from your staff. If you show a marked concern for your people; are a role model for competence, innovation and creativity; allow individuals the scope to reach their full potential within organizational goals, this will produce a motivated workforce and loyalty to the group, to you and to the organization.

## EXERCISE

This is a self-assessment questionnaire. Only you know the areas in which you are already proficient as a motivator of your team. After you have ticked in the appropriate columns below, please do not just file the results under 'bin', but keep this honest record and refer to it from time to time to see how your motivation skills are developing.

I am good at:

|  |  | *Do well now* | *Should improve* |
|---|---|---|---|
| 1. | regularly talking with employees about their work, aspirations and needs | — | — |
| 2. | taking an active interest in employees as individual people with lives outside the workplace | — | — |
| 3. | creating a supportive, caring and open environment in which we can all contribute, share and work. Have I made our section a happy/fun place in which to work | — | — |
| 4. | consulting and listening to employees' views and ideas, not just about their own jobs, but about the running of our section | — | — |
| 5. | involving people in setting realistic targets and achievements | — | — |
| 6. | ensuring that everyone knows what is expected of them; where they fit in; the importance of their contribution to the team and to the organization | — | — |
| 7. | ensuring that everyone knows how performance will be measured; regularly reviewing performance, and letting people know where they stand | — | — |
| 8. | ensuring that everyone knows and shares the organization's vision, objectives and our own sections goals and targets | — | — |

9. allowing people to plan and control their own — —
   working environment
10. encouraging individuals to set their own — —
    targets and objectives; solve their own
    problems; make decisions
11. devolving responsibility and authority as far — —
    down the organization as possible
12. providing the coaching, training and — —
    assistance necessary for each individual to
    reach his full potential
13. providing the resources necessary to perform — —
    individual and team tasks
14. praising successes and making these successes — —
    known to others
15. emphasizing team spirit — —
16. recognizing and rewarding good performance — —
17. giving (and receiving) positive, honest — —
    feedback
18. giving constructive criticism, and helping — —
    individuals to correct or eliminate poor
    performance if it occurs
19. guiding and encouraging the personal — —
    development of individuals within my team
20. arranging any interdepartmental or external — —
    contacts which would help individual or team
    effort
21. being receptive to learning; to new ideas, new — —
    possibilities; to entertain alternative opinions
22. being flexible – there is always another way to — —
    get things done
23. leading with vision, not by tradition — —
24. continually expanding my own skills, in — —
    different directions
25. recognizing my own needs. — —

Parts of this section have been adapted from UNISON/IM *Professional Management Foundation Programme* by Sue Bishop (1991). (See Further Reading.) Reproduced by permission of UNISON Open College.

# 13 Negotiation

Here we are talking negotiation with a small 'n', not the wheeling and dealing of big-time negotiators – not even the negotiating that is part of every top salesperson's day. So what is going to be covered by this chapter? We all negotiate for all sorts of things, all the time. How proficient we are at it is another matter; this section will look at the basics of good practice.

To give you some idea of the sorts of things we negotiate, I'll give you some examples from recent personal experience. I share a private footpath with five neighbours. It had fallen into disrepair, with more weeds than tarred surface, so the time came when I felt we had to agree to resurfacing the path. It fell to my lot to persuade each of the neighbours of the importance of getting the work professionally done. In other words, I had to negotiate. I wanted the work done, by a certain time, by professional people at a reasonable cost. Not all of my neighbours had the same priorities. In the event, we reached a jointly acceptable agreement, so then had to get bids from various firms and negotiate terms with them – negotiation again. Another instance was when I ran a training course where participants identified their internal customers within their organizations. They went on to look at how the work of each affected the other, and how improvements might be made – on both sides – to the overall efficiency of the organization. On returning from the training course, participants needed to communicate with other individuals/departments, explaining how their own work, as internal customers, might be improved by changes in the others' way of working. Quite a big negotiating task!

We negotiate when we decide where we will eat out – what type of food, pub or restaurant? We negotiate when we buy cars, furniture, or insurance – not necessarily over price, but on 'extras', terms or delivery dates. At work we negotiate over deadlines and workload priorities. We negotiate with family members when we decorate house, decide how to spend our summer vacation, or over the allocation of household chores. We negotiate to patch up quarrels and misunderstandings.

If both sides are in agreement about every aspect of a situation there is no need to negotiate. Negotiation takes place in any meeting where there is a conflict of interests. It is a process of getting much of what you want from others by giving others what they want. It is not about one-upmanship or getting your own way at the expense of others. That is manipulation, and is ultimately counter-productive. If the other person feels he has been browbeaten, outmanoeuvred or cheated, he will not want to do business with you again. He may even plan retribution or revenge. Respect for you and/or your organization will go out of the window. The best way to achieve the outcome you require is to ensure that the other person achieves too.

The key to effective negotiation is good preparation – knowing what you want, why you want it, what you would settle for and your best alternatives if the negotiation fails. It is also about getting into the other person's shoes, establishing his underlying interests and needs, broadening options, and enabling him to get what he wants (although that may not be the same as his demand at the beginning of the negotiation).

'The other side', whoever they might be, are unlikely to just give in to demands or accede to any request made of them without wanting something in return. The 'what's in it for me?' syndrome comes quickly into play. This section will give some pointers about how best to arrive at a win/win situation in negotiation, where both sides feel they have gained from the interaction.

# Power

The potential of the mind to influence your negotiating ability is truly powerful. Enter into a negotiation with a negative attitude – thinking that you'll never 'win' against your boss, or that the other person holds all the cards and you hold none, or that if he starts to get emotional you'll give in – the self-fulfilling prophecy phenomenon will take over. Power is what you think it is. Think positively, and the outcome will reflect this attitude. View situations from the standpoint of gain, not loss; success, not failure; positive outcome, not defeat.

In the business sense, your greatest power lies in total commitment to your organization, pride in your product, belief in your department, your people and so on. No matter what the other section head, competitor or customer says, the more confident you are about your team, company practices or products, the better negotiator you will be.

Another source of negotiating power is that of the personal relationship – a commitment to try to satisfy the interests of the other party. Show the other person from the beginning that you are dedicated to finding ways to meet his needs while not neglecting your own; build the relationship by continually demonstrating that commitment. Be honest at all times; build mutual respect. If the other person has confidence in you as an honest broker, your negotiations will be that much easier.

If you make a commitment to yourself – to achieve these terms for your section; to 'up' production within a given time; to resolve a misunderstanding etc., stick to it. Write it down, or tell someone else so that you have to proceed or lose face. There is power in making personal pledges.

# Prepare

So, you are committed to enter a negotiation. To get to your desired destination you first have to know where you are going and how you are going to get there, so planning is important. Try never to enter negotiations without forward planning, just a 'let's listen to what they've got to say and take it from there' attitude. This will result in a reactive rather than a proactive outcome. Sometimes it's necessary to negotiate from this 'seat of your pants' position, but it is by no means ideal.

One of the greatest mistakes an inexperienced negotiator can make is not recognizing that there is a difference between position (your wants) and interests (the needs and desires that lie behind these wants). For example, I want to use the car this evening; you want to use the car this evening. These are positions. If both sides concentrate on position, there is likely to be stalemate, or an argument where eventually one side wins and the other loses.

Let's look at a simplistic example of how looking at interests can achieve a win/win solution. Example: During an office reorganization two members of staff argue about who is going to have the desk by the window. Neither will give in, they have fixed *positions*. By establishing *interests*, however, it transpires that one requires the additional light for detailed work; the other wants that desk because it is next to a 'phone point, and he does much of his business by telephone. It is easy to see solutions whereby each could gain from a negotiation, e.g. angle-poise light provided for one, or an alternative desk with telephone for the other.

A further example, quoted in the excellent *Getting to Yes* by Roger Fisher, William Ury and Bruce Patton (see Further reading) is the Egyptian/Israeli peace negotiations of 1977. Both sides wanted occupancy of the Sinai desert (positional stance) but when interests were explored, Egypt wanted sovereignty and Israel needed security. They eventually agreed on a plan whereby Sinai would be ruled totally by Egypt, who agreed to a demilitarization policy, assuring Israel's security.

You will need to establish what you want to happen – ideally – as the result of a negotiation. You will probably end up with a list of wants – these are your positions, which you may or may not have to modify in the course of a negotiation. From this list establish your interests – what caused you to decide on these wants; what motivates you; what your needs and concerns are. Then do the same for the other party, try to see the situation from their position. You are negotiating because there is a conflict of interests or differences of opinion – differences defined by the disparity between your thinking and theirs. Ask yourself 'why do they want this?' 'What stops them from accepting that?' Effective negotiation is more about reconciling interests than compromising between positions.

To return to the scenario described above with my neighbours. Each set had different positions: one couple didn't see why they should pay one-sixth when they were the end house and only walked on a few feet of the communal footpath; another felt that we could do the work ourselves for far less over a couple of weekends; yet another felt the quotes were perhaps too low, and that we should go for thicker tarmacadam, longer guarantees etc. On talking with them, underlying interests were un-covered – in fact there were multiple interests to be addressed. This gave ammunition to negotiate with the contractor. We could compromise over time-scales, but not over safety. We were prepared to use the existing path as hardcore, if that could save us enough for a better quality surface. We could do a certain amount of preparation work if they could guarantee treatment of recurring weed growth over the next five years, and so on. This is a simplistic tit-for-tat list, but you can see how, by understanding interests, you have the basis for sound negotiation whereby all parties emerge winners. In the process, neighbours were asked to consider short- and long-term consequences of not resurfacing in terms of safety, cost increase and so on, and the advantages such as the aesthetic improvement to the rank of houses, adding to the value of all the properties. The contractor was extremely grateful that neighbours had reached a con-sensus view and that he didn't have to negotiate separately with each party as he had on some occasions, and that because time was not important, he could fit in our work around other contracts. Everyone gained.

So, you have your list of wants and the interests that motivate these wants, and you have assessed, as well as you can in the abstract, the positions and interests of the other person. You need now to look carefully at your lists and prioritize your wants, deciding where and in what way you can be flexible, and what your bottom line is on each issue. Prioritize wants under the headings *High importance* (must have if you are to agree at all) *Medium importance* (preferred, but not critical) and *Low importance* (great if you can get them, but no sleep lost if they have to go).

If your negotiation is to be with another head of section in your organization, for example, remember that knowledge is powerful – not just a thorough knowledge of your own team's processes and practices, but of the other department too. A little homework will pay off. Once into the negotiation, by questioning and listening you will be able better to gauge the importance of interests to the other person. An ideal solution is for you to dovetail your interests, you acceding to things of less importance to you, but of greater importance to them and vice versa. To give you an example, a father of a young teenager who is just beginning to 'feel her wings' may want her to stay at home during the week to do homework, and just go to known friends' homes at weekends to socialize. In the event of a party, dance or similar, the parent wants to know where she is going, and who she is going with. Ideally the parent would like to set a time for her to return home, and go and fetch her personally. The interests underlying these wants are mainly her personal safety. The father doesn't want her to get in with 'a bad crowd'; is anxious about the availability of alcohol and drugs at events he can't vet; he wants to maintain 'control'; he doesn't want her school work to suffer. The teenager needs to establish her independence and prove her responsibility as a young adult. She wants to be able to choose her own friends, and how she spends her time. While wanting to do well in school, she feels that socializing with her peer group is as important to her development. She resents the rules and regulations and feels that she isn't being trusted. In the course of negotiation (because that is what the ensuing conversation will be) it may well emerge that the most important factor to the daughter is her bid for independence being curbed. By careful questioning and listening, there may well be other options which allow her to achieve what she most wants from the negotiation, without the parent relinquishing anything too important to him. He may be able to achieve his main interest – her personal safety – by only slight modifications of his original ideal outcome.

Besides deciding on your wants, interests, priorities and what you are prepared to give to achieve mutual gain, you also need to consider the possibility that there might yet be stalemate, so you need to consider what your best alternative would be. I will give the example used in *Getting to Yes*, previously quoted. Imagine that you are going to sell your house. You have fixed a bottom-line price, but have aimed high (in good negotiation tradition). The house is on the market for £100,000 and you are prepared to drop no lower than £87,000. When deciding on the bottom-line price you should ask yourself not what you ought to get, but what best alternative you have, i.e. what you will do if, by a certain time, you have not got a buyer. You could rent it out privately or through an agency; let a relative live in it provided they pay the mortgage etc. It may be that one of the alternatives is better than selling for £87,000. Your best alternative is the standard against which any proposed agreement should be measured. Be realistic with 'best alternatives', but be aware that you have other options if you fail to reach an agreement. The more easily you feel you can withdraw from a negotiation, the greater your actual capacity to affect a successful outcome.

# Rapport

For negotiation to be successful, there shouldn't be an atmosphere of antagonism, animosity or competition. Rather than seeing the other person as an opponent, go into the negotiation thinking of the other as an ally. You are jointly there to look at, and discover solutions to, a problem. You are partners, looking for a fair agreement from which you will both benefit. You will discover that you have shared interests which you can advance as well as conflicting interests to be sorted out. Of course, there will always be the person who refuses to see a negotiation as anything other than a personal battle. We will look at how to deal with awkward people later in the section.

Even if you do not personally like the person with whom you are dealing, learn to act as if you do! Remember, that he is a human being with feelings and emotions – and an ego that can be dented.

Show that you care about his needs and opinions by questioning and listening carefully. You will gain his attention and respect, and in the process learn a lot more about his standpoint and underlying interests – a good negotiating ploy.

Most negotiations involve ongoing relationships, whether with family members, friends, work associates or customers, and it's important to remember that building and maintaining rapport is often as important as the successful completion of a single negotiation. If you get what you want at the other person's expense, or they suspect you of unfair tactics, you will lose goodwill that may be worth far more in the long term than a one-off triumph. Successful people work at creating rapport, and rapport creates trust, respect and confidence – essential ingredients to successful win/win outcomes.

# Communication

Negotiation is 'the process by which two or more parties attempt to achieve agreement on matters of mutual interest . . . all parties can gain something from the process' (*Collins Dictionary of Business* by Pass, Lowes, Pendleton and Chadwick, Harper Collins, Glasgow, 1991). You will need to frame each negotiation as a joint search for solutions, and this can be physically set up by sitting side by side – allies in problem-solving.

Research has shown that the process of negotiation works most smoothly when each party listens actively and fully to the other so that shared interests and points of difference can be defined precisely. Careful phrasing and choice of vocabulary, body language, tone of voice are all important to creating open dialogue, but arguably questioning and listening are the two most significant skills to employ in successful negotiating.

Negotiations can be stressful for all parties concerned. Whatever you say it is possible that the other person will misinterpret or misunderstand you. Either that or they will be so preoccupied with their next move or response, that active listening will have gone out of the window. Keep them on track by asking open questions wherever possible – questions which require some considered response. During the planning stages you will have conjectured about their position and interests. You need to test out your hypotheses, to clarify, and to gain more insight by questioning and summarizing.

Statements can produce contention but questions produce answers. They create challenges and can be used to get the other person to confront a problem area. Use questions, therefore, wherever possible. When direct questions are asked of you, rather than saying 'yes' or 'no', buy yourself thinking time by asking an open question instead, e.g. 'If I were to consider that, what further discount might be available?' If you disagree with a point made, ask a clarification question, e.g. 'What leads you to that conclusion?' It is far better to get the other person to recognize the weakness of his position than to try to explain why you think he is wrong. You might flag up your question by asking something like, 'Can I ask you about your priorities?' By agreeing, to answer your question the other person is almost duty bound to give you an informative response.

If you are not actively listening to what the other person is saying, there is no true communication. Try to concentrate on them; to see the world through their eyes, rather than thinking about how you are going to phrase your next response or argument.

Listen with eyes as well as ears so that you can pick up on underlying feelings, hidden agendas, or inhibitions (see the Calibration section in

Chapter 4) e.g. 'I feel you're uncomfortable with that; am I right?' Interrupt when appropriate with questions of clarification, e.g. 'Did I understand you correctly when you said ... did you mean?' or with summary statements, e.g. 'so as I understand it, you are prepared to ... on condition that ...' Rather than annoying the other person, he is more likely to respond well to being listened to, taken seriously, and understood.

When you summarize, reflect back what the other person has said in a positive way. Understanding their point of view is not the same as agreeing with it, and by restating their case in a strong and positive way, and then giving your response – stating your interests – you have a better chance of their accepting your position.

Some other communication tips:

- Listen and observe carefully to pick up signals that the other person is willing to modify his position.
- Some of the best negotiation you will do is when you're listening, not talking.
- Use language appropriate to the situation/person; speak to be understood.
- Avoid jargon unless you are sure that you are both/all conversant with the terminology.
- Establish a dialogue based on reason and objective criteria.
- Describe situations as they affect you; don't condemn, blame or openly doubt the intentions of the other person.
- Use silences to good effect; if you have asked a searching question wait for a response. If they have made an unreasonable proposal, don't respond – wait for them to retract/rephrase. If they attack you verbally, bite your tongue and say nothing.
- Practise self-control; lose your temper, you could lose the negotiation.
- Sometimes, in negotiation, too much communication can be a bad thing. Some thoughts are better left unsaid a) because they are provoked by anger or b) because disclosure gives the other side an unfair advantage.
- Don't interrupt; hear the other person out.
- Don't complain; offer solutions.
- Listen for a greater percentage of time than you talk.
- Summarize using neutral language.
- Generally, be non-committal about their explanations; if you need to respond, ask further questions.
- Seek and give information, but don't give too much away; 'clever' remarks can sometimes be costly.

- Listen for clues about their interests; their priorities; their worries; their commitment to positions.
- Use assertive language such as 'we need', 'I think', 'we must have' etc, rather than the waffly 'I hope', 'perhaps' 'I wish' and so on.
- Look forward, not back; talk about what can happen to progress your mutual interests rather than harp on about past problems or what someone else has said or done.

# The game

You have a given situation. You both have ideal outcomes which just happen to be different. You need to explore these differences because they will point to areas where you can make trade-offs to mutual advantage. Look on negotiation as a problem-solving game. Games have rules, and if you follow these rules, everyone should win. By seeing negotiation as a game, you will be able to detach yourself from the stress, antagonism and negative emotions often associated with it. Remember that negative thoughts hamper negotiation skills.

Opinions differ regarding whether it is best to try to lead from the front, offering your proposals first, or lead from behind: listen to what the other side wants; don't respond, but probe by open questioning to get a better idea of their commitment to the various factors which the negotiation entails. If you go for the former, make your proposal – then shut up! The other person will need thinking time, and you don't want to begin to bargain – offering more or moderating your proposal just in order to fill an embarrassing silence. If you go for the latter, learn as much as you can about the other's perspective, offering as little as possible of your own. This will give you a strong negotiating position.

Be succinct; move forward in small stages, summarizing and confirming points of agreement.

Look for mutual gain. Identify shared interests. Find bridges across points of difference; try to dovetail these. Think of the old nursery rhyme about Jack Spratt and his wife. He ate all the lean, and she all the fat from their meat – because of mutual preference – so out of difference came agreement, both parties giving up something of little value to themselves and gaining something of worth.

Focus on interests – underlying motivations and feelings – rather than positions. Think laterally; be creative; devise as many options as you can to solve each problem. State issues as you see them and invite the other person to help provide solutions without being judgemental of their suggestions. By broadening the options there is more opportunity for mutual gain. For example, if an employee demands a salary increase (position) discussion might show that what motivates his demand is a desire for a better quality of life (interests). This might not best be achieved by more money, but by offering flexitime, a shorter working week, longer holidays etc.

Once you are in the thick of the negotiation, do not suggest a counter-proposal immediately after the other person has made a suggestion. This is the time they are least likely to accept an alternative. Question and discuss their proposal. If you find fault with their idea, give your reasons first, rather than saying 'I disagree' (or even worse, 'you're wrong'!). When and if they can see the holes in their argument, then is the time for you to counter-propose. Your ideas are far more likely to be acceptable to them.

If relevant to the situation, ensure that the other person has information or ammunition to take back to their family/team/boss. If you have argued your corner well and reached a mutually beneficial agreement, the other person may now have to explain to others the reasons for concessions and gains.

When it comes to bargaining, it's not how much you concede, but *how* you concede that counts. It's not what you gained, but how you gained it that matters. I have personal experience of this. Years ago we put our current house up for sale at what we considered a fair price considering the selling price of similar properties in the area. The first viewer arrived on the same day that details were advertised, and with very little hesitation, offered us the full asking price. Were we happy? Not a bit of it! We immediately thought we could have asked more – and would probably have got it. Only after the event did we consider the extras our house had compared with properties similar in structure in our area. We were proverbially 'gutted'. Say we had aimed high and asked £150,000 with a bottom line of £125,000. We would have had good scope for negotiation. We may, in fact, have ended up with less than the asking price we actually got, but if we had worked hard to negotiate a fair price, we would have been happier because of our achievement. Human nature is a funny thing, but this is true. Most people prefer a successful barter to an outright win. The person who has to work hard to achieve a small concession leaves the negotiation more satisfied than the one who got a big discount without demur.

Some other points to remember when bargaining:

- Give a little at a time, in small increments rather than showing your hand in one go.
- Before you concede a point, always try to get something in return.

- A successful agreement is one that bears enough of the suggestions of both parties for each to feel that it is theirs.
- Attack the problem without blaming the people.
- Look for items of low cost to you and benefit to them.
- Initially, talk about preferences; don't divulge what is acceptable.
- Don't yield to pressure; only to reason.
- Aim for the 'feel good' factor for yourself and the other person.
- Give yourself space and thinking time; a good negotiator rarely makes an important decision on the spot.
- Don't risk long-term relationships for a quick 'win'.

# Pitfalls and trouble-shooting techniques

Some people will employ tactics against you. The key is in recognizing that the other person is attempting to manipulate you. With practice you will be able to spot these ploys and counter them.

Watch out for the 'what if . . . ?' negotiator. He will set you a number of hypotheses to try and ascertain what your bottom line is. He then is in a powerful position to negotiate from that point. When you recognize this ploy, play dumb, or use delaying tactics: say you don't know and will get back to him, or that you have to consult with others before proceeding.

Make sure that when you leave a negotiation you have all loose ends tied up. You may think you've done really well from a negotiation, only to find that you've agreed to a basic outline to which the other person will then add on conditions – changes which will leave you the loser.

Beware, too, of the *fait accompli*. You may have agreed a price and delivery date only to find out that when the purchase order arrives, the conditions have been changed. Or you agree that you will give a discount of 10 per cent if the bill is settled within a certain time. The time elapses, but a cheque is sent with the discount claimed. Usually 'a bird in the hand is worth two in the bush' and you will settle for the amount sent. Arguing or trying to recoup the extra isn't usually worth the trouble.

The other person may knowingly give you erroneous information. Unless you know the person well and trust and respect them, check out statements and facts before agreeing to anything.

Check out the other person's authority. Don't assume that the person you are dealing with has the final say in a negotiation. You may well agree to elements on your own behalf, only to find out that what you thought you had negotiated has to be agreed by a higher authority within the organization. You have, by then, divulged your hand, so will be, in effect, renegotiating on their terms. Try to find out as early as possible if the person you are dealing with has the authority to close the negotiation.

One way is by asking something like 'If I can XYZ can we close the deal today – right now?' Someone without the authority to close will immediately forestall, and will probably own that he needs to consult his boss first.

It is possible that you will meet someone who refuses to negotiate. The way forward here is to try to talk about *why* he is unwilling. Use lots of open questions to find out their *interests* in not negotiating – their needs, fears, motivations and inhibitions.

If you feel you have done all you can to make the negotiation work, and to make it easy for the other side to agree, yet they still vacillate, try this tactic. Say something like 'No, I don't think this is going to work – we're not getting anywhere'. If they agree, then it's probably time to cut your losses and retreat, content in the knowledge that you still have other options and your best alternative plan. If, however, they argue that there is still scope for discussion, you can continue jointly to look for bridges to span differences.

Another ploy which can work for or against you is that of documentary evidence. It's another strange aspect of human nature that we can argue with facts – even undisputed facts – on a face-to-face basis, but if we are shown a piece of paper with 'evidence' on it, generally we accept it as 'gospel'. It is there in black and white, so it must be true. A printed policy statement, a standard application form or a printed price list will be accepted where the spoken word is not.

Finally, remember your rights. There are some, especially appropriate, which you should repeat to yourself when negotiating. You have the right to be listened to and taken seriously. You have the right to be treated with respect as an intelligent, capable and equal human being. You have the right to ask for information. You have the right to ask for what you want. You have the right to be wrong, as long as you come clean and work to correct your mistakes. You have the right to take time to make decisions, and so on. Remember these; remember to respect the rights and needs of the other person while not neglecting your own; remember the power of positive thinking, and your negotiations should be a success.

## EXERCISE

Consider the following situations and suggest an appropriate response to each.

1.   The negotiation is going off course, and you feel that you are both getting bogged down in irrelevant detail.

2. The other person says 'I'm not going to the meeting in Edinburgh'. This is inconvenient as you want the whole team with you at the Scottish meeting; you have arranged a reduced price block-booking on an internal flight; you can travel there and back on the same day and therefore reconvene at the office to discuss the meeting next morning.

3. Discussion has ground to a halt. It appears to be stalemate. The other person looks to you for a way forward.

4. You are in the middle of a negotiation with your insurance broker, but he is beginning to blind you with science. You are unsure and apprehensive about the way things are progressing, and what you have already agreed to.

5. The other person is aggressive, blaming you personally for his problems.

**Suggested responses**

1. Challenge the relevancy of the current discussion. Backtrack; summarize what you feel you've agreed so far to re-establish a sound basis for further discussion. Keeping to objective criteria, resume the negotiation, keeping to relevant issues. Use open questioning and summarizing skills to keep the other person on track. Remembering your own preparation – your wants and interests – frame the discussion as a joint search for a mutually beneficial solution.

2. This is a classic case of 'I won't play'. If you stick to your position – 'I want you to be there' – and he sticks to his – 'I'm not going' – you'll both get increasingly entrenched and stalemate will result. Don't get rattled! Don't attack their position, but look behind it for reasons. Use patience and sensitive open questioning to establish his interests: to define the problem and to find out what underlies his reluctance. It could be that he has family commitments which make it impossible to work an extended day; he could be afraid of flying; he might lack confidence in his ability to contribute to the meeting; he may be afraid of letting the team down; he could have travel sickness problems – until you question you won't know. In order to negotiate a deal which suits you both, you have to find out his needs, feelings, concerns etc. Reason, and be open to reason. Explain your interests in as lively and positive a way as possible. Look for a mutually acceptable solution.

3. Decide together whether this is really the end of the line. Are you negotiating interests, or is there deadlock over positions? You could

jointly look for further options. Pose the question, 'How would a banker see the situation?', 'If you were an accountant, would you see the situation differently?', 'Seen through the eyes of a doctor, a lawyer, another team member etc, how might they perceive this situation?'. Often by looking at the problem more as an onlooker, with others with specialist points of view as the key fictional players, other options will occur to you.

You could restate your position, then require them to suggest an alternative.

You could ask the question, 'What would have to happen for this not to be a problem?' or 'Under what circumstances would you reconsider this?'.

You could try to shift them from the impasse by offering a precise bargain – on your terms – such as 'If you can agree to ABC, then I'll improve XYZ'.

You could choose to adjourn. Suggest that you both go away and think about the situation, then reconvene if there is felt to be room for further discussion. In the domestic situation, this is the same as 'sleeping on' an unresolved issue. Sometimes time and space away from the problem will be sufficient to see things in a different light, or to come up with further options for negotiation.

You might say something like, 'I don't think we're getting anywhere here'. If they disagree, throw the ball into their court by asking them to find a way around the block. If they agree, walk away from the negotiation, confident in the fact that your advance preparation has established your own best alternative to a successful negotiation.

4.  Be honest with him; explain that you want to make sure that you fully understand. Agree what you have agreed. Take the initiative; backtrack and summarize in your own words your understanding of the situation. Question, check and confirm before proceeding.

5.  Recognize that emotions are likely to run strong in negotiations – not just theirs, but yours as well. Acknowledge this openly with the other person, recognizing the legitimacy of strong emotions in potentially stressful situations. Usually this releases some of the tension, helps create bridges between you, and aids proactive discussion.

Aggressive behaviour may be a ploy to try to dominate the negotiation. Don't rise to the bait, or feel pressurized by this behaviour. Use relaxation techniques to stop the shaking hands, tremor in the voice, escalation of volume or other give-aways that you too are feeling emotionally charged. Allow the other person the space to let off steam and cool down. Don't respond or react, just listen quietly, encouraging him to continue until he has vented his spleen, and exhausted his frustration. You can then begin to build a basis for rational discussion.

If the other person's emotional outburst is in any way justified – even if only inadvertently you are the cause of the outburst – be big enough to apologize, and set to putting things right. Even if you are not to blame, an apology can often defuse the situation. Remember, you don't have to acknowledge fault; just say how sorry you are that such and such has occurred, then get down to working together to push the discussion forward.

If the other person apologizes to you, accept graciously; draw a line under the disagreement, and move on to more positive territory.

# 14 Poor performers

However good a manager you are, at some time during your career you will have a poor performer or an underachiever on your team. This can be for a variety of reasons:

- you inherit them from another manager
- misjudgment occurred at recruitment;

the individual may have:

- a lack of understanding of what is required
- poor motivation;

there may have been:

- changes in the workplace
- changes to that employee's responsibilities or workload
- changes in the individual's ability (through age or illness)
- domestic circumstances;

there could be problems with:

- the working environment
- work group/team dynamics.

There are many others. Generally, poor performance is caused by conditions to do with employees, with managers or with the organizational structure.

The employee may or may not know that he has a problem. If he has previously worked for other managers who failed to address the poor performance, or appraisal interviews have failed to pick up difficulties, then it is hardly the fault of the individual if he is underachieving.

The first step is to establish whether there really is a gap between standards and performance and whether the fault lies outside the immediate control of the employee. If the problem is work based, has the content or context of the work changed? Could this be causing the problem? Have changes to the job description put the work beyond the capabilities of this employee? Are standards and procedures laid down for the job realistic? Have your own standards changed? Are procedures and standards inappropriate to the tasks and responsibilities – or out of date?

If, after checking all of this, you find that there is sufficient gap between what is expected and what is being achieved, you will need to arrange a meeting with the employee concerned jointly to identify inconsistencies between organizational standards, those you expect of your staff, and his own performance.

The outcome of interpersonal exchanges, where each person is coming from a different standpoint, relies heavily on the active involvement of both parties. There needs to be a joint problem-solving and goal-setting – and 'ownership' if constructive progress is to be made – so involve him at every stage of the process.

If you suspect that the main cause of problem might be of a personal nature – for example, ill health or domestic difficulties – you might consider discussing the matter at his place of work rather than summoning him to your office. Wherever you decide to hold the meeting, the usual rules apply: it should be somewhere quiet, private and free from interruptions. Choose comfortable seating; offer the usual courtesies; make it as easy an interview as possible. You want to create an environment where the person feels confident to talk through his difficulties. Build and maintain rapport (see the section on Rapport in Chapter 2). The interview which follows is likely to be an enabling and helping session, so see also Chapter 6 on counselling.

It may be that the employee doesn't recognize that there is a problem. The first stage is to enable him to see that there is a discrepancy between what is expected and what is being delivered in terms of work performance, so start by asking him what he considers his role and responsibilities to be and the standards he expects to apply to the job. Depending on the problem, you could further probe by asking him how he prioritizes his workload; whether meeting client needs is more or less important than follow-up paperwork. You could ask whether he considers output to be more important than quality, or whether attention to every detail is a required or merely desired aspect of his work. You might investigate whether he can distinguish important work from urgent work, and how he prioritizes the two. This type of questioning should be leading the employee to agree that there are gaps between what is expected and his own performance.

Once there is agreement that there are discrepancies, and excuses are dealt with; reasons can be addressed and solutions looked for. You need to assess whether the poor performer's needs are being met. If, for example, he wants challenge in his work, or status, and that is not being provided, he will hardly be motivated to perform well. Does the employee really know what is expected of him? Can he place his job within the context of the whole department or organization? Is he allocated work or does he have some input in setting his own work targets and objectives? Does he get feedback on his performance? Does he get recognition for work well done? Does he receive the support and resources he needs to do his job well? Is his workload too great or too small? Either causes stress and underachievement.

You may be able jointly to agree strategies for removing obstacles to improvement, arrange for extra support or training, or if appropriate, redeployment or other means of getting the best from the individual to the benefit of the employee and the organization.

It may be that you feel the person needs additional help and a referral to an outside agency is called for. Speak with your personnel section, your boss, or look at your company rules for guidance. It could be that the fault lies with management, or even the way you've organized things. If this is the case, be 'big' enough to own that changes are called for and go about implementing them at once. If the problem lies with organizational planning, speak with your boss about this.

However, at the end of this probing type of interview a very different picture of the individual might emerge. Your poor performer may be doing his best, but floundering because of lack of information or support. He may be a frustrated high-achiever who has just got lost in the system. If this is the case, you need to reassess a number of areas within your department – or the organization as a whole – such as recruitment and selection procedures, appraisal interviews, leadership, teamwork and work allocation.

# EXERCISE

Consider this hypothetical scenario. You work in the cosmetics industry. At interview John Harris seemed to be the ideal candidate for recruiting to your sales team. Although his background is mainly in sports equipment, he has a good working knowledge of the territory – the Home Counties – and his CV indicates an excellent track record.

John is on six months' probation with your organization. While you wouldn't expect amazing results during his first few weeks while getting to grips with the work, 16 weeks into the job, John does not seem to be achieving – in fact, orders are down in his area.

List some of the reasons why John might be underachieving.

---
 

---
 

---
 

---
 

---
 

---

Consider each of the reasons listed. As John's manager, you need to do something about his poor performance. What would be your approach:

1. in general
2. to each of the possible causes for underachievement which you listed?

**Possible response**

If you did not include any of the following in your list of reasons for underachievement, consider them now. What would be your approach to solving each issue?

- Poor knowledge of the cosmetics industry.
- Inadequate induction training.
- Unrealistic imposed targets.
- Lack of support from manager.
- Insufficient product knowledge.
- Job/product doesn't relate to his personal needs.
- Incentives and rewards aren't realistic or great enough.
- Poor 'cold calling' skills.

- Lacking in confidence to 'push' or 'close' a sale.
- Poor questioning skills (to ascertain customers' needs).
- Poor interpersonal skills – doesn't listen well; upsets customers.
- Lack of motivation because of confidence in his product (cannot relate to basically 'feminine' market).

As with all hypothetical situations, there can be no 'correct' answers or responses. No doubt you questioned whether you should have spoken with John far sooner than 16 weeks into his probationary period to ascertain his progress (or lack of it) with the organization. However, given the hypothetical scenario, it is now obvious that you need to take time to talk this through with John in order to get his perspective of the situation. The usual rules apply: choose a time and place that is mutually convenient, where privacy is ensured and where neither of you will feel rushed or pressured. Remember tips about room-setting, the orientation and height of chairs, presence of barriers to communication such as desks and tables. At this stage, it is not a disciplinary interview or one where a warning is required. It is a fact-finding and counselling exchange in order to help you both find a way forward, so that warnings or failure to secure a permanent post after the probation period has expired, can be avoided. You need to be as supportive as possible.

After the obligatory settling-in small talk, you need to explain the reason for the meeting and of your concerns as clearly and succinctly as possible. Be careful that your tone of voice, facial expressions and body language all complement meaning. Ascertain whether John fully understands why he is having this talk with you. Ask him to give his views of the situation. Ask him to identify gaps between organizational standards and his performance. Listen carefully, with eyes as well as ears. Use questioning skills to: confirm facts (closed), collect detail (open), clarify (reflecting back) and verify understanding (summarizing).

Remember that John probably realizes that he is not performing well, and is just as unhappy about the situation as you are. Don't neglect his feelings in your pursuit of facts. It is in everyone's interests that John be given extra help and attention at this stage. Show empathy, offer support and suggest a positive way forward. For example, if John is lacking in confidence because he needs more experience of the cosmetics industry, this may be a very real gap in induction and product knowledge training which the organization needs to address. In the short term, John could be helped by arranging more training, visits to the factory, talks with other employees in production or marketing and so on.

In this hypothetical situation, it could be that in his previous posts, John had regular set accounts and was confident in introducing new products to well-known and established customers. However, his cold calling skills have got rusty, and he is finding it difficult to generate new customers in a field which is still new to him – cosmetics, perfumes and toiletries. He may feel that his 'macho' approach to sports equipment sales is inappropriate in his new field, and is floundering because of this. Again, good product knowledge will give him confidence. Additional assistance via traditional training, mentoring or coaching in interpersonal skills and/or sales training might be a suitable way forward.

These are possible solutions to identifiable problems. Knowing that his difficulties have been recognized and that you, and the organization, are prepared to support and help in every way possible, and given that he has the motivation and will to succeed, John should be able to gain confidence in his product and achieve well. However, it is not always easy, either to establish exactly where the problem lies, or – having established possible reasons in your own mind – getting John to recognize that he has difficulties; if he is upsetting customers by his attitude, for example. This will need skilled questioning and counselling skills.

### Example of how not to approach the problem

You: John, Ms Smith at Hammels has cancelled their account with us. She says that the sales rep – you – have an unfortunate manner. When I asked her to expand on this, the phrase 'sexual innuendo' was used to describe your sales pitch. What have you got to say for yourself?

### Example of a more suitable approach

You: John, Hammels has been a long-standing client of ours; they now want to close their account with us. Have you any idea what might have gone wrong?

John: No I haven't. I know that their buyer is a difficult person to deal with. Maybe she's the problem.

You: Ms Smith you mean? In what way is she difficult, specifically? Describe your last meeting with her.

... and so on. Keep imagining the likely conversation.

You: In what way is your approach to selling cosmetics and perfumes different from selling sports equipment?

John: Well, no different really. People are people and sales are sales aren't they?

You: You think that all people are the same and can be treated in a similar manner?

John: Not if you put it like that, I suppose. Some need handling with kid gloves – others you can have a laugh and a joke with.

You:   So you agree that your approach should differ according to circum-
       stances or the person with whom you are dealing?
John:  Well, yes.
You:   So what might have gone wrong with your dealings with Ms Smith at
       Hamells do you think?

# 15 Problem people

This section will begin with some general observations about using people skills to deal with problem people, some of which will have been described more fully in the opening chapters on communicating skills, assertiveness and NLP. It will then look at some specific types of problem and offer suggestions on how to cope effectively. It will not be possible to discuss every type of problem person you are likely to come across. Neither will some of these suggestions be suitable for you, your problem person or the situation you find yourself in. That's inevitable. I just hope that this section will show you that there are alternatives to the 'grin and bear it', counter-attack, or avoidance strategies which are the usual options when dealing with problem people.

It is a regrettable fact of life that there will be times in your career when you come across a problem person. Some people you deal with will be awkward, obstructive, angry or rude; you will not necessarily like everyone with whom you need to communicate. However, good people skills entail recognizing and coping with such difficulties. The more profoundly you disagree with someone, the more important it is to your working relationship that you deal professionally with that disagreement.

It has been argued that the best way forward is to put personalities and feelings aside, recognizing and accepting your differences, and to concentrate on working towards explicit goals. However, if you can create a good working relationship – turn an adversary into an ally – sound outcomes are more feasible. This is achieved by your exhibiting self-confident, constructive behaviour – role-modelling the kind of behaviour you would prefer the other person to display. It is all too easy, but counter-productive, to respond in kind, but this only serves to reinforce negative conduct. You can easily be drawn into a point-scoring contest where neither side wins.

There are some basic ideas about dealing with problem people which you might like to consider.

181

Use the person's name. Everyone likes to be recognized and acknowledged, so it is good practice always to learn and use the person's name while communicating with them. First names are fine if that's the sort of relationship you have, but consider using someone's title and surname if the situation warrants it (and it suits your current purpose of achieving a win/win outcome), e.g. when talking to someone who is status or power-conscious. With the difficult person, use their name whenever you want to take control or emphasize a point you are making.

Observe carefully, and focus your listening to ascertain where they are coming from. Might their problem be you? Are you their difficult person? Assess their preferred communication style, and adapt yours in order to facilitate smooth communication (see the section on communicating styles in Chapter 2). It's easy to get irritated by slow, ponderous communication if you are a quicksilver type, for example.

Recognize the strength of feelings and emotions in yourself and the other person. They may well get your back up without uttering a word – that sometimes happens in relationships – or you may be frustrated by their indecisiveness, their negativity, their tardiness etc. Some self-disclosure is often helpful. Let the other person know how you are feeling as a result of your joint difficulties. Bring things out into the open and discuss the implications. Assess and accommodate their feelings too. Often this will turn a hostile, reactive encounter into mature, proactive discussion about how to reconcile your differences.

Question your assumptions that the other person is being deliberately obstructive, hostile, or acting irrationally. Remember that each one of us brings a unique perception of the world to every situation – they may see things entirely differently from you. Question wisely to ascertain their perceptions of the situation. Take seriously, and respect their feelings. You may not agree with them, but they have a right to their views.

Match and mirror the style of the other person to build bridges across points of difference, to understand them better, and to create rapport. The words you choose to use can create or destroy rapport, but the words themselves only account for 7 per cent of the impact you have on the other person. How you speak – the tone, pace, volume, intonation, rhythm – and non-verbal communication – weight distribution, posture, facial expression, movement – have a great effect on the interaction. If you can match and mirror – get in tune with the other person – you will be able gradually to achieve mutual responsiveness.

One way of coping with destructive comments or negative behaviour is to try to see the benefits to you of what the other person is saying or doing. Pretend that they are being the way they are, not out of peevishness or ill-will, but with positive, constructive intent. This does not have to be true – rarely will it be, I'm afraid – but act as if their words or actions are intended to show you something positive about yourself. This is not easy, but with practice you will find that you can remain calm and even come out of an otherwise negative transaction with some positive feedback and ideas on which to build. Let me give you one or two examples.

1. Your boss is going on and on, in front of other members of your team, about (an admittedly silly) mistake.
   *Self-talk*: She is giving me the opportunity to stay calm; to practise my assertive response to justified criticism; to self affirm. She is giving me practice on how to deal with aggression. I have the opportunity to see at first hand how *not* to reprimand my own staff when they make mistakes.
2. One of your team is being obstructive to an idea enthusiastically agreed by the others.
   *Self-talk*: I must practice dealing rationally with seeming irrationality. Have I done everything I can to understand his point of view? Do I know where he is coming from – the reasons for his disagreement? Have I fully explained the situation to him so that we both understand each other? Is he anxious about the changes? Are there things going on his life which make further changes difficult to cope with? This is an opportunity to practise using empathetic questioning to pursue his reasoning, and if possible, bring about a mutually successful outcome. I can use my negotiating skills so that we arrive at a win/win solution.

# The loud, aggressive person

Often this person habitually gets what he wants by intimidating others. Sometimes, a senior manager may present with this sort of behaviour, but it is worth remembering that he probably got to that position in spite of, not because of his aggressive behaviour! Loud, aggressive, dominant behaviour is difficult to deal with, especially when this person is senior to you. Whoever the individual, of whatever status, there is no point in meeting aggression with aggression – the situation will just escalate. Avoidance behaviour lets the other person 'win' and reinforces the negative behaviour pattern.

So what can you do? The answer lies in your own self-perception, confidence and self-esteem. Don't allow yourself to become a victim. Here are some tips which may help:

● Ensure that you are as near eye level as possible. If you are sitting, stand up. Don't allow him to dominate by his physical presence.

- Maintain eye contact; if you are the first to break eye contact, he has subtly scored the first point. If staring him out appears hostile, keep your gaze within the triangle created by brows and chin – but don't look down or away.
- Don't let your body language give you away. Maintain an open posture and calm demeanour, no matter how you are feeling inside!
- Speak in a strong, calm voice with a downward intonation at the end of each statement. An upward lilt is not as emphatic, and could imply uncertainty.
- If there is a difference of opinion, say things like 'I disagree' or 'In my opinion' rather than 'You're wrong'. If you point the accusing finger, it will be met with defensive justifications or counter-attacks, and the situation gets nowhere.
- Use 'I' rational statements rather than 'you' blaming ones. If you intend to tell him how his behaviour is affecting you or your working relationship, use 'how I feel' sentences. Don't resort to the 'you made me' type of remark.
- Don't take his behaviour personally. He is probably rude and aggressive to everyone he can dominate. Don't you be one of them!
- Use silence to your advantage. Often the storm will blow itself out. Also, if you really have nothing to say to a torrent of abuse or unjustified criticism, don't be persuaded to join the fray.
- If possible rephrase his negative remarks into something more acceptable. Repeat this back to him, asking him if you've understood him correctly. In this way you are leading by example. You never know; some of your good practice might rub off on him!
- If the worse comes to the worst, withdraw from the situation, assertively letting him know that you disapprove of his behaviour, and that you will only resume dialogue if you can talk on a more reasonable basis.

## The power-conscious manager

It doesn't necessarily help you to deal with the power-conscious manager to know that his problem behaviour often stems from lack of confidence and the need continually to seek recognition and attention from others. This self-important and pompous individual will always have something to say, will seem to be obstructive just for the sake of it, or reject your ideas only to claim them as his own tomorrow! The power-conscious individual needs to make his presence felt wherever he goes.

Direct confrontation seldom works; neither do attempts to show him up for what he really is. His insecurity is masked by arrogance, and you will only exacerbate the situation. While it is important to present yourself as independent, self-assured and confident, if you show yourself to be too in control or self-important, he will perceive this as a threat and become more entrenched in his position. One way of dealing with the power-conscious individual is to play into his hands. Praise, flatter, be grateful for the little gems of wisdom he sends your way – whether or not they are useful. In other words, make him feel important. As long as *you* know what you are doing, and why, and are not fawning through intimidation, you may well turn a potential adversary into an ally. In all probability, everyone else in the organization can see the power-conscious person for what he is, and will assess your dealings with him accordingly.

However, if this sort of manipulative behaviour goes against your moral ethics, you might try involving him more in projects which he might otherwise block. Consult; give him the bare outline; leave gaps that he can fill in; allow elements that he can alter. Once he feels part of the scheme, and has some ownership of it, you will have more chance of seeing it through without unwarranted obstruction. If he thinks he has helped find the solution it will give him the importance he craves.

Observe and listen to ascertain his communication style, then match or accommodate it. If he is a dyed-in-the-wool direct and control style manager, he may feel threatened by the more informal style of empowered management, so adapt your style accordingly to accommodate his needs. Choose language that appeals to his values. If he is a traditionalist, fall into his style by using phrases such as 'tried and tested' or language which reflects stability rather than change and innovation: 'perpetual', 'consistent', 'regular', 'trustworthy', 'credible', 'conscientious', 'similar', 'preserve', 'retain'. Sensitivity to the language you use will make him feel more secure.

## The inert person

This could be the boss who you can never pin down to a decision, the unresponsive member of your staff, the person on your team who refuses to face up to anything and is useless in a crisis, or the colleague who is possessive over information – anyone who is 'without inherent power of action, motion or resistance' (dictionary definition of 'inert').

The problem with being on the receiving end of this sort of passive behaviour is that your own behaviour can be influenced as a result. You may initially feel sorry for, or protective towards the person who cannot stand up for himself, and as a result display similar passive behaviour, or become irritated, annoyed or downright aggressive towards your inactive colleague, or indecisive boss. The first thing you must do, therefore, after recognizing the problem behaviour and how it is affecting you, is to learn to retain control over your own feelings.

Your behaviour is your choice. No one can intimidate you without you allowing the intimidation; neither can anyone force you to remain assertive when alternative behaviour is more appropriate to the person and the situation. Acknowledge that choice and resort to behaviour that best suits your needs while respecting the other person's rights, needs and feelings.

If you can prepare beforehand, try to get into the other's shoes and see the situation from their perspective. Recognize the sort of behaviour you are likely to encounter and ensure that, through positive self-talk and by developing a sound inner dialogue, you can cope with anything that is thrown at you, be it open resistance, or uncommunicative silences. If you are caught in spontaneous dialogue with your inert person, use your spare thinking capacity to tell yourself that, for example, 'Tim is putting himself down again, putting on the "poor me" act so that I will feel sorry for him and boost his confidence by reassuring him how wonderful he is. I will not get drawn into this, or feel irritated by his behaviour, but rationally assure him and help him work through his own problems. I must encourage him to behave in a positive and constructive way.'

Dealing with the inert person can be quite tiring as you are the one who is constantly having to take the initiative. Below are some tips on helping the other person take more responsibility for their lives.

- Observe closely as their non-verbal communication will tell you a lot about how they are feeling/responding to you.
- Get the other person talking. Ensure that your own style of communication, choice of vocabulary etc. is appropriate.
- Ask open questions to ascertain their point of view.
- Adopt an approachable, friendly posture; maintain good eye contact; control silences by remaining quiet with an open enquiring look, encouraging them to take their share of air space.
- Ask probing and reflective questions and use summarizing skills to move the conversation towards something conclusive.
- State expectations; set boundaries; guide the other person into taking responsibility; don't make decisions or do the work for him.

## The doom and gloom syndrome

Then there are the people who are habitually negative; those who are continually whinging; those who find fault with your reasoning – whatever ideas you come up with – or argue against your suggestions, however sound. This person always expects the worst from any situation – and usually his views are justified. What he can't understand is the concept of self-fulfilling prophecy. Is it their attitude that produces negative situations, or the unfortunate situations that create the attitude? Quite often it is the former. The successful person is the one who confronts the difficult situation, copes with it, and moves on without wallowing in self-pity, angst or paranoia.

So how do you deal with this kind of problem person? First, differentiate between the genuine grievance and moody whinging. Discover, through questioning, if there is a real problem behind the whinging. Talk about the negative attitude; guide the other person to looking for solutions to his problem. If you try to solve his problem for him by suggesting things he might do, the practised whinger will always have a reason why he can't do what you suggest, or why your solution won't work. Make him take responsibility for solving his problems, emphasizing that you will offer support if he is willing to help himself, but that you do not intend to take on his problems for him.

If you have tried to help the whinger through his problem in the way suggested and he won't budge from his negativity, or if the whinging is habitual and unwarranted, don't commiserate or let the negative attitude get to you. Remember, behaviour is infectious, and it's all too easy to let a conversation degenerate into a doom and gloom session. Instead, ignore the negative statement as if it hadn't been said. When the whinger meets with silence or a change of subject every time he starts to moan, he will eventually get the idea that this sort of communication is having no impact on you. Make it clear that you won't discuss the issue again unless the whinger has a positive contribution to make.

This can solve the problem for you, but may not for him. The negativity is still there, and there may well be an underlying reason for it. If you are in the position to offer some counselling help, either on an informal basis between the two of you if you have the skills, or by referring him to an expert, this may well be the best way forward. He may well have long-term problems, trouble at home or on a personal level which is affecting his view on life. Training is another option – a course such as assertiveness training which will enhance confidence and self-esteem and improve effective communication, or transactional analysis where he will learn to communicate on an 'I'm OK/You're OK' basis.

At whatever stage you return to full communication with the (hopefully ex-) whinger, without going over the top, reinforce positive behaviour. If there becomes a danger of him returning to his old ways, revert to ignoring his unhelpful remarks, while acknowledging positive contributions. If necessary, you could introduce a rule that no complaint or moaning about a problem is allowed unless accompanied by possible, positive solutions.

## The nitpicker and the apathetic

You may well have either of these types of people in your team. The perfectionist and the lazy worker represent two sides of the same coin – both are time-wasters. Their work will affect the rest of the team. Let's look at the nitpicker first.

He is the sort of person who pays minute attention to every detail, checking and double-checking. He will have set himself very high standards, and it is quite likely that in his eyes, he will never achieve these standards. His work will never be good enough. Invariably he will feel that he has too much work on his hands to do justice to any of it. He will feel pressured and anxious. It is unlikely that his output will compare favourably with other members of your team.

I admit that I was in danger of becoming this kind of employee early in my career. Luckily I had a boss who recognized what was happening; told me 'you're not overworked, you're just confused' and helped me prioritize and realize that sometimes 'good enough' really was just that. I avoided the nervous breakdown and learned to enjoy doing an adequate amount of good work as part of a motivated team rather than a few near-immaculate pieces as a neurotic individual!

You need to talk to the nitpicker on a one-to-one basis, and the usual rules of interviewing apply. Allow sufficient time, at an appropriate time of day; choose a location which is quiet and free from interruption. Extend the usual courtesies and put him at ease by maintaining a good rapport. Explain to him that time is money, and that your organization, while recognizing the need to strive for excellence, sometimes has to settle for efficient and effective working. Help him recognize that while close attention to detail is a desired, it is not required if deadlines are threatened, and/or other people's work is affected. You will need to use patience and empathetic reasoning with him, communicating in a style he understands and will respond to (see the section on communicating styles in Chapter 2).

Time management training will help the perfectionist to prioritize his work. If this is not feasible, you could get him to keep a log about what he does and when throughout the day, and go through this regularly with him, offering support and advice. Be patient, as it will take a lot of persuasion and encouragement before the nitpicker will become comfortable with letting go of some of the detail and concentrating on task completion within the allotted time. If the problem is deeply entrenched, you may need to resort to breaking down each of the perfectionist's tasks into sections, giving deadlines for each. In this way you can each frequently check on progress; he will get a lift each time he achieves within the allotted time.

There are many reasons why the lazy person is apathetic at work. Why isn't he motivated? Is there a way you can find out what 'makes him tick' and capitalize on that?

Again, the usual rules about arranging a meeting apply. Spend some time initially creating an atmosphere of empathy and trust so that the other person can talk freely to you. Don't switch off the rapport when you begin to confront the problem, but take care to maintain it throughout the interview. Listen and question carefully to try to establish why he is underachieving. Bear the following in mind:

- Does the problem lie within or outside the control of the person?
- Has the context or content of the work changed?
- Is the work beyond his capabilities?
- Does he know what he is doing, why and where his contribution fits in within the work of the team/department/organization?
- Is the work challenging enough? Is he bored?
- Are procedures realistic?
- Am I giving him sufficient information/support?
- Has he problems of a personal nature which is affecting his work?
- Is he afraid of failure?
- Are there problems with other members of staff or with the work itself which are affecting his performance?
- What could be stopping him from doing a good job of work?
- Is his time-wasting a way of getting attention? If so, why does he need that attention?

The answers to these questions will direct how you need to proceed. However, if the apathetic person has no reason for his underachieving except laziness you have to decide on a plan of action whereby he is given the chance to improve. This will need time and support from you. As with the perfectionist, get him to use a time log. Set tasks and deadlines, and meet regularly to discuss progress. Don't allow the lazy person to pick and choose the tasks he prefers to do, but help him prioritize and manage his time. Celebrate successes and reinforce positive behaviour. If necessary, spell out the consequences of failure to improve. (See also Chapter 14.)

## EXERCISE

This exercise is only appropriate if you currently have a problem person on your team, and is more of a suggestion for you to consider the difficulties you are facing and a possible way forward in turning this person into an effective and motivated member of your team.

PROBLEM PERSON'S NAME:

DEFINE THE PROBLEM: (Whiner, antagonistic, 'wet blanket' etc.)

NAME THE SYMPTOMS: (What does he do? What doesn't he do?)


NAME THE POSSIBLE CAUSES:


HOW DOES HIS BEHAVIOUR AFFECT ME?


IS THERE ANYTHING I HAVE DONE (OR NOT DONE) TO CONTRIB-UTE TO THE PROBLEM? (How does he see me? Have I given enough information/training/support? Have I confronted the problem or talked it through sufficiently with him? Do I use an appropriate communication style?)


WHAT SHOULD I DO TO IMPROVE THE SITUATION? (Should I change my approach? Adapt my communication style? How will I plan my next meeting with him?)


WHAT OBSTRUCTIONS TO PROGRESS CAN I FORESEE?


HOW CAN I OVERCOME THEM?

# 16 Redundancy

Because this book is about people skills, this section will concentrate on the one-to-one practicalities of conducting a redundancy interview. It will not get bogged down with legal matters, union involvement etc., and assumptions have been made that the resolution to make redundancies has been preceded by the usual organizational decisions regarding re-allocation of jobs, natural wastage, early retirements and so on. It makes a further assumption that you will be carrying out the termination interviews with staff.

## What you need to consider

First, you need all the facts of the situation at your fingertips (although you will not necessarily need to discuss these with the person who is to be made redundant). For example, what events led to the decision of unavoidable redundancies? You will need to know the selection criteria used for redundancy, e.g. whether a 'last in first out' policy was decided upon. Will pay be offered in lieu of notice? Will the person's last day of service be the same as his last day of work? You need details of severance terms. These will include things like outplacement, financial counselling, insurances and pension plans. You will have to liaise with the Personnel Department to take advice on procedures, to know where their role begins and ends, and to obtain severance letters, cheques etc. which need to be given to staff at the termination interview.

Then there are the practical details to be considered. Will there be prior warning of redundancies? (It may be that management has already made an announcement about 'important decisions regarding the company's future', or some such wording. Wherever possible, however, do not tell individuals, in advance, what the interview is about.) Who, in the company, *needs* to know about the planned redundancies prior to formal announcements? (The fewer the better is the obvious answer.) Where will you be holding the interviews? (Somewhere quiet, private and guaranteed free from interruption is required.) How many termination interviews will you be giving? How long should each interview take (between 5 and 10 minutes – no longer). In what order should you call staff for interview? (Generally, you should see more senior staff first.) What happens to individuals after the interview? Will they be handed over immediately to outplacement counsellors? Will they return to their departments to work out notice? If they are to return to their desks, what about other people in the section still to be seen by you? Who will tell the team about the redundancy? If severance is to be immediate and/or there are security issues involved, can arrangements be made at evenings or weekends for staff to return to clear their desks?

What can the employee be offered to lessen the blow? Will he be free actively to pursue other job opportunities and to attend interviews while working notice? Can he ask for secretarial help to type a CV and letters of application? Can he use the company facilities such as photocopier and telephone? Will he be offered outplacement counselling, or financial counselling? If he has a company car, can he keep it until the last day of service, whether or not that's the last day of work? Can he keep it beyond that date with certain provisos regarding maintenance, fuel etc.? What about medical insurance? Will he still be covered for a reasonable time after severance, or until the annual renewal date? Can life and accident insurance cover be maintained for a reasonable period, or can interim cover be obtained via the company's insurance brokers? Will there be an *ex gratia* payment? If early retirement is an option, can the pension be enhanced?

There is also the issue of when to hold the interviews. Try to ascertain whether individuals have birthdays or anniversaries around the preferred time of the termination interview. It would be a kindness to avoid these dates. Similarly, don't make redundancy announcements on a Friday, immediately before annual leave or public holidays. Also avoid 'busy' work days. Especially if the individual has no prior warning of the content of the meeting, it is essential that he can give priority to the interview date and time.

Now you need to get yourself in the correct frame of mind to undertake this difficult task. Remember that management decisions to reduce the size of the workforce are usually taken after all other possibilities have been exhausted, and will be for the good of the organization as a whole. This is not a personal vendetta against certain members of staff; it is a necessary pruning for the growth – often survival – of the company. Although the individual may not always see it this way, redundancy doesn't carry the stigma it once did. Gone are the days of a job for life. Keep reminding yourself that it is *the job* which has become redundant. There is no reflection on the individual's skill or competence.

You will need to be firm and calm, yet sensitive to the other person's feelings and reactions. Be prepared for the 'shoot the messenger' syndrome; you may have to deal with angry or emotional outbursts. Loss of employment is like any other form of bereavement, and you may have to deal, in microcosm, with the well-documented stages in the bereavement process: disbelief and denial, anger, guilt and so on. Help avoid this by keeping the interview professional and succinct. Don't prevaricate or try to sugar the pill. Have a clear structure for the meeting; be systematic and efficient in putting your points across in the allocated time. Give details about why the situation has arisen, stress that the decision is irreversible, and explain what will happen next. You will need to include the following:

- employment with your organization is at an end
- there is no possibility of internal transfers or redeployment
- the decision is final; there is no appeal
- last day of service; last day of work
- details of redundancy package/severance terms
- the handing over of duties and responsibilities
- the handing over of keys, laptop computers, cars etc.
- where they go from here – back to desk; on to outplacement counsellor etc.
- references.

While explaining all this, be clear and concise in your language and ensure that your facial expression, gestures and body language are congruent with what you say. Whether the redundancy was foreseen, welcomed or dreaded, the other person is likely to be hurting to some degree. Be aware of their needs and rights. Don't try to justify your or your organization's position. Avoid statements such as 'I'm finding this really difficult' which is likely to evoke a negative response from the other person – 'You're finding it difficult! Well poor old you! At least you've still got a job to go to. What about me? I've a mortgage to pay and three kids to feed . . .' etc. Another comment to avoid is 'I know how you're feeling'. Even if you have experienced redundancy at some time, you are presently speaking from a position of power (and employment). Everyone brings a unique experience of the world to any given situation, so you can't possibly know how another individual with different circumstances, commitments, feelings and drives is reacting to the present situation.

You will need to allow time in the interview for questions. If you followed a well-organized plan as suggested above, most obvious questions will have been answered, but at times of stress it is often difficult for the other person to take in and retain information, so be patient if there needs to be some repetition. Prepare by considering answers to some of the most typical questions which are as follows:

'Why me?'
'Who else is going?'
'Might senior management reconsider?'
'Do I have to work notice?'
'If I accepted a drop in salary/status/position, could I keep working for you?'
'Who else knows?'
'If the situation changes in the future, would you re-employ me?'
'What about perks like my medical insurance – that covers the whole family?'

You may also get the rhetorical type of question which I would advise you leave open-ended. The sort of 'How can I tell my wife' question is typical. You need to stress that the post became redundant (because of restructuring or streamlining) and that the individual's competence has not been questioned.

## EXERCISE

Practise giving a severance interview by asking a colleague (whose critical opinion you trust) to role-play a member of staff who has to be made redundant. Ask him to get as much into role as he can, but at the same time, to make a mental note of your performance so that he can give you constructive feedback.

Make the situation as real as possible, starting right from the beginning by asking him to 'Come in and take a seat'. (Do you smile ... shake hands? Just because the situation is formal and serious, doesn't mean that you shouldn't be friendly and show care. Shake hands only if you have this kind of formal relationship with this member of staff.)

To come straight to the point or not? Yes; this is not the place for small talk, or to ask him why he thinks has been called to see you. Be up-front about the situation and the organization's decision to make compulsory redundancies. Give a definite leaving date. Don't take this personally and over-apologize for having to be the bearer of bad tidings; don't blame others; don't justify what is, after all, a management decision for the benefit of the company as a whole.

Show a caring, yet determined professional approach through choice of words, tone of voice and congruent body language.

When the role-play interview is complete, ask your colleague for his honest opinion of how you handled it. What went well? How could you have improved the interview? Was he left with no doubt about the finality of his employment with you? Was he sure about what happens next? Were all his questions answered adequately?

Before leaving the subject of redundancies it is well to remember that job losses can have a knock-on effect on the morale of those left – the survivors.

# EXERCISE

Make a list of what their concerns might be. Try to come up with at least six. Next consider how you, as their manager, might address these concerns to ensure that productivity, efficiency and effectiveness doesn't suffer as a result of lowered morale.

1. _____

2. _____

3. _____

4. _____

5. _____

6. _____

Survivor feelings/concerns may be:

- initially altruistic; concern for colleagues who no longer have employment
- guilt at having survived the axe when colleagues haven't
- that these are just first round redundancies: 'I may be next'
- that the company is in financial difficulties; if the receivers are called in, I may not get as good a deal – or a redundancy package at all
- that I would *love* to be made redundant, but may not get offered it!

- envy, if redundancy package is generous
- jealousy, if those who got a reasonable hand-out and severance deal also easily find new employment
- who is going to take on the departing employees' workload?
- will I be able to cope with additional work?
- will I be able to handle additional responsibility?
- the general atmosphere will suffer; morale will be low
- can't work well/won't be happy in an unsettled environment
- (if colleagues are working notice) ditto, plus the embarrassment/ awkwardness of still working side by side for the notice period
- should I start looking for another job, just in case?
- if I find another job, might I be missing out on a possible redundancy package here in the future?
- bitterness against organization which might have better organized affairs by earlier adopting a policy of early retirements, voluntary redundancies or natural wastage.
- can I ever trust the company again . . . will I ever feel secure?
- the company culture is bound to change . . . will I like the new set-up?

Look carefully at each of the items on this list. What would you do to allay the concerns of the team and of the individuals who comprise your team?

As manager you need to move quickly to raise morale and motivate your remaining staff. This means being open and honest, explaining fully the reasons for reducing the workforce, and the implications for the new working structure. You will need to apply all your leadership skills to reassure, and to generate the enthusiasm to make the restructured organization a success.

# 17 Selection interviews

In spite of the fact that one-to-one selection interviews are one of the least reliable methods of predicting which candidate is the most suitable for a job, most organizations use this kind of interview for at least part of the recruitment process; in some companies, it is still the only method of choosing between short-listed candidates.

Why is it so unreliable? There are a number of reasons. Often, managers, supervisors and employees are interviewed by managers unskilled in interviewing techniques. They have not been trained in the sort of questions to ask to elicit relevant information; they may not have given the interview sufficient forethought, so rather than having a structure to work to, they 'fly by the seat of their pants' or rely on instinct. When the successful candidate subsequently proves unsuited for the appointment, it could well be because the wrong questions were asked at interview, or the right ones omitted which would have given a more accurate picture of the candidate's suitability.

Also, unless working in a personnel section where interviews are frequently undertaken, for most managers selection interviews are few and far between – managers do not get much practice. Interviewers who are nervous or unsure of themselves will pass on this tension to candidates, and not get the best from them. Neither does it give candidates a good impression of the organization.

With inexperienced interviewers (and with some experienced ones too, I'm afraid) prejudice and bias get in the way of judgement. They might instinctively favour a candidate even before meeting them because they like the way the application form was filled in, or feel a rapport through their style of writing in the covering letter. The interviewee will be at a distinct advantage, because the interviewer will want to prove his initial judgement to be sound. Similarly, even if the interviewer has no prior feelings about the candidate, first impressions can create a 'halo' or 'cloven hoof' effect. These rather flippant terms are used to describe what happens when you are influenced by the physical appearance of a candidate, their mannerisms, accent, personality or lack of it, and so on. It is easy to be 'conned' by the neatly dressed, attractive, smiling candidate, or put off by the scruffy, unappealing interviewee who has a marked accent, or hesitant manner. These intuitive leaps can result in the interviewer subconsciously deciding to accept or reject a candidate very early in the interview. All of the subsequent discussion will serve to support the decision they have already made. In fact, research has shown that most interviewers make up their minds about candidates within the first four minutes of the interview.

On the plus side, the one-to-one interview allows the manager and candidate to meet and get an initial impression of each other. The manager will be able to assess the candidate's suitability for the position, especially if good verbal communication skills are required, for example – skills which cannot be tested by other means. The candidate will be able to get a feel for the organization and find out more about the job.

The other plus is that even if you are a manager unskilled in selection interview techniques, you can be trained relatively easily. It is an area of management where people skills are very important. The rest of this section will give you some guidance in improving your chances of selecting the right person for the job through the one-to-one selection interview.

## Job descriptions and person specifications

When a vacancy occurs, the first thing the organization should do is to conduct a job analysis to ascertain what the position entails (if it is a new post) or what has changed, or needs to be restructured (in an existing job). This is a specialist field; we will assume that someone in your organization has conducted a job analysis (having consulted you, of course) to ascertain the content and context of the work, the tasks, activities and processes involved, and the responsibilities and type of authority carried by the position. From this a job description or job profile can be written up. This will usually include:

- the job title
- function/division
- main purpose of the job
- to whom responsible
- for whom responsible
- main duties/results areas
- occasional duties

- job context
- job scope
- control of resources
- extent of authority
- performance standards
- other information relevant to that particular position.

The next step is to produce a person specification – a profile of the sort of person you want to recruit. This will list the knowledge, skills, abilities and attributes that an ideal candidate would have. Like the job analysis and job description, compiling a person specification is likely to be done by the Personnel Department, but to give you an idea of the criteria used, some will have been trained to follow the seven-point plan designed by Professor Alec Rodger:

1. Physical make up
2. Attainments
3. General intelligence
4. Special aptitudes
5. Interests
6. Disposition
7. Circumstances.

Another well-established formula is the classification system devised by John Munro Fraser in the 1950s, still used a lot today in selection interviews:

1. *Impact on others* – appearance, speech and manner
2. *Qualifications and experience* – education, knowledge, skills, vocational training, work experience
3. *Innate abilities* – how quickly and accurately an individual can comprehend; aptitude for learning
4. *Motivation* – what kind of work appeals; consistency and determination; success rate
5. *Adjustment* – emotional stability; stress tolerance; ability to get on with people.

As previously stated, unless you are working for a small concern, or it is company policy for managers to write job descriptions and person specifications for their own recruits, it is probable that the Personnel Department will deal with these issues. However, if you are to be the one interviewing for a position, you will need to be aware of the above in order to structure your questions so that all criteria are fairly tested with each candidate. More later of how you evaluate against criteria.

So, you have your job description and person specification. We will assume that the recruitment process has so far successfully run its course and that a short-list has been drawn up. It's now down to you to organize the selection interviews.

Preparation is all important. It is your task to match the job, as described in the job description, with the candidate who most successfully matches all criteria (although increasingly there is a tendency to match the person with the job – if that person is 'right' for your organization). Examine the job description, and using this as a guide, list person specification qualities on a 1–10 scale of importance. For example, if you are recruiting a receptionist check out the tasks, duties and responsibilities. Your list might look as follows:

| | | |
|---|---|---|
| 1. | Impact on others | 10 |
| 2. | Qualifications and experience | 5 |
| 3. | Innate abilities | 4 |
| 4. | Motivation | 2 |
| 5. | Adjustment | 9 |

You now have criteria against which to assess each candidate fairly. We will look at how to use this in your final assessment later in the section.

By going through this exercise you are also less likely to be influenced by the 'halo' or 'cloven hoof' effects. You will have established, for example, that the first category *Impact on others* is not important if you are interviewing for a workshop machinist, but would be if the candidate is for a receptionist or an up-front sales position.

## Questions

Now you need to formulate your questions. Whereas it would be foolish to suggest that you ask exactly the same questions, in the same order, to each candidate, you have to ensure that you cover similar ground with each, and that your questions are fair, are not discriminatory and are related to the job. You will need to have a structure to the interview and your questioning will loosely follow this pattern. One such structure might be:

- put candidate at ease; build rapport
- explain structure and timing of interview
- opening questions
- question against application form/CV/resume
- previous career and current/most recent job
- why candidate should be considered for this post

- ending questions
- information to applicant *re* organization, job, terms and conditions
- ask for questions from candidate
- conclusion – what happens next.

Your questioning might be based on something similar to the following, used to interview for an executive position. By the end of this sort of interview you will need to have assessed:

1. *Acceptability* – experience, manner, speech, appearance
2. *Motivation* – what he has made of his opportunities
3. *Drive* – how well he applies himself
4. *Experience* – relevance; achievements
5. *Intelligence* – what level he seems to have; hard evidence?
6. *Interest* – why is he interested in this job? Why is he changing jobs
7. *Ambition* – his short- and long-term plans
8. *Personality* – his overt personality traits
9. *Management style* – will his style fit in with the organizational culture?
10. *Perception* – what he sees as the key elements of the position; how he would go about his new role if offered to him.

In the course of the questioning you will also discuss things like his education, home life, health, social and recreational activities etc.

When compiling your questions, remember to use open questions to draw the candidate out, closed questions to ascertain facts, check and clarify. Avoid multiple questions which will only confuse, and leading questions to which the candidate will obligingly give you the answer you want to hear rather than what he truly feels. Use probing questions to draw him out; reflect back if necessary to clarify meaning.

The form and extent of questioning will depend on the position applied for, of course, but continuing with the executive example, these are the sort of questions you might ask.

## Opening questions

- This appointment would be a change of direction for you. What interests you about our industry, specifically?

## Checking against CV/résumé/application form

- What can you tell me about yourself that makes you think you're a good ... ?
- In your capacity as ... what exactly did you do? Tell me in detail.

- How do you feel about your career progress so far?
- What would you say is the logic behind your career progression?

## Most recent post

- What do you look upon as your major achievements in recent years?
- What changes were you able to make?
- What was the most demanding aspect of the job?
- What was your greatest challenge and how did you meet it?
- What were the best/worst aspects of the job?
- What are the qualities you look for in your manager?

## Reason for leaving

- . . . it sounds really interesting, so why are you leaving?
- Why did you decide to move on?
- Why are you looking for a position outside XYZ?

## Why this position?

- Based on what you know about this organization, why do you want to work for us?
- Why do you want this position?
- What elements of the world of work are important to you?
- Tell me about your experience in . . .
- Why do you think you'll succeed in this job?

## Ambition

- What does success mean to you?
- What are your goals/hopes/aspirations for the future?
- How do you see your career developing over the next five/ten years?
- What are your plans to help you achieve this?

## The difficult ones!

- Did you ever fail in any job you tried to do? . . . What happened?
- Are you considering other positions at this time? . . . How does this one compare?
- We have had several excellent applications for this post. Why should we appoint you?

- Actually, this position is below your ability isn't it?
- What are your particular strengths?
- What are your weaknesses/areas for improvement?

## Concluding questions

- What are your best qualities?
- What else do you think I should know about you?

This gives you some idea of how to phrase questions for this type and level of interview. You will also need to probe into the intelligence, aptitudes and knowledge of the candidate by questioning about education and training. This will also give insight into attitude, disposition and character (choice of college/university/subject; vacation work; societies joined; post-college training etc.). Home life, too, can greatly influence performance, but question with care (see 'Discrimination' below). Health is another area to investigate, but with tact.

When you question about recreational and social activities, it shouldn't just be out of idle curiosity, or as a means of establishing rapport, but you should seek to determine the standards the candidate sets for himself, the level of motivation, the social interaction involved, leadership qualities and so on – aspects relevant to the job applied for.

You will also need to consider what candidates are likely to ask you. What information do you need in order to answer them? Interviewee questions are likely to fall into the following categories:

- *Job description* – e.g. can the job described be altered/upgraded?
- *Job history* – e.g. why did the previous post holder leave? Why isn't this an internal appointment?
- *Personnel* – e.g. who will be my immediate superior? What is the average age of the people in the section I would be working?
- *The department* – who controls the department's budget? Is there anyone on the existing staff who applied for this post, but was bypassed?
- *The organization* – how will I become familiar with company policies? Does the company offer training opportunities?

# Discrimination

Beware of questions which might get you and the organization into difficulties regarding contravention of the Sex Discrimination Act or the Race Relations Act. This is not the time or place to go into detail – your

Personnel Department can advise you – but be conscious that this legislation exists. For example, you shouldn't question a woman about child-care provision, or whether her spouse/partner's work might mean a change of location in the future. You shouldn't ask a black candidate if he thinks he would fit in because all his colleagues would be white, or an Asian whether he might need to take long vacations to visit family back home.

So, you now have your questions sorted out, and will have some idea how long it will take to interview each candidate. (Allow enough time to write up notes on each interview before seeing the next candidate.) You now have the domestic arrangements to sort out. You will need a room which is comfortable, quiet, and will be free from interruption. You will need to give reception a list of candidate names, interview times, and where the interviews are to be held. Is there an area where candidates can wait? Does it have company literature available for interviewees to read? Where can candidates leave coats, umbrellas, briefcases etc. Will you be offering tea or coffee, and if so, who is going to arrange it? What about after the interview; are you going to show candidates the building/office/site where they might be working? Who is going to give the guided tour? How are travel expenses going to be claimed/paid?

Having done all this, and having brushed up on your questioning skills, you are ready to hold the interview itself. Although a formal situation, you need to create an atmosphere which is friendly and relaxed – one which encourages trust and participation and where the candidate feels able to respond freely.

Greet the candidate with a smile and a handshake. Offer him a seat. Begin with something like:

> 'Thank you for coming to see me. I see you're from . . . how was your journey here?

Continue to put him at his ease, and build rapport by brief small talk. Try to get on his wavelength by mirroring his speech preferences, selecting appropriate vocabulary and using body language to create a feeling of empathy. You are in control of this dialogue; you direct the pace and flow, and it is your job to give each candidate every opportunity to excel. You could choose something from his CV to chat about – something non-threatening like a shared experience (e.g. both lived in Liverpool at some time) or a hobby or pastime:

> 'You've an interesting resume. I see one of your pastimes is . . . I've never tried that – what's involved?

Remember that everything a candidate tells you could be important in your analysis of his suitability. For example, if he had a dreadful journey from his home to the place of work, might this be a potential future problem? If one of his pastimes is house renovation, might he have difficulty prioritizing between work commitments and a demanding hobby? On the positive side a pastime such as arranging 'twinning' visits between his home town and one in France might indicate all sorts of abilities and attributes useful to the job. Ensure that your judgements are made on job-related issues however, i.e. that they are relevant to the position for which you are interviewing.

Next, outline what is going to happen – the form the interview is going to take and how long it is likely to last – something like the following:

> 'What I want to do over the next hour is to find out a bit more about you: your career so far, your education and training and so on, then we'll discuss why you want to come and work for us. I'll explain a bit more about the organization, what the job involves and terms and conditions, then answer any questions you might have. Does that sound OK? I'll be taking a few notes here and there, but don't let that put you off.'

Kick off with your questions, always actively maintaining rapport. Maintain good eye contact, use encouraging noises, smiles and nods of the head to compliment your questioning and to encourage the candidate to speak. In an interview situation, you should aim at speaking for no more than one third of the time. It's the candidate who has the stage most of the time.

Try not to do anything distracting. Note-taking, though an essential part of interview practice, can stultify discussion, so don't further upset the candidate's concentration by unnecessary paper shuffling, looking out of the window, searching in desk drawers for pens and the like. Use body language to show that you are interested; watch their non-verbal behaviour for any tell-tale clues.

When you need more detail about an aspect of the interview important to the job and person specification, probe with appropriate questioning, but don't bully or harass. If the candidate begins to waffle or stray off the point, nudge the interview back on line by comments such as:

> 'You mentioned earlier ... I was interested in why you chose to ...'
> 'So what factors led you to decide ... specifically?'
> 'I'd like to move on to look at ...'

The flow and direction of the interview is up to you. You want to allow each candidate every opportunity to give of his best. Don't forget that silences are important too. Candidates will need a few seconds thinking time to consider your question and formulate a sound response.

When you have exhausted your questions, and given the candidate the opportunity to tell you anything else he thinks might be relevant, not already covered by the interview, close by thanking him for coming and explaining what will happen next; something like:

'I'll be interviewing for the rest of this week. I should have reached a decision by the . . . and will be in touch then.'

See the candidate to the door, ensuring he is delivered into the hands of the person who will sort out his travel expenses, show him around the workplace, or see him off the premises. Remember that successful or not, this candidate will want to leave with a favourable impression of the organization. The finer points make all the difference.

# Follow-up

You will probably have made cryptic or one-word notes, which will mean something to you now, but will be gobbledegook by tomorrow – especially if you are seeing more candidates. Take some time to write up your notes in a legible format.

When you have seen all candidates you might want to go back to your five-point plan against which you graded criteria for the job. Mark candidates according to how well they meet the attributes. Your list will look something like this:

|  | | Chris Smith | Jo Green | Laurie Brown | |
|---|---|---|---|---|---|
| 1. | Impact on others | 8 | 7 | 9 | (10) |
| 2. | Qualifications/Experience | 5 | 4 | 8 | (5) |
| 3. | Innate abilities | 3 | 4 | 4 | (4) |
| 4. | Motivation | 1 | 2 | 4 | (2) |
| 5. | Adjustment | 10 | 8 | 7 | (9) |

The figures in brackets on the right were the original assessment, importance to the job being graded on a 1–10 scale.

By comparing the candidate scores with the ones you selected, you will have an objective means for appointing. This approach is advocated by Viv Shackleton in her book *How to Pick People for Jobs* (see Further Reading). She suggests you tally the scores for each candidate, first multiplying each score by the marks you gave to each area of the plan, so Chris's tally would be

$$
\begin{array}{rcr}
8 \times 10 & = & 80 \\
5 \times 5 & = & 25 \\
3 \times 4 & = & 12 \\
1 \times 2 & = & 2 \\
10 \times 9 & = & \underline{90} \\
& & 209
\end{array}
$$

Make similar calculations for each candidate and you have them ranked in order of preference. All else being equal, the highest scorer gets offered the job. I have deliberately 'rigged' the figures to show one disadvantage of using this final tally method of grading candidates. The highest score went to Laurie Brown, but compare the individual scores with those you decided were suitable for the job of receptionist and you will see that in fact Laurie is over-qualified in some areas, perhaps too ambitious, and has poorer people skills than the other two – in fact lower than those identified as ideal for the post of receptionist.

| | | |
|---|---|---|
| Impact on others | $9 \times 10 = 90$ | (Speech, manner, appearance OK) |
| Qualifications/ experience | $8 \times 5 = 40$ | (Position below candidate's ability?) |
| Innate abilities | $4 \times 4 = 16$ | (Quickness of comprehension and aptitude for learning fine, but combined with over-qualification?) |
| Motivation | $4 \times 2 = 8$ | (Will the candidate be too ambitious, set personal goals beyond remit of post?) |
| Adjustment | $7 \times 9 = 63$ | (Ability to cope with clients suspect?) |
| | 217 | |

'Noddy guide' – check for over-qualification by seeing which figures in the left-hand column exceed those decided appropriate for the job (right-hand column).

On balance, although the highest scorer, Laurie should probably not be offered the post. However, in principle, this is a good way to use rational thought and objective processing in selecting the candidate who best fits the person specification. It obviates bias, and gives something tangible to justify your decision should you be required to do so.

Besides telephoning/writing to the successful candidate, other follow-up skills could involve giving constructive feedback to unsuccessful candidates. This is obviously useful to their pursuit of employment, and also gives a good impression of your organization.

# Other types of selection interview

You may be involved in panel interviews. The same good people skills practices apply, but you will need to communicate well with fellow panel members prior to the interviews regarding which areas of questioning you are to cover. Yours may be one in a series of interviews conducted by several interested parties. While there is bound to be some duplication of questioning which can be annoying to candidates, it is sensible for interviewers to agree beforehand an area on which each can concentrate. Ultimately, you will all have to agree on the most suitable candidate. The danger is that the most senior or persuasive person's choice will get appointed, so it is important to have facts and figures 'up your sleeve' in order to choose the most suitable candidate. Another aspect of people skills is assertively stating to less skilled colleagues and bosses that selection should be based on objective criteria!

# EXERCISE

Selection interviewing centres around the ability to ask well phrased, relevant, open questions. Consider the following closed questions and suggest better ways of phrasing them to draw out a fuller response from the candidate.

1.  Are you able to motivate staff?
2.  Are you satisfied with the progress made in your career?
3.  Did you have any problems with your last job?
4.  Have you ever had to do a selection interview?
5.  What university did you attend?

**Possible responses**

1.  What qualities are required to produce a motivated team?
2.  How do you feel about your career progress so far?
3.  What was the most difficult aspect of your last job?
4.  Tell me about you experience in selecting personnel.
5.  Why did you choose to go to ... University? (You will know which university he attended from his CV.)

# 18 Team-building

Chapter 9, on empowerment, looks at teamwork in some depth, and considers the changing role of today's manager in this process. This chapter will concentrate on building and developing teams.

Unfortunately, truly effective teams still seem to be a rarity. There are work groups who *think* they are teams, and teams where personal relationships are excellent, but which are too insular or competitive to be of the greatest use to the organization as a whole.

In some organizations, outside, expert professionals are employed to facilitate the process of forming and developing teams. However, this chapter will assume that it is down to you, as manager to either set up new teams, to build a team from a work group, or to enliven existing teams to increase their effectiveness. It should be stressed that team leaders do not necessarily have to be managers, 'the boss' or the person of highest status. You may well find yourself a team member if that role best fits the current needs of the team and the organization. However, in order better to explain the principles of effective team-leading, I will assume that you will be 'taking the reins' initially. If this means facilitating an existing team, you will have to redefine your role as team leader rather than manager, openly discuss your feelings (and concerns if you have them) of taking on this role, and reassure that open discussion will be welcomed and not have negative consequences for anyone. As manager, you have certain powers over your subordinates – at appraisal for instance – and team members must feel confident that what they say and do as part of the team will not have adverse affects – on their promotion chances, for example.

## The effective team

An effective team is a group of people, enthusiastic, motivated and willing to give of their best to each other, the team and the organization.

There is a mutually supportive and challenging environment, a focus on process as well as task, clear agendas and a clarity of vision and mission. Team members recognize their interdependence and are committed to goals they helped to establish. There is a high standard of output, strong performance, with the right mix of strategic thinking, technical know-how, creativity, co-ordination and implementing skills. The effective team will have appropriate leadership from a person who will not seek to dominate proceedings but who is prepared to take responsibility for decisions. The team leader will be able to get the best from the available talent in the team.

# Choosing your team

It is important that each team has within it the right mix of skills and abilities to function effectively. A colleague of mine was once called to an organization which was committed, in principle, to teamwork, but was having great difficulties in turning groups of people into productive teams. The first 'team' he met with comprised of eight people of similar status and role within the company, of similar cultural backgrounds and education; all creative people of high intelligence, bursting with ideas – but squabbling rather than achieving. He began to solve the problem by disbanding the existing group and creating a new team with a spread of talents and mental abilities. The new team comprised a writer, an administrator, technical staff, the catering manager and so on. During team meetings status was dropped; everyone had equal air space; everyone's views and ideas were listened to and respected. They bonded well and each brought added value to the team through their own special skills and attributes.

In this instance, the number of people in the team was eight – which is about the top limit. More than that and the more reticent will find it difficult to fully participate. Fewer than four and you are unlikely to get all the skills required for a fully effective, functioning team.

No section on team-building would be complete without mention of the work of Dr R. M. Belbin who developed a team role theory. His first work on this subject, *Management Teams: Why They Succeed or Fail* (see Further reading), was the culmination of nine years of research and study. His approach to building effective teams lies in choosing or creating a balance of strengths within the team. His research disclosed that many teams were formed from people who were like-minded, as in the anecdote above. This is not surprising as we generally gravitate towards, and like people, who are 'like us'. However, such teams are seldom as effective as ones comprised of diverse talents and personalities. Put several individualistic, 'ideas people' together, and you could have the recipe for conflict. Have more than one person with strong leadership abilities in one team, and you could have internal power struggles to contend with. To create synergy, you need balance, where individual strengths complement each other and the combined energy of the team outdoes the sum of individual efforts. Individual weaknesses can be both tolerated and compensated for provided there is someone else in the team with the relevant strength.

Since the first publication of Meredith Belbin's book in 1981, the impetus of team role theory and the use of team roles to describe working relationships, has escalated. Ideas changed regarding the validity of some of the methods used to assess team roles of individuals. The result of this evolution is a new book by Belbin, *Team Roles at Work* (see Further reading), where he no longer advocates one single method of assessing team roles. Whether predictions are made using questionnaires, test batteries or psychometric testing, Belbin asserts that what matters most is how team role profiles are used once the information has been collected.

The nine team role profiles are as follows:

1. *Co-ordinator* – the person who focuses the group, pulls things together, delegates and motivates. He recognizes and knows how to use ability in others. This person will have a strong sense of overall objectives, will clarify goals and promote decision-making. He may not be an 'ideas' person or show creativity, but will be good at controlling and co-ordinating resources. He will encourage participation, but be prepared to make decisions and take responsibility for them. He will direct the efforts and activities of others towards an overall goal or objective.

2. *Shaper* – a natural leader in some ways as this person has drive and enthusiasm and can command respect and generate energy in others. This person likes to see his own ideas implemented – and quickly. He will be impatient of complacency and lack of progress; his highly strung nature will give a strong sense of dynamism and urgency. He has the energy and determination to overcome obstacles He has a strong preference to 'lead from the front' with an inner need to control decisions and actions personally. On the down side, he can be provocative or insensitive to others' feelings.

3. *Plant* – an ideas person, the Plant is creative. He is likely to be a dominant individual, yet a serious-minded introvert. He has imagination and intellect; will be innovative with flashes of inspiration, and a good problem-solver. Often seen as having his head in the clouds, he can be tactless in the pursuit of his ideas and lack sensitivity towards others. He may shun the orthodox, be impatient of doing things 'the

proper way' and not be concerned with the practical implications of his ideas, some of which may lead to success, some may not. An individualist, he tends to be self-sufficient, can be uncommunicative, and as such, can be a 'difficult' team member. In some ways he is child-like in that he loves to be flattered, and doesn't like his own ideas criticized.

4.  *Monitor evaluator* – a person who can process information in a logical, analytical and objective way. He will take a calculating approach to issues and ideas, providing an objective outlook and cool judgement. He is naturally cautious, and highly critical of flawed thinking in others. He is a realist who could be seen as a 'wet blanket' as he will damp down enthusiasm if the team is in danger of being swept away in its enthusiastic pursuit of an idea. He is the rational 'brakes' of the team, suggesting they consider alternative actions, or refuting unsound proposals. Although unable to inspire and motivate others, his role is essential to effective team outcomes.

5.  *Resource investigator* – is the team's ambassador, never happier than when on the telephone or meeting new people, making and developing contacts outside the team, exploring anything new. An extrovert, with low anxiety levels, he is resourceful and outgoing and will respond to anything new with enthusiasm, but can lose interest quickly if progress is slow or once the initial 'buzz' begins to weaken. He will stimulate thinking within the group and be involved in lively discussion, but be prepared for his 'grasshopper' mind as he will hop from subject to subject very rapidly. He will find it difficult to follow anything through as he is only interested in pursuing the latest ideas and challenges.

6.  *Implementer* – a stable personality who is self-disciplined, organized and hard-working. He will be able to foresee how the team's ideas and plans will work out in practice. He will take some convincing that a new idea is practical and of genuine worth to the organization, but once committed he will be systematic and thorough in his work. Happy when involved with, or designing, rules and procedures for implementation he tends to be less effective when procedures and objectives are unclear.

7.  *Team worker* – a person who works well with different people, promoting good team atmosphere. He helps the team to bond, and encourages team spirit. He is diplomatic – often 'the wit' of the group, yet sensitive to the feelings and needs of others. He is interested in developing good relationships, is perceptive, and will be the one most likely to be aware of others' personal problems or crises. He will be a good listener and have the ability to recognize and avert friction. His

ability to 'read' others and to recognize differing abilities promotes high morale and a good sense of co-operation.

8. *Completer* – an anxious introvert who is likely to be a perfectionist, attending to detail, and expecting the highest standards for himself and others. He will give tasks his complete attention, and will produce work of a high standard, on time, but not without stress. His nitpicking and worrying may lower team morale but his persistence can prevent careless mistakes and omissions being made.
9. *Specialist* – a self-motivated team member who provides knowledge, skills and ability in a specialized area. He will be dedicated to and enthusiastic about his own area of expertise, but may choose to remain unenlightened about factors outside his own specialism.

Do you see yourself in any of these roles? As member of this team, would you be the natural leader? Would your talents be better used as Plant, or Completer? If you are to be team leader, who would be your ideal deputy? (The team profile may well show that the person best suited to cover in your absence is not necessarily the most senior on your team.)

You will find that one of the above categories is your dominant role. You may have one or two other roles strongly in your profile. The same may be said for other members of your team. Wide team-role coverage is a feature of successful teams because you can draw on a fuller range of strengths. Where there is duplication, develop a secondary strength of one of the team to fill any gaps you have. You may have more than one Team worker. This is fine because the more morale boosting members you have, the better. You may have more than one Monitor evaluator – again fine if they can work together to keep the team's feet on the ground and not have too dampening an effect on the whole. Difficulties arise when you have two or more strong Shapers or Resource investigators in the team. They will both come up with ideas, but their thinking may not be compatible. Other difficulties can arise where natural leaders such as Team workers challenge Shapers or Co-ordinators as team leaders. It should be decided who should assume their dominant role, and who should develop a secondary role to fit the needs of the team. It is sound practice to develop strengths so that team members are able to perform different roles as and when they are required by the team.

Trainers, practitioners and other writers on team-building have adapted Belbin's approach, and advocate using a team role theory as a sound basis for effective teamwork. Provided you have the right strengths within your team, and an appropriate mix to avoid personality clashes, you should have the basis for effective team working. The basic requirements of an ideal team are one person to give focus and direction; who will be willing to take the lead and make decisions where there are blockages or lack of progress; who will co-ordinate the work of the team. One person to be the team's eyes, ears and mouthpiece outside the team, making contacts, checking out new ideas and developments. One creative 'ideas' person. At least one person whose feet are firmly on the ground; who can be objective about ideas and evaluate the work of the team. At least one person who will get on with the task in hand, turning ideas into reality. At least one person who is concerned with detail, will check work for mistakes and ensure that deadlines are kept. Hopefully, every team member will develop into the equivalent of Belbin's team worker, functioning well with a range of different people, motivating, supporting and promoting good team atmosphere.

# Team-building

If you are setting up a new team, or want a fresh start with an existing team, your first meeting might follow the following format.

You will have chosen an appropriate room and seating arrangements for your meeting, and informed everyone of the date, time and likely duration of the meeting. As they arrive, set the tone (informality), and help create the climate you need, encouraging rapport through small talk.

Maintain this informal approach as you then explain the purpose of the meeting. Ensure everyone understands, then either suggest the process you would like to use to achieve objectives, or begin team-building by involving the group in deciding the process. Whichever method you choose, involve everyone; asks questions, but be prepared at this initial stage to get either little response, or blanket agreement, because at this point everyone is still unsure of the situation and will be looking to you to take the lead.

Because of this, it is important, early on, to get everyone involved, through brainstorming or some other low-risk activity, such as an ice-breaking activity or one to introduce the concept of creative thinking (see *50 Activities for Interpersonal Skills Training* by Sue Bishop and David Taylor, Gower, Aldershot, 1991). At this initial meeting it is important for you to talk for no longer than 15 minutes. This time should be devoted to acknowledging uncertainties, explaining your role as facilitator rather than controller or director, your vision for an effective team, and sharing information – creating an atmosphere of openness and trust.

'Formal' input over, introduce a group task – such as brainstorming (see below) – after which everyone should begin to feel they belong to a group which is to be democratic, challenging – and fun. Then move on to discussing the task or 'mission' explaining the context and content, but paying more attention to process – the 'how' you are going to achieve results. Have some idea of how this might be achieved, but let the group do the thinking and deciding. Be flexible enough to alter or modify your original ideas '*en route*', and skilled enough to guide the team if they go too far off course. They must feel that they have ownership of the task and involvement in the process.

Finish the initial meeting by summarizing what has taken place, getting agreement from your fellow team members. Agree any actions resulting from the meeting – who is going to do what and by when. Agree the time, place and objective of your next meeting.

At subsequent meetings, whenever a 'meaty' question is asked, return to brainstorming or team problem-solving sessions to come up with alternative actions to improve performance. Where individuals have setbacks or difficulties, encourage them not to come to you, but to call in the team to help solve the problem. It should be said, however, that there will be occasions when *someone* has to be accountable for the team, so if there is a real crisis, or a snap decision has to be made, the team leader will be that person.

Team leaders must address three needs: organizational needs, team needs and also individual needs. Another respected approach to team-building is John Adair's (see his *Effective Teambuilding* – Further reading). The basis of his theory is that whereas each team, like each individual, is unique, there are shared needs common to all teams. These are as follows:

- to achieve the task
- to build the team
- meeting the needs of individuals.

The reason for building the team is primarily so that the task in hand can be achieved more effectively. The team needs to be aware of the resources available to it, and the process involved in achieving the task. Team needs cover such things as personal relationships, bonding; the team developing a life and strength of its own. Individual needs can be seen in terms of Maslow's hierarchy of needs (see Chapter 12) – security, belonging, self-esteem etc. Most teams tend to focus too much on the task and not enough on team or individual needs. If the team ensures that wherever possible individuals' needs are met – although not at the expense of the task or team needs – the team will be more productive.

As an effective team leader you will need to:

- have belief in yourself and in the power of teams
- have faith in your team members' potential for success

- beware of abusing positional power
- think team = us, not team + me
- share vision and mission
- support openness
- manage confrontation
- create a climate or trust, empathy and respect
- facilitate agreement of clear objectives and goals
- listen well and question effectively
- motivate others to think for themselves
- ensure that co-operation and conflict are used constructively
- manage the process in order to achieve the task
- be honest and open, communicating clearly.

Regarding this last point, if you used some sort of questionnaire or psychometric testing to obtain a team profile, don't keep the results to yourself. It is important to set the tone of open and honest communication by sharing the findings with the team. Discuss together the implications of gaps or duplications of role within the team, and how you are going to handle discrepancies. Brainstorming might be a good way of creating team spirit and achieving this end. You might brainstorm how to achieve/improve your team effectiveness.

# Brainstorming

Brainstorming is an important aspect of teamwork, and it would be a good idea to introduce the concept to the team at the earliest opportunity. It is a good team-building tool as it encourages participation, on an equal footing, and helps new teams quickly to bond. It can move existing teams from a static situation to a more dynamic and proactive level. Brainstorming capitalizes on the idea that two heads are better than one. Involve the whole team in your brainstorming sessions. You need to define the purpose of the brainstorming, then assign someone the role of facilitator. This could but need not be you. The facilitator's role is to keep the session on track, to ensure that everyone has their share of air space, to enforce the ground rules, and latterly to encourage discussion of the ideas presented by asking questions – closed for clarification, open, probing etc. to stimulate debate.

The idea of brainstorming is to produce as many ideas as possible – sound, feasible, outlandish, silly – to solve the problem in hand. Participants in the brainstorming should be encouraged to contribute any idea – however way-out – the ground rule being that the facilitator will record (preferably on flip-chart paper) *all* contributions. Neither the facilitator nor other team members should criticize or evaluate ideas at this stage. This ban on criticism includes implicit comment through body language. In this way wild ideas are encouraged. (It is useful to have a few wild ideas up your sleeve to offer if your team is taking the operation too seriously, only coming up with a few obviously rational ideas.) Even if these way-out suggestions are not practicable or even remotely feasible, other team members may get the germ of an idea from the outlandish one that *may* be possible.

For brainstorming to be a success, it is best done away from the office or usual workplace. Choose a congenial meeting room appropriate to your needs – in other words, don't choose the board room with high backed chairs and oak panelling. If the room is formal, the atmosphere is likely to be stilted and formal too. Arrange the seating so that team members are sitting side by side, or in a gently curved line, facing the flip-chart. Psychologically, you are all then on an equal footing, confronting a common problem together.

In order to create the right atmosphere for team members to feel at ease and able to let their innovative minds run riot, try doing something like taking off your jacket and tie and encouraging the others do the same, or having refreshments available and perhaps some sweets to hand round – anything to encourage the right climate for relaxed spontaneity and creativity. Although it has a serious intention, brainstorming should be fun.

To begin the session, the facilitator reminds the team of the problem in hand, and of the ground rules of no criticizing or evaluating at this stage. He then invites contributions, questioning only if necessary for clarification, and writes up contributions. When one sheet of newsprint is full, this should be pinned up where it can be seen by the team. One idea often stimulates another, and duplication is avoided if contributions are always visible.

When everyone's imagination has been exhausted, the next step is to discuss all ideas, this time criticizing, evaluating and probing further. The facilitator should mark any promising ideas for further consideration. The object of the exercise is not to come up with one preferred solution, but with a list of feasible options.

It is sometimes useful to do some reverse brainstorming at this stage – brainstorming reasons why preferred ideas might not work. In this way you have a full range of things which might go wrong – the most pessimistic scenario. If you can come up with ways of coping with these problems, and still have a good option, you may be on to a winning solution. A more positive alternative is to take each of the preferred ideas and try to enhance them further, inventing ways to improve the proposal, to make it more realistic, and suggesting ways of implementing the idea.

The facilitator can help this process by asking members what it is they like best about the idea, or how it might be enhanced.

## Stages of team development

New teams always go through various stages of development before becoming fully functional, effective and 'motoring'. As with the processes of grieving (at the death of a loved one, or loss of a job, where one goes through stages of disbelief, anger, denial, guilt and so on before acceptance and progress towards a new life) these stages are invariably unavoidable. As team leader you must recognize that it is normal to experience some negative feelings and reactions – all teams go through growing pains – and that these can be worked through successfully.

These stages in team-building are described in various ways by exponents of different approaches to teamwork. 'Forming, Storming, Norming, Performing' is one way of describing these developmental stages. The words are self-explanatory: the first stage is when the group is forming – getting together for the first time – and members will either be on their best behaviour, saying little and agreeing with the leader or strongest member of the team, or feeling anxious, reluctant, sceptical etc. The next stage, 'Storming', describes the stage when individuals begin to get the measure of each other but are as yet unsure of their ground or the changes required of them. There may be splinter groups within the team; individuals may feel unsure of their roles, or isolated from other team members; they may suspect hidden agendas; they may feel frustrated at lack of action or anxious that things are moving too rapidly for personal comfort. Conflict often ensues. With careful handling by the team leader, the team should be able to move on to the next 'Norming' stage, where the group settles down, members are more comfortable with each other and the team bonds. The crucial point, of course, is not to get lulled into a false sense of security, basking in the success of team cohesion, but to progress to the 'Performing' stage where the sum of the parts exceeds individual endeavour, and the teamwork advances in leaps and bounds.

In his book, *Building your Team* (see Further reading), Rupert Eales-White explains that when new teams pass from immaturity to maturity they can experience six different stages, Confusion, Conflict, Co-operation, Commitment, Control and Consensus – the six Cs. Again, the words are self-explanatory, so I will just put a little meat on the bones regarding your role as team leader during each of these stages.

At the *Confusion* level, you will be confronted with a group of individuals thinking in terms of their own insecurities, doubts, vulnerabilities etc. – in Maslow's terms, the survival and security levels. They will be looking to you for structure and purpose. You will need to acknowledge, and be understanding of their uncertainty, and the fact that each will be experiencing different feelings about being there at all, the need for a team, where it will be going and what is going to be expected of them etc. Model good practice, listening well and respecting the needs and feelings of others. You may need to reassure about your role – that you are there to support team effort and manage the process, not to tell them what to do – and explain the content and context of the team task ahead of them. If you are working with an existing or ongoing team, the task might be to achieve better teamwork or you might have a particular goal or target to meet or exceed. Agree the objectives for this at your first meeting. Share knowledge and information (for example, if you have used team profile questionnaires, now is the time to discuss this). Encourage participation and joint responsibility for team cohesion.

According to Maslow's Hierarchy of Needs, once survival and security needs have been met, individuals work towards 'belonging' needs. Your new group will begin to bond; individuals will feel they belong, and you have the makings of a functioning team. However, the next need – for self-esteem – brings with it individualism, so there is likely to be *Conflict* as individuals jostle for position while attempting to gel as a team. It is up to you as leader to concentrate the team's efforts on process – the 'how' of achieving tasks. Again, brainstorming helps to create the right environment for bonding.

The level of *Control* is where there is too much dependence on the leader. This can result when individuals are locked into the security level, needing guidance and leadership and looking to you for inspiration, or where the group's cohesion only exists through the leader – perhaps from too powerful or status-conscious leadership. It is your task to motivate others to think and act for themselves, be involved in goal-setting and the decision-making process. Look at your own leadership style. Are you too dominant? Are you doing everything you can to empower your team?

*Co-operation* can be reached quickly if you create an appropriate environment of trust, respect and support, and if you handle your first couple of meetings well. Team identity becomes a reality. Individuals are prepared to work together, listen to each other; modify their opinions, and accommodate other team members' views. As team leader you will have modelled good questioning and feedback skills. These will developed by individuals in the team. Conflict will be seen as an opportunity for debate and problem solving within the group.

*Consensus* is the stage where the team thinks it has 'arrived' but in fact is locked into a cosy situation where relationships and team identity are all-important. No one 'rocks the boat'; everyone enthusiastically supports others' ideas or suggestions. There is no conflict because in fact there is very little dynamism, challenge or drive. As Rupert Eales-White writes, 'getting things done can take forever – as the group flows in one direction and then another – all together, but not focused on or committed to task achievement.'

*Commitment* is the stage teams should be aiming for. Like the Performing stage in the 'Forming, Storming, Norming, Performing' cycle, it is the exciting moment when the team 'takes off', everyone enthusiastic and motivated, coming up with new ideas, accepting challenges, seeing individual or team setbacks as temporary, and opportunities for mutual problem-solving. It is when there is evidence that individuals are performing beyond capabilities they themselves thought possible, and team effectiveness exceeds expectations. It is your role, as team leader, to maintain the momentum by ensuring that the team is challenged and motivated by new missions and goals, providing opportunities for individuals and the team to continue to grow.

The six Cs are possible features of group dynamics. As has been stated, you need to be aware of the stages a team may find itself in so that you can recognize difficulties and blockages for what they are, realize that this is quite a normal occurrence in the life of a team, and help the group to move on to more productive territory.

# EXERCISE

How effective a team leader are you? Having read the chapters on empowerment, motivation and team-building, you will not need a score sheet to interpret your answers to the following questions. This questionnaire is designed purely to make you consider your leadership style for strengths and weaknesses.

1.  Are team meetings held at workstations, or do you find a comfortable room where you will not be disturbed?

2.  What do you do to make the meetings informal and fun, yet productive?

3.  Do team members come to you with problems or setbacks or do they put them to the team for discussion?

4.  Are you part of team creativity, or would you prefer to be set apart from 'action thinking' sessions?

5.  Do you consider yourself a co-ordinator or controller of your team?

6. Do you ever offer your point of view with a 'Does everyone agree?' type conclusion?

7. Do you encourage a genuine exploration of different points of view to seek an answer that satisfies everyone?

8. Do you facilitate productive brainstorming sessions which generate a multitude of choices, or are the sessions little better than a tentative offering of a few obvious ideas?

9. Do you recognize seniority or status within your team, or does everyone feel equal and able to participate fully in every way?

10. Do you openly express your thoughts and feelings, and encourage others to do the same?

11. Do you avoid conflict, or do you see it as a healthy difference of opinion and opportunity for debate?

12. Do you think a team functions best if it ignores competition and rivalry between its members?

13. Do you encourage the team to develop its own analyses and strategies for development?

14. Do you encourage feedback as a team activity, ensuring that it is given in a positive and constructive way?

15. Do you ensure that discussion focuses on future action rather than 'post-mortems' of past events?

16. Is blaming discouraged? Do you help the team to concentrate instead on problem-solving?

17. Can you be disinterested and objective with each team member?

18. If there is conflict between two members of your team, how would you go about resolving it?

19. If a member of your team leaves, and is replaced, what do you do to help integrate the new member?

20. If a member of your team leaves, but is not replaced, what implications has this on the rest of the team, and how do you cope?

The last three questions need some comment, as these aspects of team-leading were not covered in the chapter. I would suggest that if there is conflict between two members of your team, and they are not resolving it between them, you must recognize that this relationship will affect the whole team. It is therefore up to the whole team to look for solutions. Invite them to offer suggestions about how to progress from the stale-mate. If this doesn't produce positive results, get the team to offer ideas on how the situation can best be managed. Ensure that the way forward is a team decision.

Regarding the team member who is a replacement; he is in an unenviable position if the team had previously gelled. The team will expect this new member to fill the departed member's shoes – to think behave and react as he did. As this is an impossible situation for an individual with opinions, ideas and feelings of his own, the most appropriate course of action is for you, the team leader, to go back to square one and rebuild the team as if it were new.

If a team member leaves, but is not replaced, the role he filled within the team and the tasks he undertook will have to be taken on by the remaining members of the team. Again, the best way to deal with this situation is to return to basics and rebuild your team from scratch, developing strengths to fill the gaps left by the departing member.

# Further reading

Adair, John. *Effective Teambuilding*, Aldershot: Gower, 1986.

Armstrong, Michael. *Management Processes and Functions*, London: Institute of Personnel Management, 1990.

Back, Ken and Kate. *Assertiveness at Work*, Maidenhead: McGraw-Hill, 1982.

Bandler, Richard and Grinder, John. *Frogs into Princes*, Utah: Real People Press, 1979.

Belbin, R. Meredith. *Management Teams: Why They Succeed or Fail*, Oxford: Heinemann, 1981.

Belbin, R. Meredith. *Team Roles at Work*, Oxford: Butterworth-Heinemann, 1996.

Bishop, Sue. *Develop Your Assertiveness*, London: Kogan Page, 1996.

Bishop, Sue. *Motivation : Unit MHR.122 Professional Management Foundation Programme*, London: UNISON/IM, 1991.

Bishop, Sue and Taylor, David. *50 Activities for Interpersonal Skills Training*, Aldershot: Gower, 1991.

Burley-Allen, Madelyn. *Managing Assertively*, New York: John Wiley and Sons, 1983.

Cava, Roberta. *Dealing with Difficult People*, London: Piatkus, 1989.

Clark, Neil. *Team Building – a Practical Guide For Trainers*, Maidenhead: McGraw-Hill, 1994.

Davies, Philippa. *Personal Power*, London: Piatkus, 1994.

de la Bedoyere, Quentin. *Managing People and Problems*, Aldershot: Gower, 1989.

Dell, Twyla. *How to Motivate People*, London: Kogan Page, 1988.

Dilts, Robert, Cameron-Bandler, Leslie, Bandler, Richard, Grinder, John and DeLozier, Judith. *Neuro Linguistic Programming*, Capitola, CA: Meta Publications, 1980.

Eales-White, Rupert. *Building Your Team*, London: Kogan Page, 1995.

Fisher, John, Ury, William and Patton, Bruce. *Getting to Yes*, London: Century Business, 1992.

Graham, H T. *Human Resources Management*, London: M and E Handbooks, 1990.

Harrison, Rosemary. *Employee Development*, London: Institute of Personnel Management, 1992.

Heron, John. *Helping the Client*, London: Sage Publications, 1990.

Hodgson, Philip. *A Practical Guide to Successful Interviewing*, Maidenhead: McGraw-Hill, 1984.

Honey, Peter. *Problem People And How To Manage Them*, London: Institute of Personnel Management, 1992.

Honey, Peter. *Face to Face Skills*, Aldershot: Gower, 1996.

Hudson, Howard. *The Perfect Appraisal*, London: Century Business, 1992.

Hunergager, S.G. and Heckmann, I.L. (eds). *Human Relations in Management*, 2nd edn, Cincinatti, OH: South Western Publishing Company, 1967.

Karrass, Gary. *Negotiate to Close*, London: Collins, 1985.

Kennedy, Gavin. *The Perfect Negotiation*, London: Century Business, 1992.

Knight, Sue. *NLP at Work*, London: Nicholas Brealey, 1995.

Laborde, Genie. *Influencing with Integrity*, California: Syntony Publishing, 1984.

Leigh, Andrew and Maynard, Michael. *Perfect Communications*, London: Arrow Business, 1993.

Maddux, Robert B. *Team Building*, London: Kogan Page, 1988.

Maddux, Robert B. *Effective Performance Appraisals*, London: Kogan Page, 1987.

Meighan, Michael. *How to Design and Deliver Induction Training Programmes*, London: Kogan Page, 1995.

Moon, Philip. *Appraising Your Staff*, London: Kogan Page, 1993.

Nelson-Jones, Richard. *Practical Counselling and Helping Skills*, London: Cassell, 1988.

O'Connor, Joseph and Seymour, John. *Introducing NLP*, London: Aquarian/Thorsons, 1993.

Rawlinson, G.J. *Creative Thinking and Brainstorming*, Aldershot: Gower, 1986.

Shackleton, Viv. *How to Pick People for Jobs*, London: Fontana, 1989.

Smalley, Larry R. *Effective Induction Training*, London: Kogan Page, 1995.

Stanton, Nicki. *What Do You Mean 'Communication'?* London: Pan, 1982.

Stewart, Valerie and Andrew. *Managing the Poor Performer*, Aldershot: Gower, 1988.

Weightman, Jane. *Managing Human Resources*, London: Institute of Personnel Management, 1990.

Wheeler, Marilyn. *Problem People at Work*, London: Century, 1994.

# Index

Absenteeism (as grounds for
    dismissal) 97, 99
Active listening 5–6, 14, 15–16, 17, 28,
    31, 38, 48, 86, 92, 116
  during negotiations 163–164
  see also Listening skills
Adaptive behaviour 26
Advice giving 85
Affirmations 17, 35
Aggression 31, 32, 33, 34–35, 42–43,
    170, 183–184, 185
  negative effects 33
  responding to 51–52
Anchoring (in NLP) 67–68, 135
Anxiety 8, 9, 10, 11, 84, 87, 115
Apathy 99, 153, 188–189
Appraisal of staff 71–81
  planning for 74–76
Appreciation of other points of view
    12, 16, 37–38, 81, 125, 132–133,
    159–162
Apprehension 36, 40–41
Arguments 37, 39
  see also Conflict
Assault (as grounds for dismissal) 97,
    98–99
Assertiveness 10, 21, 31–53, 108, 187
Attention 5, 6, 15, 16, 24
Auditory stimuli 4, 61
Availablity/approachability (to
    colleagues) 85–86

Bargaining see Negotiation

Behaviour styles 26, 29, 33–35, 38–39,
    49, 56–57, 119, 140–148, 181,
    184–186
Belief systems 13, 32, 56, 57, 133–134
Body language 5, 13, 14, 28–29, 32, 40,
    42–43, 47, 48, 52, 56, 76, 81, 85, 87,
    101, 126, 129, 163, 177, 184, 186,
    193, 195, 204, 205, 217
  see also Non-verbal communication
Brainstorming 130, 214, 216–218, 219
Broken record (technique) 44–45

Calibration in communication 60–61
Cause and effect considerations 65
Chairing meetings 127–130
Change 33, 58, 86, 108139, 174
  management of 113, 115, 116
Choice of words 5, 6, 21–23, 24, 31, 37,
    39, 40, 41–42, 48, 62, 81, 185, 186
  during counselling 87–88
  during negotiations 133, 163, 164
  during redundancy meetings 193,
    195
  when refusing requests 46
Closed questions 19
Co-operation stage in team
    development 218, 219
Co-ordinator (team role) 211
Coding of messages 5
Colour of attire 43
Commitment stage in team
    development 218, 220
Communicating skills 11–29, 35, 108

Communication 3–10, 31–32, 37–38, 40,
61–62, 97, 102, 105, 116, 125,
151–152, 153
blockages 10
by empowered staff 112
during counselling 87
during negotiations 131–132,
163–165
with problem people 181–182, 185,
186, 187, 188
within companies 7, 9, 10
within teams 216
Communication styles 24–26
Comparators (in language) 67
Comparisons 63
Competition 33, 107, 139
Completer (team role) 213
Comprehension *see* Understanding
Compromises 46
Concentration 15, 16
Confidence 10, 28, 32, 34, 35, 39, 43,
53, 101, 153, 184
Conflict 32, 34, 35, 39, 81, 84, 141, 211,
218, 219, 221, 222
Conflict stage in team development
218, 219
Confusion 6
Confusion stage in team development
218–219
Conscious competence (concept) 11
Conscious incompetence (concept) 11
Consensus stage in team development
218, 219–220
Constructive dismissal 106
Control stage in team development
218, 219
Counselling 83–90
Criticism 31, 35, 36, 47, 48–49, 72, 73,
78, 129, 217
handling of 49–50, 183
Crossover mirroring of actions 59

Decision making 17, 34, 110, 116, 168,
211, 219
Decoding of messages 6, 11–12, 14
Delegation *see* Empowerment
Direct questions 19
Disagreement 6, 16, 51
Disapproval 37
Disciplinary interviews 91–95
Discouragement 29

Discrimination considerations in staff
selection 203–206
Dishonesty (as grounds for dismissal)
97, 99
Dismissals 92, 97–106
reasons for 97–98
Double-talk phrases 22
Drinking (as grounds for dismissal)
97, 98–99

Ego *see* Self-esteem
Emotional stability 83, 199
Empathetic communication *see*
Rapport
Empowerment of staff 107–116, 139,
148
Encoding of messages 5
Encouragement 17–18, 29, 42, 72, 75,
80, 87, 89, 93, 108, 152, 211
during counselling 87–88
Excellence (copying of) 56
Excuses 46, 175
Eye contact *see* Body language
Eye movements (as an indicator of
thinking processes) 60

Facial expressions *see* Body language
Facilitator role 103, 107, 109, 115, 139,
209, 214, 216–218
Failure to match minimum standards
(as grounds for dismissal) 97, 98
*see also* Underperformance
False claims of qualifications (as
grounds for dismissal) 97, 98
Fears 36, 40–41
Feedback 6, 7, 8, 31, 46–50, 72, 80, 92,
116, 175, 221
Feel Good factor 12, 35–36, 167
Forming stage in team development
218
Forward planning 48–49

Generalizations 65, 66–67
Genuineness (during counselling) 87
Gestures *see* Body language
Grievance procedures 78, 106

Harmony (in human contact) 59, 61
*see also* Mirroring of actions
Health (effects of behaviour at work)
33, 34
Helping skills 84, 85, 86–90
*see also* Counselling

Herzberg's Two Factor Theory of Motivation 147
Hidden messages *see* Metacommunication
Humour 41

Imagery 24–25
Imperative questions 21
Implementer (team role) 212
Induction of staff 117–123
Inefficiency/incapability (as grounds for dismissal) 98, 99–100
Inferiority (feelings of) 34
Influencing skills 125–137
Innate abilities 199
Insubordination (as grounds for dismissal) 98, 99
Internal communications 7, 9, 10
Internal dialogues (within self) 12, 36, 37–40, 44, 45, 48, 53, 186
Interpersonal skills 11, 31, 79
*see also* Rapport; Relationships
Interruptions in communications 14–15
Interviews 126–127, 197–208
Intimidation 38, 185, 186
Intonation *see* Tone of voice
Intuition 65–66
Irrational fear 36

Jargon 7, 22, 41, 164
Job descriptions 75, 174, 198–200, 203
Job satisfaction 71, 109, 147, 150, 153
*see also* Empowerment
Job security 107, 146
Judgemental observations 41, 48, 49, 64, 73, 81, 91

Kinesic communication 26–27, 61

Language (use of) 6, 23, 56, 58, 46, 62, 185
during counselling 87–88, 89
*see also* Choice of words; Neuro Linguistic Programming
Lateral communication 9–10
Leading questions 21, 77
Learning ability/needs 56, 72, 78–79, 115
Linking questions 20
Listening skills 5–6, 13–17, 24, 48, 51
during counselling 87

Loaded questions 21

Managerial in-fighting 33
Marathon questions 19–20
Maslow's theories on motivation 143–147
McGregor's Theory X and Theory Y 147–148
Meaning of words 5, 14, 23, 28, 50, 62, 66, 88, 89
Meetings 127–131
Meta Model (of language) 62–66
Metacommunication 27–28
Mirroring of actions 13, 28–29, 59, 132, 182, 204
Misconduct *see* Disciplinary interviews
Mission statements 9
Misunderstanding 8, 11, 17, 32, 158, 159
*see also* Understanding
Modal operators of necessity and possibility 64
Monitor evaluator (team role) 212
Morale 10, 110, 119, 152, 153, 213
Motivation 10, 47, 71, 107, 139–155, 165, 173, 199
Mutual understanding 89, 101, 159, 182

Needs (of individuals) 6, 15, 25, 32, 92, 120, 140–148, 162, 215
Negative self-image 34
Negativity (in people) 182, 186–188
Negotiation 131–135, 157–171
communication factors 163–165
preparation 159–162
rapport 162
Nervousness 40–41, 126
Neuro Linguistic Programming 24, 55–68
Nit-picking 151, 188–189, 213
NLP *see* Neuro Linguistic Programming
No (saying and meaning the word) 31, 45–46
Nominalisations (verbal nouns) 64
Non-assertive behaviour *see* Passive behaviour
Non-verbal communication 5, 6, 7, 14, 16, 26–29, 31, 32, 40, 42–43, 46, 85, 129, 152, 182, 186
*see also* Body language

Norming stage in team development 218
Nouns 66

Objective setting 110
Observation skills 24
One-way communication 8
Open questions 19
Organizational change 84, 107, 108, 115
  *see also* Change
Organizational goals and effectiveness 7, 107, 139, 140, 148, 153, 177, 196
Organizational inefficiency (as grounds for dismissal) 98, 99
Outcomes 37, 38, 56, 57, 61, 73, 125, 128, 130, 135
Outplacement counselling 192
Over-qualification 207

Pacing (behavioural technique) 59–60, 132
Panel interviews (in recruitment) 208
Passive behaviour 32, 33–35, 43, 84–85
  dealing with 52–53, 185–186
Passive listening 17
Performance standards 9, 199
Performing stage in team development 218
Person specifications (for recruitment) 199–200
Personal Construct Theory 142
Personality 140–142, 151
  clashes 52, 81, 213
  effects on behaviour 140–148
Plant (team role) 211–212
Poor performing staff 93, 173–179
  *see also* Underperformance
Positive thought 32, 48, 56, 57, 67–68, 168
Posture *see* Body language
Power 184–185
  in negotiation 158–159
  *see also* Empowerment
Power-conscious managers 184–185
Praise 47
Prejudices 15
Presentation (of self) 43
Presuppositions 65
Probing questions 20
Problem people 181–190

Problem solving 17, 39, 211
  *see also* Counselling
Problem solving 215
Put-downs 35, 41, 49, 50

Qualifications 97, 98, 199, 200, 207
  false claims regarding 97, 98
Quality standards 9
Questioning skills 11, 18–21, 31, 41, 48, 51, 116, 177
  during appraisals 77
  during counselling 87–88
  during negotiations 163–164
  during recruitment interviews 200–203

Rapport 12–13, 16, 23, 24, 56, 59, 61, 76, 83, 84, 119, 125, 126, 127, 128, 132, 135, 174, 182, 188, 189
  in negotiations 162
  in selection interviews 200, 204, 205
Recruitment of staff 175, 197–208
Redundancy 191–196
Reflection (during counselling) 87
Reflective questions 20–21
Rejection (fear of) 37
Relationships 4, 13, 16, 31, 32, 33, 37, 56, 87, 128, 159, 167, 212, 215, 219, 222
Relaxation 32, 40–41
Request making 44
Resource investigator (team role) 212
Responsibility 22, 83, 89–90
  during counselling 889–90
Reverse brainstorming 217
Rudeness 52, 181
Rule breaking (as grounds for dismissal) 98, 100
Rules 66, 122
Rumours 10

Sarcasm 33, 41
Sarnoff Squeeze (technique) 40
Satisfaction of needs 140–148
Selection interviews 197–208
  discrimination considerations 203–206
  questions 200–203
Selective attention 5
Self-actualization 145, 148
  *see also* Empowerment
Self-confidence 25, 32

Self-delusion 37
Self-esteem 12, 32, 34, 35, 36, 83,
    144–145, 219
Self-fulfilling prophecy (concept) 36,
    56, 57, 64, 187
Self-help 84–85
Self-presentation 43
Senses (human) 56–57, 58, 67
Sensory preferences in language use
    24–25
Shaper (team role) 211
Social contact as a motivating force
    144, 145
Space and silence (during counselling)
    89
Speaking up to superiors 50–51
Specialist (team role) 213
Statement questions 20
Stimuli (sensory) 4, 61
Storming stage in team development
    218
Stress 40, 84, 126, 170, 175
    tolerance of 199
Summarizing questions 21
Suspension of staff 102
Syntonic learning (in NLP) 67–68, 135

Talent recognition 56
Team building 209–222
    role theory 211–213
    selection of members 210–214
Teamwork 7, 10, 71, 111, 113, 116, 127,
    209–222
Technical language 41
Temperament as a consideration in
    language use 25
Temporary staff 100
Tension 40, 126

Thinking process 58, 62
    *see also* Neuro Linguistic
        Programming
Thought encoding 5
Time management 188, 189
Time orientation of individuals
    134–135
Tone of voice 17–18, 20, 22, 28, 31, 32,
    40, 42, 48, 52, 59, 163, 177, 182,
    184, 195

Uncertainty 10, 130, 214, 219
Unconscious competence (concept) 11
Unconscious incompetence (concept)
    11
Unconscious mind 56
Underperformance 91, 99–100, 144,
    152, 173–179, 189
Understanding 3, 4, 5, 6, 13, 16, 17, 18,
    20, 23, 52, 56, 62–63, 88, 89
    lack of 173
Unfair dismissal 100, 101
Unsatisfactory performance 91–95
Unspecified nouns 63
Unspecified verbs 63

Value systems 13, 32, 57, 133–134
Verbal communication 5, 24, 198
Verbal nouns 64
Verbs 66
Violence (as grounds for dismissal) 97,
    98–99
Visual stimuli 4, 61
Vocabulary *see* Choice of words
Voice intonation 22, 28, 31, 32, 42, 48,
    52, 59, 163, 182, 184, 195

Waffling 41, 165

# Counselling for Managers

## Nigel MacLennan

*Counselling for Managers* takes a sympathetic and highly practical look at workplace counselling. All managers find themselves counselling staff occasionally: few receive training in this very demanding aspect of managing people. Yet when the need arises the skills need to be there already - preparation time is not an option.

Dr MacLennan, himself a qualified psychologist, makes counselling accessible as a performance management tool, and explodes many of the cherished myths with which the counselling profession surrounds itself along the way. He shows the reader how to harness the counselling skills they already, unknowingly, have. Workplace problems are often the result of some kind of skills deficit, and MacLennan describes a detailed system for resolving them on that basis. His eight stage model of counselling is based on eight simple counselling rules and the skills training model. These rules are designed to enable anyone to counsel with a high degree of effectiveness.

*Counselling for Managers* is an exceptionally honest book about the realities of counselling, which will be warmly welcomed by people-managers everywhere. Cartoons, humour and interactive exercises add to MacLennan's accessible writing style.

# Gower

# Developing Your Business Through Investors in People

## Second Edition

Norrie Gilliland

• What does Investors in People involve and how would it benefit
my organization?
• How can I make sure that our training and development
activities will help achieve our business objectives?
• How can I encourage employees to "take ownership"?
• How do I prepare for IIP assessment?

These questions and many others are addressed in this revised
edition of Norrie Gilliland's highly acclaimed book. Drawing on
experience acquired working on Investors in People with more
than 50 organizations, the author describes the business benefits of
developing employees through systematic communication,
involvement and training.

He examines the IIP national standard in detail and suggests
numerous ways of meeting it, showing how to align training and
development with business objectives, how to assess individual
development needs and what should be the role of managers in the
process. For this new edition the text has been enlarged and
improved to reflect the revisions to the national standard
introduced in 1997.

For managers in every kind of business, for HRD specialists and for
consultants, Norrie Gilliland's book will continue to be the best
available source of reference and guidance in its field.

Gower

# Diary of a Change Agent

## Tony Page

Tony Page is a 40-something management consultant, wrestling with the conflicting demands of a growing business and a growing family. For three years he kept a diary to which he confided his hopes and fears, his triumphs and setbacks. With painful honesty he analysed his working and business relationships as he strove to add value to his clients' businesses and to improve his own abilities.

The diary captures a unique personal journey and by including further commentary, analysis and exercises Tony Page both challenges the reader and emphaizes the human component in managing change.

Tony Page's book:

- introduces diary-keeping as a method for continuous professional and personal learning
- demonstrates ways of gaining control over personal performance
- shows how to conduct conversations that empower other people to change and learn
- provides an example and a direction for leaders who want to 'walk the talk'
- uncovers why corporate change programmes fail and how to mobilise people in an organization.

This honest account will have immediate appeal for anyone serious about business performance improvement, change and learning.

# Gower

# The Empowerment Manual

Terry Wilson

Most thinking managers would probably claim some knowledge of empowerment - the underlying philosophy, the potential benefits, perhaps some of the techniques involved. But how do you turn that knowledge into action that will match the specific needs of your own organization and the people who work in it? How do you measure their readiness to embark on an empowerment programme? How do you choose the best starting point and the most appropriate policies?

Terry Wilson's manual is based on his experience helping many organizations to empower their staff - and it can help you to do the same. Part I will enable you to decide on the most suitable type of programme and the best way to introduce it into your company or unit. Part II contains a series of activities through which you can assess your existing level of empowerment and then develop a detailed scheme for increasing it. The final Part tells the true story of how a successful company adopted empowerment to help it achieve its business goals. Throughout the text you will find questionnaires, checklists, exercises and action plans designed to help you map out the best way forward.

If you're serious about empowerment, but need a guiding hand to support planning and implementation in your organization, this Manual is for you.

Gower

# The "How To" Guide for Managers

John Payne and Shirley Payne

• Encourage your team to suggest their own objectives
• Prevent fires rather than fight them
• Decide! You'll never have all the information you would like

These, and another 107 'ideas', form the basis of John and Shirley Payne's entertaining book. Whether you're newly promoted or an old hand at managing, it will help you to improve your performance and avoid some of the pitfalls you may not even have been aware of.

Written in a practical, no-nonsense style, the Guide focuses in turn on the eleven key skills of management, including setting objectives, decision making, time management, communication, motivating, delegating and running effective meetings. A questionnaire at the beginning enables you to identify those chapters that will give you the maximum benefit. Or read through the whole book - as the authors say, using their ideas can't guarantee success, but it will increase your chances.

# Gower

# It's Not Luck

*A Gower Novel*

## Eliyahu M Goldratt

There has been a shift of policy at board level. Cash is needed and
Alex Rogo's companies are to be put on the block. Alex faces a
cruel dilemma. If he successfully completes the turnaround of his
companies they can be sold for the maximum return: if he fails
they will be closed down. Either way Alex and his team will be out
of work. It looks like lose-lose, both for Alex and for his team. And
as if he doesn't have enough to deal with, his two children have
become teenagers.

As Alex grapples with problems at work and at home, we begin to
understand the full scope of Eli Goldratt's powerful techniques.
*It's Not Luck* reveals more of the Thinking Process-techniques that
consistently produce win-win solutions to seemingly impossible
problems.

# Gower

# Mind Skills for Managers

## Samuel A Malone

How good are you at managing multiple tasks? What about problem solving and creativity? How quickly do you pick up new ideas and new skills?

Managers in the '90s are measured against some tough criteria. You may feel that you're already doing everything that you can, and you're still being asked for more. But in one area you've got over 90% of unused capacity ... your brain.

*Mind Skills for Managers* will help you to harness your mind's unused capacity to:

- develop your ability to learn
- generate creative ideas
- handle information more effectively
- and tackle many of the key skills of management in new and imaginative ways.

Sam Malone mixes down-to-earth ideas with techniques such as Mind Maps, checklists, step-by-step rules, acronyms and mnemonics to provide an entertaining, easy-to-use guide to improving your management techniques by unleashing the full power of your mind.

The skills in this book need to be practised. The best approach is to take one idea at a time and apply it. By following the book you will learn a whole range of 'mind skills' and be rewarded by measurable improvements in your performance.

Use and implement the ideas and you will think better, think faster and work smarter.

# Gower

# New Leadership for Women and Men

## Building an Inclusive Organization

### Michael Simmons

What are the key attributes of successful leaders in today's organization? The answer to this question is of course hotly debated. But Michael Simmons' ground-breaking book is the first to place the development of a new leadership for women and men at the heart of the argument. In particular, it is the first to focus on the benefits of helping leaders to overcome the negative effects of gender conditioning on the quality of their leadership.

The author proposes that leaders must transform their organizations by learning how to manage a turbulent environment, increase productivity and quality, and build an "inclusive organization". Achieving these aims requires that *everyone* is involved in planning the future direction of the enterprise and contributes to its continual improvement. But gender conditioning leads many managers to put up barriers to the full involvement of all their people. Transformation means reaching beyond equality to an organization where boundaries and limitations are not placed upon anyone. It needs a new kind of leadership capable of harnessing the intelligence, creativity and initiative of people at all levels, especially those who have traditionally been excluded.

This timely book provides much more than a searching analysis of women and men's leadership. Using real-life examples and case studies, it sets out strategies, programmes and techniques for improving organizational performance, and describes in detail the type of training needed. In short, it is a book designed to inspire not just thought but action.

# Gower

# The New Time Manager

## Angela V Woodhull

Why is it that, when there are exactly 168 hours in everyone's week, some people accomplish so much more than others? Often they're the same people who appear least stressed and enjoy both personal and professional lives the most.

Dr Woodhull's absorbing book explains the key principles of modern time management and shows how to apply them in our day-to-day activities. Traditional time management revolved mainly around to-do lists and delegating. *The New Time Manager* is concerned far more with factors like developing good working relationships and establishing a healthy lifestyle. For example, new time managers:

- prioritize
- communicate effectively
- give constructive feedback
- take time to play
- act to prevent burnout.

The result is a life in balance, with sufficient time for what is important to *you*. Whatever your objective, Dr Woodhull's book, with its practical guidance on every aspect of time, will help you.

# Gower

# The New Unblocked Manager

## A Practical Guide to Self-development

Dave Francis and Mike Woodcock

This is unashamedly a self-help book, written for managers and supervisors who wish to improve their effectiveness. In the course of their work with thousands of managers over a long period the authors have discovered twelve potential 'blockages' that stand in the way of managerial competence. They include, for example, negative personal values, low creativity and unclear goals.

By means of a self-evaluation exercise, the reader first identifies the blockages most significant to them. There follows a detailed explanation of each blockage and ideas and materials for tackling the problem.

This is a heavily revised edition of a book that, under its original title, *The Unblocked Manager*, was used by many thousands of managers around the world and appeared in ten languages. The new edition reflects the changed world of management and owes much to the feedback supplied by practising managers. In its enhanced form the book will continue to provide a comprehensive framework for self-directed development.

# Gower

# Practical NLP for Managers

Ian McDermott and Joseph O'Connor

It is almost a truism to say that your success as a manager depends on the quality of your communication.

NLP (Neuro-Linguistic Programming) is based on the study of excellence and provides the most powerful tools currently available for improving communication skills. There are many books setting out the relevant techniques; this is the first to show them at work in a practical management setting. The authors, both of them experienced NLP trainers, look in turn at each of the key elements in the management process and show how NLP can help. They explain:

- how to capture other people's attention and trust
- how to motivate
- how to use language (including body language) to maximum effect
- how to handle staff appraisals
- how to develop a consistent set of organizational values.

*Practical NLP for Managers* is a powerful communication skills tool for every manager who wants to improve their powers of persuasion and leadership.

Gower

# Project Leadership

## Second Edition

Wendy Briner, Colin Hastings and Michael Geddes

The bestselling first edition of this book broke new ground by focusing on the leadership aspects of project management rather than the technical. This radically revised edition is substantially reorganized, to introduce much new material and experience and bring the applications up to date.

Project leaders now exist in many different types of organizations, and they and their projects extend far wider than the construction work where traditional project management began. This new edition begins by explaining why the project way of working has been so widely and enthusiastically adopted, and provides new material on the role and key competences of project leaders in a wide range of different organizations. The authors provide invaluable guidance to senior managers struggling to create the context within which project work can thrive as well as be controlled. A new section, 'Preparing the Ground' reflects their increased emphasis on getting projects off to the right start, with new insights into the scoping process designed to ensure all parties agree on objectives. It also demonstrates the importance of understanding the organizational and political factors involved if the project is to succeed in business terms.

Part III shows how to handle the issues that arise at each stage of the project's life including a whole new section on the critical process of project team start up. The final section contains a thought-provoking "action summary" and a guide to further sources of information and development.

# Gower

# Takeover

*A Gower Novel*

## Sam Volard

Over the elaborate Christmas festivities at the Human Ethicals
Division of AgriBus International falls a shadow in the shape of an
alarming rumour. Can it be true that the Division is being sold?
And if it is true, what will it mean for the staff of HED? In
particular, how will it affect the heroes of Sam Volard's novel - the
assorted but loyal group of friends who we meet in the opening
chapters at their traditional Christmas holiday together? Their
friendship is about to be put under intense pressure...

For the one-year period covered by the story we follow the
reactions of scientists Brian Curtis, Britt Berghoff and Armand
Hernier and lawyer Tony Johns, together with their partners and
their colleagues. We see how they survive - or fail to survive - the
turmoil of redundancies and restructuring until the Division has
been fully integrated into the new parent company. At the same
time we come to understand the problems of the new divisional
chief and his head office team as they deal with the initial trauma
and then, with the help of a detailed change model, set about
creating a High Involvement Workforce.

*Takeover* can be read for its fast-moving story and colourful
characters. But as we follow the process of the takeover from
initial rumour to total integration, we see it from all angles, with
good and bad management practice, and all the hopes and fears
brought in its wake. The author also provides a chapter-by-chapter
commentary analysing the action and underlining the lessons to be
drawn. Senior managers will find this a stimulating and rewarding
read; one to which many will relate from their own past or current
experience.

# Gower

# The Vision

Richard Israel and Julianne Crane

In the new global economy, where wealth is information and the rules of business have been turned inside out, a new force is emerging. It weighs three pounds, works 24 hours a day and has unlimited potential. Sounds like you should find out more? Well, you're already the proud owner of one. In fact, you are using it now.

Recent research has begun to reveal the mysteries of the human brain and its almost infinite capacity. *The Vision* provides a step-by-step guide to using more of your creative genius. It tells the fast-moving story of Sandy Stone, as she struggles to boost the performance of her sales team, battles with her unhelpful boss, teaches – and learns from – her young son. As you share Sandy's experiences you will learn with her:

- how to create and achieve a peak sales vision for more sales
- how to harness the power of your brain
- how to use multi-sensory thinking
- how to mind-map for improved memory and recall
- how to become a visionary leader
- how to change limiting belief systems (your own and other people's)
- how to enhance self-esteem, and how to manage your time more effectively
- how to master the visionary process for future growth.

The story is followed by a commentary in which the authors explain the key learning points in more detail.

# Gower